Psychology of Running

Psychology of Running

EDITOR
Michael H. Sacks, M.D.

Associate Director of Resident Training, Payne Whitney Clinic, New York, NY
Lecturer in Psychiatry, Columbia Psychoanalytic Center for Training and Research, New York, NY
Associate Professor of Psychiatry, Cornell University Medical College, New York, NY

ASSOCIATE EDITOR
Michael L. Sachs, Ph.D.

Assistant Professor, Department of Physical Activity Sciences, University of Quebec at Trois-Rivieres, Quebec, Canada

PUBLISHER

Human Kinetics Publishers, Inc.
Champaign, Illinois

Publications Director — Richard Howell
Copy Editor — Margie Brandfon
Typesetter — Carol Luckenbill
Text Design and Layout — Denise Peters
Cover Design and Layout — Jack Davis

Library of Congress Catalog Card Number: 81-82450
ISBN: 0-931250-23-4

Human Kinetics Publishers, Inc.
Box 5076
Champaign, Illinois 61820

To Judith and Timothy
MHS

To Mom, Dad, Irene, Fay
My deepest and everlasting love
MLS

ACKNOWLEDGEMENTS

"Running Through Your Mind" by J. H. Greist et al. is from the *Journal of Psychosomatic Research*, 1978, **22,** 259-294. Copyright 1978 by Pergamon Press, Inc. Reprinted with permission.

"'The Running Treatment': A Preliminary Communication on a New Use for an Old Therapy (Physical Activity) in the Agoraphobic Syndrome" by A. Orwin is from the *British Journal of Psychiatry*, 1973, **122,** 175-179. Copyright 1973 by The British Journal of Psychiatry. Reprinted with permission.

"The Running Meditation Response" by E. Solomon and A. Bumpus is from the *American Journal of Psychotherapy*, 1978, **32,** 583-592. Copyright 1978 by the American Journal of Psychotherapy. Reprinted with permission.

"Anxiety Reduction Following Exercise and Meditation" by M. S. Bahrke and W. P. Morgan is from *Cognitive Therapy and Research*, 1978, **2**(4), 323-333. Copyright 1978 by Plenum Publishing Corporation. Reprinted with permission.

Parts of "Running, Anorexia Nervosa, and Perfection" by J. A. Sours are from *Starving to Death in a Sea of Objects: The Anorexia Nervosa Syndrome.* Copyright 1981 by Jason Aronson, Inc. Reprinted with permission.

"A Case Study of a Woman Jogger: A Psychodynamic Analysis" by B. G. Berger and M. M. Mackenzie is from the *Journal of Sport Behavior*, 1980, **3,** 3-16. Copyright 1980 by the United States Sport Academy. Reprinted with permission.

"The Anxiety of the Runner: Terminal Helplessness" by W. F. Graham is from *The Christian Century*, 1979, August 29-September 5, pp. 821-823. Copyright 1979 by the Christian Century Foundation. Reprinted with permission.

"Running and Other Vices" by J. Epstein is from *The American Scholar*, Spring 1979, **48**(2). Copyright 1979 by the United Chapters of Phi Beta Kappa. Reprinted with permission.

"Body and Soul" by G. Sheehan is from *The Physician and Sportsmedicine*, 1980, **8**(2), 43. Copyright 1980 by George Sheehan. Reprinted with permission.

"The Second Second Wind" by A. J. Mandell is from *Psychiatric Annals*, March 1979, **9**(3), 57-69. Copyright 1979 by Insight Publishing Company, Inc. Reprinted with permission.

"The Athlete's Neurosis" by J. C. Little is from *Acta Psychiatrica Scandinavica*, 1969, **45,** 187-197. Copyright 1969 by Munksgaard International Publishers Ltd., Copenhagen, Denmark. Reprinted with permission.

The addendum to "The Athlete's Neurosis" by J. C. Little is an excerpt from "Neurotic Illness in Fitness Fanatics" by J. C. Little from *Psychiatric Annals*, March 1979, **9**(3), 55-56. Copyright March 1979 by Insight Publishing Company. Reprinted with permission.

TABLE OF CONTENTS

SECTION FIVE. PSYCHOBIOLOGY OF RUNNING

SECTION SIX. PSYCHOPATHOLOGY AND RUNNING

PREFACE

unning has become the sport of the 1980s. Everywhere people are jogging, more than 25 million by some estimates. This immense popularity is partly due to the ease with which one can become a runner. Unlike most other sports, running doesn't entail acquiring new and often difficult skills, finding a partner, or scheduling court space. Runners simply put on their running shoes and begin to run.

But the ease in becoming a runner cannot be the only reason for the phenomenal growth in running. Efforts to explain its attraction have resulted in a large literature, most of it in the popular press. Enthusiasts have proclaimed it as a source of mental well-being, elation, and even euphoria. It has been proposed as not only an easy and efficient means of maintaining physical fitness but also as a cure for chronic fatigue, obesity, depression, phobias, anxiety, insomnia, schizophrenia, heart disease, high blood pressure, and a long list of other ailments. For some, running has become a new religion. Many of these born-again runners have abandoned traditional medicine and psychology, claiming that these professions are too exclusively concerned with the diseased, and that they base their standards for physical and mental health on populations which should be regarded as abnormal because they consist of sedentary spectators rather than the active and physically fit (Sheehan, 1975, p. 91).

This in turn has produced a counter-literature which regards the running movement with skepticism and even alarm. One outstanding physician views it as a sign of the pathology of our time (Thomas, 1975); another sees it as part of a new narcissism (Lasch, 1978), an example of turning to the inward world of our bodies and away from the external world, where the threats of political and ecological destruction seem so beyond our control; and finally, Epstein (see Chapter 16 in this volume) sees it as yet another smug and vain manifestation of the consciousness movement.

Sides are being drawn, and polemics have become a substitute for scientific investigation. This is unfortunate for two reasons. First, this controversy neglects the work of many who have studied the psychological and therapeutic effects of running in a careful and meticulous manner (see

Chapters 1 and 21 in this volume). In part, this may be the result of the general unavailability of these studies, for many are still unpublished or available only in scientific journals that are difficult to obtain. Second, the debate fails to appreciate the range of behaviors in runners, from the intermittent jogger who runs 3 miles two or three times a week, to the heavily committed runner who runs 10 miles twice a day, every day. The motivations and experiences of these different runners may be as different as their total weekly mileage. To lump them together may be to lose important and significant distinctions.

We have edited this book to provide a readily available selection of important articles on running therapy for psychiatrists, psychologists, physical educators, and other professionals so that they might begin to form their own judgments regarding the current state of knowledge. In this way they can make informed decisions about the role of running and, by extension, other endurance sports. We view running as one form of exercise and, in part, see the running boom as an incentive to review some of the cherished beliefs regarding health and the relationship between body and mind. Hippocrates recommended exercise, and William Osler included exercise with food, rest, and fresh air in his "quadrangle of health." And, of course, the Greek saying, *mens sana in corpore sano*—a sound mind in a sound body—remains a traditional ideal. Until recently, however, there has been no evidence for causality. The relationship between mind and body has proved elusive.

The *Psychology of the Runner* is divided into six sections, each covering a different topical area in running therapy. The first section, Running Therapy, provides an introduction to how different therapists have integrated running into their treatment of patients. Psychodynamics of Running, the second section, explores the unconscious significance of running for some of its participants.

Running Addiction, the third section, explores positive *and* negative aspects of different states of commitment to running. In the fourth section, The Mind of the Runner, the psychological state of the runner is examined from the different perspectives of a theologian, a female runner, an ultramarathoner, and a commentator on the consciousness movement.

The chapters in Section 5, The Psychobiology of Running, provide an overview of the rich contribution of the study of running to our understanding of the mind-body relation in psychology. Finally, Section 6, Psychopathology and Running, identifies several subgroups of runners who are either drawn to running or secondarily use running as a means of coping with psychiatric difficulty.

Most of the papers in these sections were presented at the Cornell University Medical College seminars on the Psychology of Running held in 1978, 1979, and 1980. We have added other previously published articles in order to provide a more complete view of these topics.

To those authors and publishers who permitted us to reproduce their articles, we are indebted. Our thanks to Rainer Martens and Margery Brandfon for providing helpful remarks about the manuscript. We also wish to acknowledge the secretarial help of Ms. Ruth Pollock and Ms. Marie Sirois for their assistance in preparing the manuscript.

References

Sheehan, G. *Dr. Sheehan on running.* Mountain View, CA: World Publications, 1975.

Thomas, L. The health care system. *New England Journal of Medicine,* 1975, **293,** 1245-1246.

Lasch, C. *The culture of narcissism.* New York: Norton, 1978.

ABOUT THE AUTHORS

Victor A. Altshul, MD, is an associate clinical professor of psychiatry at Yale University School of Medicine in New Haven, Connecticut.

Michael S. Bahrke, PhD, is an assistant professor in the Department of Health, Physical Education, and Recreation at the University of Kansas in Lawrence, Kansas.

Bonnie G. Berger, EdD, is an associate professor in the Department of Physical Education at Brooklyn College, City University of New York in Brooklyn, New York.

Ann K. Bumpus is a research assistant who lives in Carver, Massachusetts.

Edward Colt, MD, is an assistant attending physician at St. Lukes Hospital as well as a clinical assistant professor at Columbia University in New York, New York.

Arnold M. Cooper, MD, is a professor of psychiatry at Cornell University Medical College in New York, New York.

James M. Crabbe, PhD, is an associate professor in the School of Health, Physical Education, and Recreation at the University of Nebraska in Lincoln, Nebraska.

Zira DeFries, MD, is an assistant clinical professor in the College of Physicians and Surgeons at Columbia Presbyterian Medical Center in New York, New York.

Richard A. Dienstbier, PhD, is a professor in the Department of Psychology at University of Nebraska in Lincoln, Nebraska.

David L. Dunner, MD, is chief of psychiatry at the Harbor View Medical Center and professor of clinical psychiatry at the University of Washington, in Seattle, Washington.

Roger Eischens, MS, is a running shoe store owner, running therapist, and yoga teacher in Madison, Wisconsin.

Joseph Epstein, AB, is in the Department of English at Northwestern University in Evanston, Illinois.

John Faris, MD, is a psychiatrist who is in private practice in Madison, Wisconsin.

Ronald R. Fieve, MD, is a professor of clinical psychiatry at Columbia University College of Physicans and Surgeons in New York, New York.

W. Fred Graham, BA, MDiv, ThM, PhD, is a professor of religious studies at Michigan State University in East Lansing, Michigan.

John H. Greist, MD, is a professor of psychiatry at the University of Wisconsin in Madison, Wisconsin.

Alan S. Gurman, PhD, is a professor in the Department of Psychiatry at the University of Wisconsin in Madison, Wisconsin.

Glen O. Johnson, PhD, is an associate professor in the School of Health, Physical Education, and Recreation at the University of Nebraska in Lincoln, Nebraska.

Kathleen Hall is a doctoral candidate in the Department of Movement Sciences and Education at Teachers College, Columbia University, in New York, New York.

Julie A. Jorgensen is ascertainment and audience research coordinator at the Nebraska Educational Television Commission at the University of Nebraska in Lincoln, Nebraska.

Paul Joseph, PhD, is with the Department of Sociology at Tufts University in Medford, Massachusetts.

Marjorie H. Klein, PhD, is a professor in the Department of Psychiatry at the University of Wisconsin in Madison, Wisconsin.

Thaddeus Kostrubala, MD, is a running therapist in Bishop, California.

Dennis C. LaVelle is a graduate student in the Department of Psychology at the University of Nebraska in Lincoln, Nebraska.

Daria Linn, MS, is at the University of Wisconsin in Madison, Wisconsin.

J. Crawford Little, MD (Bristol), FRCPsych, FRCP (Edin.), DPM, is director of clinical research and consultant psychiatrist at Crichton Royal Hospital in Dumfries, Scotland.

Marlin M. Mackenzie, EdD, is a professor in the Department of Movement Sciences and Education at Teachers College, Columbia University, in New York, New York.

Arnold J. Mandell, MD, is a professor of psychiatry at the University of California, San Diego, in La Jolla, California.

Paul Milvy, PhD, is staff scientist on the Council on Environmental Quality in Washington, DC.

William P. Morgan, EdD, is a professor and director of the Sport Psychology Laboratory in the Department of Physical Education at the University of Wisconsin in Madison, Wisconsin.

Carole A. Oglesby, PhD, is a professor of physical education and is in the PsychoSocial Interactions and Movement Laboratory at Temple University in Philadelphia, Pennsylvania.

Arnold Orwin, MD, FRCPsych, DPM, is consultant psychiatrist at the Queen Elizabeth and Midland Nerve Hospital in Birmingham, England.

Samuel Perry, MD, is an associate clinical professor of psychiatry at the Cornell University Medical College in New York, New York.

Charles E. Riggs, Jr., PhD, is in the Department of Movement Science and Physical Education at Florida State University in Tallahassee, Florida.

James Robbins, PhD, is a staff sociologist with Jewish General Hospital and is in the Department of Sociology at McGill University in Montreal, Canada.

Michael L. Sachs, PhD, is an assistant professor in the Department of Physical Activity Sciences at the University of Quebec at Trois-Rivieres, Quebec, Canada.

Michael H. Sacks, MD, is an associate professor of psychiatry at the Cornell University Medical College in New York, New York.

Mitchel M. Sadar is a graduate student in the Department of Psychology at the University of Nebraska in Lincoln, Nebraska.

George Sheehan, MD, is a runner and author in private practice in Red Bank, New Jersey.

Lloyd R. Sherman, EdD, is director of the Secondary Education Through Health Program at Mount Sinai School of Medicine in New York, New York.

Earl Solomon, MD, is a staff psychiatrist at Massachusetts General Hospital and Harvard Medical School.

John A. Sours, MD, is on the Faculty of the Columbia University Psychoanalytic Center for Training and Research in New York, New York.

William G. Thorland, PhD, is an assistant professor in the School of Health, Physical Education, and Recreation at the University of Nebraska in Lincoln, Nebraska.

SECTION ONE

Running Therapy

Claims for running as a therapeutic modality are so frequent that they have become part of the popular psychological folklore. Enthusiasts, most of them runners, affirm the marvelous effects of running on their anxiety, depression, work performance, self-image, assertiveness, etc. At times the claims seem so extravagant that one is tempted to speculate more about the apparent self-proclaimed instability of runners than about the therapeutic effects of running.

Interest in the mental well-being associated with exercise is not new. The Greek ideal of physical and mental excellence is well known, but less familiar are other periods in history in which physical fitness was highly valued for its presumed effect on the psyche. During the 1850s, in the United States and England, a movement called Muscular Christianity emphasized the importance of intense physical activity for the development and maintenance of both moral and mental well-being. Oliver Wendell Holmes, a leading advocate, regularly criticized his contemporaries for their neglect of physical activities and stressed the importance of vigorous exercise for the achievement of physical, mental, and moral health. In England, Thomas Arnold introduced athletics into the public school system at Rugby in order to improve the character of young boys. Other historical instances of the relationship between physical activity and character development are found in *The Saga of American Sport* by John A. Lucas and Ronald Smith (1978).

Despite tradition and popular folklore, the relationship of physical activity and health to mental health still remains only a hypothesis. It has never been definitively established whether physical and mental health are connected and, if so, whether the relationship is causal or simply an association. The contributors in this section are concerned with this problem and approach it in a number of ways. They conduct controlled experiments (Greist et al., Bahrke and Morgan), prescribe running to their patients and observe the results (Solomon and Bumpus), or deliberately do not prescribe running but observe its effects in those patients who do run, as well as in themselves (Altschul). Finally, a group of therapists run with their patients. Foremost in this group is Thaddeus Kostrubala, who is represented in Section 2 on psychodynamics.

Despite the variety of approaches, the problems of experimental or clinical verification of the efficacy of running therapy are immense. The illnesses being treated—depression, anxiety, and the phobias—are often difficult to diagnose reliably. For example, depression can be a disease in itself, a symptom secondary to another disease such as physical illness, or a normal response to a misfortune, such as the depression of the bereaved. Similarly, anxiety is found in a great number of dissimilar psychiatric conditions. A second difficulty is the necessity of controlling for the naturally remitting course of many of the disease processes for which running is claimed as a cure. Depression left to itself will eventually remit spontaneously. Finally, there is a problem in establishing a causal link between the running and the proposed therapeutic effect. Are the findings of therapeutic benefit the results of chance, experimenter bias (the "evangelical attitude" of many running therapists), a nonspecific aspect of the intervention, or do they represent the effects of the running itself. None of the articles in this section avoid all of these pitfalls; they are pilot studies, preliminary efforts to delineate whether running is an effective therapy and, if so, the mechanisms of its action.

In the first chapter, Greist presents an excellent overview of the relationship between exercise and depression, and offers his own controlled attempt to compare jogging with psychodynamic psychotherapy. He found that jogging produced a more immediate antidepressant effect than the control treatments, which persisted during the follow-up period. His results are encouraging but, as he is careful to point out, the number of subjects was small and it was difficult to control the nonspecific antidepressant effects of the jogging instructor, as well as the novel aspects of the running prescription itself. Nevertheless he makes the interesting clinical observation that the running effects seem to be sudden, more like those of antidepressant medication than those of psychotherapy. This suggests that the mechanisms of action might be more physiological than psychological.

Chapter 2, by Arnold Orwin, on the treatment of agoraphobia with running is one of the first published attempts to use running as a treatment for a specific phobia. It rests on the perceptive clinical observation that agoraphobics often increase their walking speed when they approach or are within the phobic situation. This increased physical activity, Orwin suggests, might in itself be the cause of breathlessness, pounding heart, perspiration, and other signs of physical arousal which the patient mistakenly confuses with anxiety. By prescribing running into the phobic situation, he provides the afflicted individual with an opportunity to acquire a sense of mastery over the sensations associated with running, which generalize to the similar sensations experienced in anxiety. His is a clever strategy and provides a possible paradigm for the antianxiety effect of running. Unfortunately, other clinicians have not attempted to replicate his findings or, if they have, have not reported them. Solomon and Bumpus, in Chapter 3, report on their use of running with 50 patients. They detail different ways in which running can be combined with hypnosis and meditation to produce a pleasant euphoria or peak experience, to provide an opportunity to focus on particular psychological problems, and finally to serve as a warm-up for the therapy session. Although their conclusions on its efficacy as a treatment itself or as an adjunct to other treatments must be regarded with the caution that one would attach to the clinical experiences of one therapist, the authors do provide a useful scheme for integrating meditation, running, and self-hypnosis into patient practice.

The enthusiasm of Solomon and Bumpus for utilizing running in a therapy practice contrasts with Dr. Altschul, who, in Chapter 4, does not advise his patients to run even though he himself is a committed runner. With humor and honesty, he explores the running in his own mental economy and the role it played in the psychodynamic treatment of a runner who was his patient. As a psychoanalytically oriented therapist, Dr. Altschul emphasizes the capacity of running to facilitate fantasy, as well as how this process can be used adaptively, defensively, or metaphorically both by patients and their therapists. He nicely illustrates the complexity of evaluating running treatment when the therapist-observer is himself deeply involved with running. Once the patient learns of this involvement, and the therapist's anonymity is lost, the running becomes a complex means of communication between patient and therapist. Altschul does point out that this need not result in a therapeutic impasse but can be very helpful in the treatment.

Finally, in Chapter 5, Bahrke and Morgan establish the importance of good controls in the study of running. Their demonstration that taking time out to rest from one's daily activities is as effective as jogging in reducing anxiety is an important one. It suggests that the psychological aspects of jogging might be nonspecific; that it is not the running itself that is the active antianxiety agent, but the time taken to do it. Perhaps running provides a justification or an opportunity for distraction and recuperation from the stresses of work and family, and it is similar in that regard to playing bridge, going to a movie, or just setting aside time to do nothing.

With the possible exception of Solomon and Altschul, each of the authors finds that running is a symptomatic cure in that it does not deal with the causes of the stress or the symptom formation. Although in many cases this may not be necessary, in others it may be more important. Perhaps in the latter instances, one would expect a relatively high relapse rate. What are needed are follow-up studies to investigate the persistence of the treatment's success and its dependence on continuing to run. In other sections of this book, we will explore the possibility that running might be a symptom substitution in certain individuals who become addicted to it, or a source of biochemical and physiological change within the body that might have profound effects upon the metabolism and the functioning of the brain.

Reference

Lucas, J.A., & Smith, R.A. *Saga of American sport*. Philadelphia: Lea & Febiger, 1978.

CHAPTER 1

Running Through Your Mind

*John H. Greist, Marjorie H. Klein,
Roger R. Eischens, John Faris,
Alan S. Gurman, and William P. Morgan*

Mens Sana in Corpore Sano
Homer

For centuries Man has had strong opinions about the importance of exercise in the maintenance of physical and mental health. Unfortunately, very little systematic study has been conducted to determine whether there is a relationship between exercise and mental health and, if a positive relationship exists, what specific factors under the broader rubric of "exercise" are responsible for its effectiveness in the maintenance and restoration of health.

The Physical Consequences of Exercise

While recognizing that the distinction is conceptually naive, it is heuristically useful to differentiate physical from mental health because there is a substantial body of evidence concerning the positive physiological consequences of regular exercise in contrast to a paucity of data concerning psychological changes associated with exercise. The substantial interest in the effect of exercise on

5

physical health has produced evidence that exercise reduces the risk of coronary artery disease, obesity, hypertension, and associated risk factors of cigarette smoking, elevated blood lipids, and "type A" personality characteristics. All of these factors influence life span to some extent and though prospective statistical proof is difficult to obtain, it appears ever more certain that exercise *per se* reduces the risk of life-threatening physical disease and thereby increases longevity.

A recent study of 43 men, age 45 to 55, highlights the physiological implications of jogging (Kasch, 1976). Two-thirds of these subjects were previously sedentary. They all participated for 6 to 10 years in a thrice weekly, 30 to 40 minute jogging program. At the end of that time, subjects showed consistent decreases in resting heart rate and increases in maximum oxygen consumption, a reversal of the "normal" decline in maximum oxygen consumption with age. Another study of 66 sedentary middle-aged men (mean age 47) who participated in an exercise program found similar results (Paolone, et al., 1976). Thus, deconditioned, sedentary middle-aged men can reverse the expected decline in physical functional capacity through participation in a regular exercise program.

The Psychological Consequences of Exercise

Avoid exercising either mind or body without the other, and thus preserve an equal and healthy balance between them. So anyone engaged on mathematics or any other strenuous intellectual pursuit should also exercise his body and take part in physical training. By such moderate motion he can reduce to order and system the qualities and constituents that wander through the body. (Plato, trans. 1971, p. 117)

Most studies of the effects of running on mental health have been uncontrolled or conducted on analogue populations. They will be described in the context of the population examined.

Developmental Delay in Childhood and Adolescence

Among the most impressive studies reporting a positive relationship between fitness and emotional health are those of Johnson and co-workers (Johnson, 1962). They found improvement in fitness in handicapped children (mental retardation and various neurological disorders which caused visual and speech problems) to be associated with improvement in various aspects of emotional health. With improvement in physical fitness, they reported improvement in social adjustment, school work, finger skills, speech, functional intelligence and response to various forms of psychotherapy. Holden (1962) reported evidence of significant improvement in body images of 69 physically handicapped children as a result of a 2-week camping experience. Schultz (1961) found statistically significant superiority in the body image of high school girls of high physical fitness as compared with girls of low fitness. Bonniwell (1962) obtained measures of body image of 16 children with various neuromotor problems before and after individualized physical developmental programs. He reported a definite relationship between improvement in confidence, classroom performance, and social adjustment.

These studies suggest beneficial psychological and intellectual effects of exercise, but do not allow the relative contribution of increased physical fitness, improved motor control, and therapist-child relationship to be untangled. They do, however, support the general observation that when physical functioning of large and small muscle groups is brought under better control, the person's intellectual and emotional components have greater opportunity for maturation and expression. The American developmental sequence of gross motor development followed by fine motor manipulation succeeded by predominantly symbolic verbal manipulation without actual physical movement obscures the importance of physical activity in adulthood. Even at earlier ages there is evidence that the television has replaced the playground as a major source of entertainment. Our sedentariness has come back to haunt us in the pandemic of coronary artery disease now afflicting all industrialized nations of the world. In this regard Morgan (1976) has shown that despite the significantly more positive attitudes toward physical activity in former athletes as compared with former nonathletes, the two groups did not differ significantly ($p < .05$) in their reported frequency, duration of intensity of current exercise patterns, and these self-reported activity levels were confirmed by similar weight, percent of body fat, and maximal aerobic power in the two groups. To summarize: In a number of uncontrolled studies, children seem to respond to improved neuromuscular control and fitness with generalized improvement in many intellectual and psychological spheres.

Adolescence

Jankowski (Note 1) treated 208 inpatient and outpatient adolescent boys having problems with learning, running away, alcohol, or other drugs with either thioridazine (3-4 mg/kg body weight), eclectic psychotherapy, or kinesitherapy (2 hours, twice weekly "*intensive* athletic training or *hard* physical activity—mainly *sports* activity" (emphasis added). No difference in outcome was observed. We speculate that the competitiveness of the activity employed and the failure to individualize exercise intensity may have limited any possible benefits.

The Geriatric Population

Powell (1974) used a randomized block design to examine the cognitive and behavioral consequences of 21 weeks of exercise therapy on institutionalized geriatric mental patients. Significant improvement in the Ravens

Progressive Matrices Test and Wechsler Memory Scale was found in the exercise group as compared with an untreated control group and a group participating in scheduled social activities. No effort was made to document possible increased physical fitness. Stamford, Hambacher, and Fallica (1974) exercised nine male geriatric mental patients daily for 12 weeks. Physiological training effects were documented in this study as evidenced by decreased resting heart rate and decreased systolic blood pressure. Significant improvements on both the general information section of the WAIS and a standardized questionnaire used at the Woodville State Hospital were demonstrated by the experimental patients versus a control group.

Buccola and Stone (1975) studied men between 60 and 79 years of age who jogged or cycled for 10 to 40 minutes 3 days per week for 14 weeks. Similar weight and blood pressure decreases in both groups were observed while maximum oxygen consumption increased. Based on the Cattell 16-Personality Factor Questionnaire, the walk-jog group became more sober and self-sufficient, a change not found in the cyclers. If one discounts improvements attributable to the Hawthorne effect (a subject works hard simply on behalf of the experiment and consequently improves), each of these studies support the concept of improved psychological functioning as measured by cognitive tests accompanying increases in physical fitness.

Drug Addiction

Sheehan (1975) clearly recognized the addictive properties of running and Glasser (1976) aptly described running as a "positive addiction" for regular adherents. For these "addicts," running represents a daily activity that they feel compelled to perform. When unable to run, a withdrawal syndrome much like a drug withdrawal syndrome sets in. This was strikingly illustrated when Baekeland (1972) attempted to study changes in sleep EEG's of steady exercisers deprived of their exercise for long periods. Daily exercisers refused to join the study despite substantial monetary inducements to do so and he finally had to settle for subjects who exercised only 3 days a week. He concluded that even in this group the month-long period without exercise resulted in impaired sleep, increased sexual tension, and an increased need to be with others.

Observations of running's addictive potential suggested that regular exercise might be an effective replacement therapy for the common addictions and Guthrie (Guthrie & Gary, 1972) reported that a group of hospitalized alcoholics who jogged 1 mile per day for 20 days improved their cardiovascular fitness, self-esteem, and slept better when compared with a group of nonexercising controls who continued usual ward activities.

Dodson and Mullens (1969) studied the effects of jogging on 18 Veterans Administration Hospital inpatients with a variety of psychiatric disorders including alcoholism who ranged from being "well-oriented" to "out of contact." Three weeks of daily jogging resulted in increased fitness as reflected in a decreased resting pulse rate and increased respiratory capacity. There was a significant decrease in the hypochondriasis (Hs) and psychasthenia (Pt) scales of the MMPI during jogging while no change was observed on these dimensions in a control group. The most provocative aspect of the study was that only 10 of the 18 study patients were still in the hospital 6 months later, a significant decrease in the normal length of hospitalization for the ward studied. However, the authors were concerned that, "we had no way to measure how much of this effect was halo, that is, more positive attitudes toward the patients."

Anxiety Neurosis and Phobias

In an uncontrolled study, Orwin (1973) described the successful treatment of eight agoraphobic patients using the vigorous physical exertion of running to compete with the anxiety response of the agoraphobic. Orwin (1974) also reported using strenuous running in the successful treatment of a specific phobia. The running was usually "close to the limit of toleration . . . at her best speed" and produced "breathlessness for several minutes . . . gasping for air," although one of the agoraphobic patients ran at a "jog-trot." Orwin (1974) explained:

> In the running treatment the anxiety response may be inhibited at a physiological level of competition from an already activated autonomic system coping with the urgent metabolic needs of vigorous physical activity. Moreover, the internal excitation is matched by appropriate external behavior, established before the anxiety can be produced. The patient only enters an 'anxiety zone' when in urgent need of breath and with rational external cause for the obvious inner activity, so that cognitive labeling is now appropriate. If an anxiety response is produced, it may not be recognized, being overshadowed by other needs, eg, to breathe.

Muller and Armstrong (1975) used running as the major intervention in the successful treatment of a single patient with elevator phobia.

A recent report by Driscoll (1976) concluded that exertion (running in place) plus pleasant fantasies produced a significant reduction in self-reports of examination anxiety, comparable to a reduction obtained by tape recorded desensitization. When administered alone, exertion and fantasies also significantly reduced anxiety, though not as much as when used in combination.

In a series of experiments, Morgan (1973) has assessed anxiety by means of the State-Trait Anxiety Inventory (STAI) before and after vigorous exercise. He found that state anxiety initially fell below the preexercise base line with moderate to heavy exercise whereas no such drop was found after light exercise. When 15 adult males ran aerobically for 15 minutes, anxiety decreased below the base line immediately after running and remained diminished 20 minutes later. Six male anxiety neurotics and six normal males were tested before and following maximal treadmill testing to complete exhaustion, and a similar finding resulted. Neither anxiety nor symptoms were noted in either group and postexercise lactate levels were identical in both groups, indicating comparable exercise efforts. Thus vigorous exercise was found to reduce state anxiety as measured by the STAI in both normals and anxiety neurotics.

Kostrubala (1976) describes a thrice weekly running-group psychotherapy treatment which has had positive results in two uncontrolled studies. Individuals with depression, schizophrenia, anorexia nervosa, and "life style changes" have all reported symptom reduction and improved functioning in important roles. Kostrubala feels that running immediately before psychotherapy "stimulates . . . openings into the unconscious and is a valuable tool in the therapeutic process."

Schizophrenia

Linton, Harelink, and Hoskins (1934) found that schizophrenic patients scored significantly lower than normals on exercise tests designed to measure cardiovascular fitness. McFarland (McFarland & Huddleson, 1936), who investigated schizoid adults and Nadel (Nadel & Horvath, 1965) who studied schizophrenic children reported similar results. Schizophrenics scored significantly lower than normals on standard tests of muscular strength and endurance. However, hospitalized schizophrenics have been found to be quite similar in fitness to nonschizophrenic patients who have been hospitalized for prolonged periods. Thus the decreased physical fitness in schizophrenia might reflect sedentary institutional life styles rather than debility attributable to schizophrenia. The contribution of the decreased fitness to schizophrenic symptoms or severity of illness is at present unknown.

"Normal" Adults

Here we are dealing with that large population of individuals who often appear to function "normally" in major life roles (student, worker, parent, spouse, etc.) and may or may not manifest symptoms and signs of emotional distress. Valliant (1976) reported that athletic success in high school was not subsequently correlated with more mature psychological defense patterns. However, he did find that 76% of 45-year-old males with mature defense patterns engaged in "competitive athletics" while only 23% of those men with immature defense patterns did so. Folkins, Lynch, and Gardner (1972) measured aspects of physical and psychological "fitness" in college students at the beginning and end of a semester-long jogging course (the control group participated in archery or golf). They found significant increases in physical fitness as measured by decreased heart rate and improved running time in a 1.75 mile course. At the outset of the study, women in the jogging course were found to be less psychologically fit than women in the control group. In a within group analysis, significant improvement correlated with improved physical fitness was noted for the women in the jogging course. Subjects in the poorest physical and psychological condition show the greatest improvement. Gutin (1966) also concluded that the beneficial psychological effects of physical fitness programs are most pronounced in those persons with the lowest initial physical fitness scores. Ismail and Trachtman (1973) studied a group of 60 middle-aged men who jogged three times a week for 4 months using the Cattell 16-Personality Factor Questionnaire. High and low physical fitness groups were isolated and the low fitness group showed significant increases in emotional stability, imaginativeness, guilt proneness, and self-sufficiency on completion of the program and approached the pretest scores of the high fitness group on these measures. These studies suggest that unfit "normals" begin to approach fit normals in certain psychological characteristics and functioning as a result of progressive exercise training. Deconditioned "normal" individuals show evidence of more psychological distress and dysfunction than conditioned individuals. In general the more deconditioned people are, the less "normal" their psychological test scores and the more change they demonstrate as they achieve an improved level of physical fitness.

Tillman (1965) maintains that basic personality structures do not change as a result of improved physical fitness. However, he holds that mood variables in particular do appear to be altered by changes in fitness. In a recent review, Morgan (1976) discusses the "personality versus mood" dichotomy in terms of state versus trait variables emphasizing that physical activity can demonstrably modify state variables such as anxiety and depression but did not modify trait variables such as extroversion-introversion in his study.

Work efficiency is also susceptible to change through increase in physical fitness. Reviewers of cardiac reconditioning programs in West Germany cite a study in which absenteeism decreased 68% for workers with cardiovascular symptoms following an exercise program (Raab & Gilman, 1964). Petrushevski (1966) reported increased efficiency in teletype operators following a physical fitness program.

An interesting universal phenomenon in normals engaged in exercise programs is the "feel better" sensation experienced during and after exercise. To date no psychometric correlates have been discovered for this commonly reported experience and its significance vis-a-vis mental well-being has not been investigated.

Depression

Morgan (1968) compared grip strength, muscular endurance, and reaction time in populations of depressed and nondepressed adult male psychiatric patients. Two groups differed only in muscular endurance. Because endurance was measured only for small muscle activity, the significance of this difference was hard to evaluate. But Morgan also made the interesting observation that strength of grip and endurance measured at the time of admission to the hospital were inversely correlated with the length of hospitalization.

Thus the short-term (and presumably less ill) group possessed significantly higher levels of fitness from the outset. Utilizing a bicycle ergometer test to measure physical work capacity, Morgan (1969) showed that depressed male patients had significantly lower capacity than nondepressed male patients. While a later study compared depressed female patients versus nondepressed females failed to extend this observation to women, Morgan (1970) did report that hospitalized female patients of all diagnoses were significantly less physically fit than nonhospitalized adult females.

Morgan et al. (1970) studied the relationship of depression to a variety of parameters in a "normal" adult population consisting of 67 college faculty members. He concluded that depression and physical fitness were not correlated in normal adult males. However, 11 of this group scored in the depressed range on the Zung depression scale at the outset of a 6-week physical activity study. Each of these 11 men increased their physical work capacity and scored in the nondepressed range on the Zung scale at the end of the study. None of the other 56 subjects had fallen into the depressed range at the study's completion.

Morgan (1976) recently reported two additional studies with 100 adult male volunteers from each of two different prison populations. Subjects were free of recognized mental or medical problems and adequate psychological data was available on the 54 subjects from each study (subjects excluded were discharged from prison, transferred to another prison, injured, withdrew themselves from the study, or had high probable response distortion). Jogging problems of different frequency and individual session duration produced a subjective improvement in sleep and sense of well-being as well as subjective reductions of tension and depression when compared with sedentary control groups. These individuals scored in the normal (nondepressed) range on psychological instruments before, during, and after termination of the study.

Brown (Note 2) investigated the relationship between thrice weekly exercise and depression in 167 college students. Students rated themselves on the Zung Depression Inventory before and after 8 weeks of either wrestling, tennis, "varied exercises," jogging, or softball. Joggers were unsupervised and averaged 1.24 kilometers per session. The softball players and 6 control individuals who did not exercise showed no reduction in depression scores, while all other subjects did, with joggers showing the greatest reductions. Subjects who initially scored in the range of clinical depression (Zung score greater than 50) also showed a significant reduction in depression with activity $(p < 0.001)$.

Kavanaugh (Kavanaugh, Shephard, & Tuck, 1975) administered the MMPI to 101 patients 16 to 18 months after myocardial infarction. He isolated a population of 56 with severe depression and followed them for 2 to 4 years. In a regular running program these patients showed significant improvement in the D (Depression) score of the MMPI Scale, while the other indices remained unchanged. "There seemed to be a correlation between improvement in depression, adherence to the program and increase in physical fitness" (Kavanaugh, Note 3).

Running As Treatment For Depression: A Pilot Study

In a pilot attempt to determine whether running might have beneficial effects for actual patients seeking treatments for neurotic or reactive depression, 13 men and 15 women patients were assigned randomly either to running or to one of two kinds of individual psychotherapy (10-session time-limited or time-unlimited). Entry criteria required that patients be between 18 and 30 years old, have prominent depression as the first target problem, Symptom Checklist-90 (SCL-90) depression cluster score at the 50th percentile or above, minor depression according to the Research Diagnostic Criteria (National Institute of Mental Health, Note 4), and absence of psychosis, significant suicide risk, or need for antidepressant medication. Patients in the running group were interviewed in detail regarding symptoms of cardiopulmonary distress and received a resting electrocardiogram and maximal stress exercise treadmill test. No patients had to be excluded from the running group. Ten patients received running treatment, six patients time-limited psychotherapy, and 12 patients time-unlimited psychotherapy in this pilot study.

Running Therapy

The running leader initially met individually with his patients three to four times per week for 1 hour. Occasional running in small groups (2 to 4 individuals—some of whom were not in the study) was done when such groups formed spontaneously, but this accounted for no more than 25% of the runs for any patient. During the 5th week of treatment, only two sessions were scheduled with the leader, and during the 7th and 8th weeks, only one session was planned. Patients were encouraged to run at least three times weekly either with the leader or on their own. The intention in this sequence was to ensure that patients participated in treatment, learned the correct approach to running and became independent runners, capable of continuing treatment by themselves after the 10-week study ended.

During each session, the leader ensured that patients ran and walked comfortably and taught them to use their breathing rate and ability to converse while running as feedback and guides to a comfortable pace. Pace and distance covered increased gradually and steadily as treatment progressed. The emphasis was on avoiding pain and fatigue by interspersing walking periods with runs of varying length. Discussion during the runs focused on running itself (sensitivity to biofeedback, foot strike, stride, arm carry, body lean, diet, running equipment, etc). No discussion of depression per se was encouraged or reinforced either during the running session or after. This approach worked well since depressive cognitions and affect seldom emerge

Table 1

SCL-90 Depression (D) and Additional Items (A)

AVERAGE SCORE		Weeks of Treatment							Follow Up Months	
		0	2	4	6	8	10	12	1	3
Extremely	4-									
Quite a bit	3-D									
	D									
	DA					A	D			
Moderately	2-DA					DA	DA			
	DA	DA				DA	DA			
	DA	DA				DA	DA			
A little	1-DA	DA	D	DA	DA				DA	A
	DA	DA	D	DA	DA	DA			DA	A
	DA	DA	DA	DA	DA	DA	DA		DA	DA
Not at all	0-DA	DA	DA	DA	DA	DA	DA		DA	DA

during running, and when they do, they are virtually impossible to maintain. On those occasions when depressive affect and ruminations persisted during a run, the leader suggested a sequential focus on breathing, the sound and feeling of foot falls, and an awareness of the spine in an erect position. This technique of concentrating on separate physical elements of running was successful in breaking through depressive ruminations in all of our patients.

Case History

Ms. X, a 28-year-old professional student who had previously completed a master's degree in another field, complained of a 2-year depression characterized by depressive mood, a sense that nothing could or would change, a lack of meaningful relationships (she lived at home and seldom went out), difficulty going to class and studying, and excessive cigarette smoking (three packs per day). She scored at the 91st percentile on the depression cluster of SCL-90.

Within three weeks of beginning running, her mood subjectively improved and both depression and additional items (largely vegetative symptoms and signs of depression) cluster scores on the SCL-90 began to fall (see Table 1). These improvements continued until she hurt her ankle during week 5 while exceeding her recommended distance and running frequency and had to stop running until week 8 to recover. Her depression promptly returned with cessation of running, but when her ankle had healed and she could run again, depression again rapidly disappeared and she said, "I'm out of shape, but I know I'll get back in shape again, and I felt better (less depressed) the first time I ran."

She has remained in remission to the present (by subjective report on SCL-90 scores), and we often encounter her running and smiling along a lake path.

Results

> Better to hunt in fields for health unbought
> Than fee the Doctor for a nauseous draught.
> The wise for cure on exercise depend.
>   Dryden, circa 1675

There were two dropouts from the running group. One patient never ran since he moved away before completing the initial assessment and the second patient was an individual with a protracted psychiatric illness including a 6-month hospitalization and a strong sociopathic flavor in his relationship who dropped out after 3 weeks. Dropout rates for the two psychotherapy groups were very similar: one of six patients in time-limited psychotherapy and three of 12 time-unlimited treatment dropped out (terminated before the sixth session).

Results of Running

Of the eight patients who remained in running treatment for 10 weeks, two women showed little improvement. One had scheduling difficulties early in the treatment and did not participate actively. She was also unable to run because of a very low fitness level but did initiate a regular program of walking during the 6th week of the treatment program. She had a dramatic remission of symptoms during the 6th week of the follow-up period. The second woman who failed to improve while running never felt that running "could be treatment" though she ran regularly and had a marked increase in physical fitness as measured by maximum oxygen uptake (all eight patients who ran demonstrated this training effect). After 10 weeks of running, this woman had four sessions of exploratory psychotherapy which strongly suggested an underlying oedipal problem of attachment and separation from significant males. When her male friend returned to town, her depression promptly remitted. While this single case shows that completion of 10 weeks of running treatment is not always effective for moderate depression, it also suggests that the therapist, a likable and physically attractive male, did not provide a "transference cure" for the running group, and that elements of the running itself are probably therapeutic.

Running Compared with Psychotherapy

Outcome comparisons for the three pilot study groups indicated that the running treatment was as effective in alleviating depressive symptoms and target complaints as either the time-limited or time-unlimited psychotherapy treatments. However, some procedural problems that emerged with the pilot study made us reluctant to base firm conclusions on these data, and we have turned to an on-going study of psychotherapy of depression for outcome comparisons with the pilot study running patients.[1]

Procedures in the second study were essentially the same as for the pilot study except that the time-limited and time-unlimited psychotherapy were both carried out in the outpatient clinic under close supervision, with care taken to see that time-limited therapists set time-limited contracts. Also, patients were selected only if their depression scores exceeded the 65th percentile (as compared to the 50th percentile for the pilot study) on the SCL-90 depression scale, yielding groups more comparable to the runners. In all other respects procedures were identical to that for the pilot study.

Results on change outcome measures taken at 2-week intervals for the eight running patients from the pilot study and 16 patients from the later psychotherapy study (nine time-unlimited and seven time-limited) are shown in Figures 1-3. For Depression Symptom Checklist scores (Figure 1, running and the time-limited treatment groups show quite similar levels of improvement over 12 weeks. Similar patterns are apparent for changes in the initial target complaints (Figs. 2 and 3). The lesser change of the time-unlimited group probably reflects the fact that treatment is not complete.

To summarize, in our pilot study of running as treatment for moderate depression, running was at least as effective in alleviating depression symptoms and target complaints as either time-limited or time-unlimited psychotherapy.

Discussion

Patients should have rest, food, fresh air, and exercise—the quadrangle of health.

William Osler

In our clinical practice, we had observed several moderately depressed individuals who responded to a simple increase in physical activity with prompt alleviation of their symptoms. It was our impression that this response was more prompt and dramatic than that obtained with psychotherapy alone and similar to that which follows a positive response to antidepressant medication in major ("psychotic-endogenous") depressive illness. We wondered

---

[1]Some of the therapists doing time-limited therapy had failed to set clear time-limited contracts. Some of the psychotherapy was not as closely supervised as had been planned. Despite random assignment, the runners as a group had depression scores somewhat higher than either of the two psychotherapy groups.

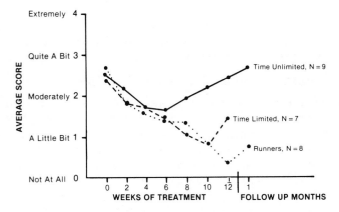

Figure 1. Depression—SCL-90

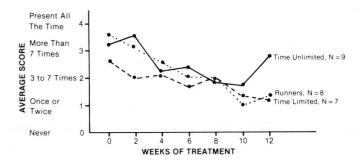

Figure 2. Frequency of first target problem.

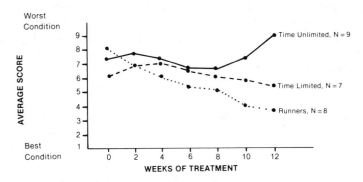

Figure 3. Intensity (at worst) of first target problem.

whether running treatment for moderate depressions might prove more effective than psychotherapy in alleviating symptoms, just as antidepressant medications are more effective than psychotherapies for *symptomatic* treatment of major depression (Weissman et al., 1976).

Possible Explanation of a Therapeutic Effect

This approach to the treatment of depression can be conceptualized as graded skill training or practice with built-in positive reinforcement. By regularly filling time with comfortable, rhythmical movement of large muscle groups, the positive reinforcements of physical adaptation (cardiovascular-pulmonary capacity and musculoskeletal strength) and psychological benefits follow. Movement within adaptive limits is easily monitored by the ability to talk while running and modeled by the running therapist who starts to walk before the patient grows fatigued. Injuries from running occur when people cannot control their feet and legs as signaled by loud flapping during the foot strike. In conditioned runners, this occurs either during very fast or very long runs, conditions found most often in racing. With most deconditioned individuals, the possibility of injury occurs at much lower levels of speed and distance than with fit runners. Part of the success we have had in getting depressed people to become independent runners (runners who will continue running by themselves after the active treatment is completed) lies in avoidance of serious injury. Emphasis is placed on a gradual increase in physical capacity, patience necessary to achieve increased capacity without injury, and sensitivity to individual feedback from breathing rate, gait, and footfall, upper extremity, fatigue, and pain. This graduated and gentle approach to frequent running produced an 11% dropout rate in depressed individuals who often have difficulty initiating and sustaining any activity. Dropout rates of 30% to 70% are commonly reported for jogging groups of normal individuals, with most attrition occurring in the first 6 weeks (Morgan, 1977; Pollock et al., 1977).

Several other hypotheses may each partially explain the beneficial effect running appears to have on depression:

1. *Mastery* — Individuals who become independent runners develop a sense of success and mastery of what they correctly perceive as a difficult skill. Many people in our society try to become runners and fail, usually because they push too hard and expect too much of themselves too soon.

2. *Patience* — To become an independent runner takes time, and one learns again the necessities of patience and making regular efforts until running becomes a habit.

3. *Capacity for change* — Our subjects also learned, often dramatically, that they can change themselves for the better. Running improves their physical health, appearance, and body image with concomitant increases in self-acceptance.

4. *Generalization* — Some subjects who described a new and positive image of themselves as competent at running explicitly stated that this change

helped them feel capable of becoming competent in other areas.

5. *Distraction* — Subjects noticed new and very real bodily sensations which distracted them from preoccupations with minor but annoying physical symptoms of depression.

6. *Positive habit or "addiction"* — Many of our subjects recognized running as a positive activity and seemed to substitute it rather consciously for more negative and neurotic defenses and habits.

7. *Symptom relief* — Running provided a reliable means of lysing symptoms of anger and anxiety as well as depression. All subjects who ran reported some kind of "good feeling" during the run. There was a pleasure and satisfaction in the functional act of running which became for most a sufficient justification to keep running.

8. *Consciousness alteration* — There is often a consciousness altering component associated with protracted running (more than 15 to 30 minute duration). While not available to the beginning runner, this state is described by experienced runners as a very positive, creative, less conscious, and more insightful interlude which is so addicting that many runners find it difficult to skip running for even a single day.

9. *Biochemical changes* — The biochemical hypotheses which have been advanced as explanations of depression were well summarized in a recent survey article (Akiskal & McKinney, 1975). While none of these hypotheses is firmly established, and it has been shown that some biochemical changes in depression are secondary to changes in physical activity (Post et al., 1973), nevertheless it seems certain that biochemical correlates of clinical depression will eventually be found. How running may interact with the "biochemical depression" is undoubtedly complex and the subject of present inquiry by Brown and Goodwin (Brown, Note 2).

Before the actual treadmill stress test, we found an abnormal anticipatory blood response during a practice walk in 7 of our subjects. Blood pressure rose out of proportion to the increased physiological demands of walking. This response was not present in any subject at the time of the second treadmill test. If this substantial sympathetic dominance characterizes the depressed individual's response to minor stress, it may have implications for patient selection, monitoring change and outcome and biochemical mechanisms underlying moderate depression.

Problems of Present Study

There are a number of factors which could vitiate the apparent comparability of running and psychotherapy as treatments for depression. 1) The experience level of the psychotherapists was not great (most were second year psychiatry residents) in contrast to the running leader who had 7 years of experience helping people learn to run. 2) The psychotherapists may not have been committed to the kinds of psychotherapy they were using. We attempted to control for this effect by having each therapist provide both kinds of psychotherapy, but there is obviously some confusion in the minds of these young therapists about how to proceed in a training setting with strong advocates for different psychotherapies. 3) Knowing that these patients were in a "research study," the therapists may not have developed as great a sense of responsibility for their patients. 4) The running therapist may have been an effective "psychotherapist." 5) The runners had more contact with their therapist than the patients did with their psychotherapists. 6) There may have been group interaction effects which are more important than the running itself. 7) Patients who ran may not have been as ill as patients in psychotherapy. Actually, the reverse is true if one uses as a criterion a widely employed 35-item symptom self-report instrument (Kelman & Parloff, 1957). Running patients had a mean score of 78.7 versus 62.3 (higher score indicates greater psychopathology) for patients in psychotherapy. All of our treatment groups were more symptomatic than 150 patients treated in 5 private psychiatric clinics (mean score 36.8). The private clinic patients were in turn more symptomatic than individuals who applied to growth centers (mean score 23.3), national training laboratories (19.0), and a normative population (9.8). 8) In this pilot study we have looked only at the most immediate measures of symptomatic change. While symptoms of depression have been shown to be largely unresponsive to psychotherapy (Lipman & Covi, 1976; Weissman et al., 1976). Weissman et al. were able to demonstrate improvements in social adjustment as a result of 8-month-long psychotherapy in depressed female patients who remained symptomatically well.

These and other variables will require more careful control in subsequent studies. Nevertheless, the rate and amount of improvement we observed in these depressed patients who ran compares favorably with outcomes we have observed clinically with a variety of therapies and therapists. Unfortunately, this "clinical experience" criterion remains largely unchallenged in a field where we as well as other workers "were not able to find a single systematic published report of the psychotherapy of depression that included more than 12 reported cases or described any attempt at a quantitative measure of outcome (Klerman et al., 1974).

Why Running?

Moderate depression, like anxiety neurosis, is a common problem in Western society and one that is often managed by general practitioners (Shephard et al., 1966). While diazepam has become a mainstay in the management of anxiety (Blackwell, 1973), there has been no comparable medication for the treatment of moderate depression which is usually managed with supportive psychotherapy until spontaneous remission occurs. Although there is now some evidence supporting the use of tricyclic antidepressants in moderate (neurotic or reactive) depression (Klerman et al., 1974; Lipman & Covi, 1976), most psychiatrists have believed and prescribed as though the use of antidepressant medication in moderate depression is not indicated and may even prove dangerous in suicidal patients who are thus provided with a potentially lethal drug. If other studies replicate the findings of our pilot study, running would provide an alternative somatic treatment for minor depression which could be made available at low cost to large numbers of patients.

While there has been something of a backlash of criticism against walking-jogging-running by some who do not run or have run in such a way that it is unpleasant, running, which differs from walking in that both feet leave the ground at some part of the movement cycle, shares with walking its very naturalness. Walking and running are eminently natural activities for human beings and most people can still find satisfaction and even pleasure in having their bodies function in the regular rhythmical activities we call walking and running. Since we learn these activities very early as a part of our normal growth and development, and can continue them as long as we are physically able to do so, this familiar activity can legitimately fulfill many purposes. Running can be done at any time of the year, in any weather, indoors and out. It can be done alone and with others and at a pace that is comfortable for everyone.

The actual salary paid to the running leader for treatment of these 10 patients was $850. While treadmill tests were provided at no cost, they can be obtained privately in our community for $30 each or $300 total. If one assumes that 10 sessions would be a reasonable average for outpatient psychotherapeutic treatment of depression (as it is in our clinic and larger psychiatric community), and that psychiatrists charge at least $50 per session (as they do in our community), the relative cost of treating one depressed patient is $115 for running versus $500 for psychotherapy. If the treatments are equally effective in terms of outcome of depression, running is 4 times more cost effective as a treatment for this common health problem. (Whether any treatment is cost effective in this characteristically self-remitting illness is a larger and more complicated question) (Weinstein & Stason, 1977).

Running also has beneficial side effects in contrast to some other treatments where side effects can be deleterious or even dangerous, e.g., drug treatment. This treatment also emphasizes the role each individual can play in treating illness and maintaining health—thereby utilizing the largest untapped health resource available—the patient.

If effective in the treatment of acute illness, this approach may also have prophylactic value against recurrence of depression since one goal of the treatment (and a frequent outcome in our pilot study) is to help individuals become independent and continuing runners.

The physiological benefits of aerobic running are well documented. If the psychological effects of running are also demonstrated to be beneficial in actual patients, the whole area of physiological-psychological interaction may yield valuable insights into the therapeutic process. The implications of this psychosomatic relationship for the psychological fitness of our sedentary population as well as the possible contributions of physiological "unfitness" to emotional problems and mental disorders will require additional investigations.

Because of the simplicity of this form of therapy, the patient's style of performing in running is also highlighted. Thus, the impact of various styles of
running (hard-driving and aggressive, meticulous and obsessive, hypochon-
driachal, etc) on the psychological consequences of the activity may also provide fruitful variables for further study.

Conclusion

Running is a melody of my life, of all my life: to sweat out anger, to concentrate
on the tasks of life, to feel the pleasure and delight of loneliness and freedom, to
be all of a human being.

Fritz Schreiber, a runner for 70 of his 80 years

In our opinion, running as treatment for depression remains experimental,
in need of replication by additional controlled studies and potentially
dangerous to depressed individuals.

While most analogue studies of exercise treatment of nonpatients who
scored in the "depressed range" on self-report measures have shown
statistically significant reductions in depression with exercise and anecdotes
and uncontrolled studies in clinical populations also support running's effectiveness as a treatment for moderate depression, we believe this report is the
first controlled study of running in depressed individuals who present
themselves for treatment.

Our results suggest that running is as effective as two kinds of
psychotherapy for moderate depression. Because of the problems of research
design (psychotherapist inexperience, single running leader, small populations, limited age range studied, possible group effect, etc.) one cannot draw
firm conclusions about running's effectiveness from this single study. As Hans
Zinser said, "Two mice are no mice at all." We feel the results of this pilot
study warrant carefully designed studies which can define the roles and limitations of this approach in the treatment of depression.

We are concerned that too widespread application of this technique, for
whatever reasons, may actually be dangerous to depressed individuals.
Beyond the obvious risk of cardiovascular misadventure which can be largely
eliminated by exercise testing with electrocardiographic monitoring and a
gradual increment in physiological stress, there are other problems with the
casual advocacy of running as treatment for the complex process we label
depression.

First, we have no evidence that running would be at all helpful in the
management of major (psychotic-endogenous) depressions—the kind of
depression which seems to have a life of its own. In our view, major depressions are best managed at this time by somatic therapies (antidepressant
medications or electroconvulsive therapy) or, when indicated by psychosocial deficits, by a sequence of first somatic and then psychosocial therapies.

Second, there is the possibility that the treatment prescription will be incorrect or that patient adherence will be poor, leading to treatment failure as still another proof that s/he is hopeless, helpless, and worthless. Expertise is required to assure that the running prescription is individualized, adhered to, and monitored for effectiveness. Most physicans know a great deal about illness, but very little about health and the healthy activity of running. People over the age of 12 are not intuitive runners—they usually expect far more running of themselves than they can produce—occasionally they expect less than they are capable of. Those who overdo exceed their adaptive capacity, find running unpleasant, get sore, injured, quit, and chalk up another failure. Those who underdo (either in frequency, intensity, or duration) fail to increase their adaptive capacity, feel "running isn't helping," quit, and add running to their list of failures. To the extent that running proves beneficial as a treatment for depression, we predict that it will be for those individuals who run within the "therapeutic window" of their adaptive capacity. Both above and below critical threshold levels for each individual, the treatment will probably not be helpful and may even make depression worse.

Even if the treatment plan is correct and the patient follows it to the letter, depression may not abate, as it did in one of our patients. It is very seldom that a single treatment is successful for all cases of a particular disorder (often because of imprecision in diagnosis) and it is necessary to remain alert for signs of failure so that alternative treatments may be employed. Psychiatry remains an inexact science, a problem in probabilities performed within the many potentialities of human psychopathology and the therapeutic interaction.

Our bias (and we purposely label it as a bias which requires additional evaluation) is that running may prove to have antidepressant properties for many individuals with moderate depression; that running treatment itself will be adequate for some patients; that it will facilitate psychotherapy in others; and that even an ideal running program either alone or in combination with ideal psychotherapy will be ineffective for some patients.

Acknowledgement

Exercise treadmill tests were provided by Francis J. Nagle, PhD, Director of the Biodynamics Laboratory at the University of Wisconsin. We are also indebted to Sandra Bass, MS, and Ms. Joy Danks for assistance in the performance of this work. This investigation was supported by grants 133-A253, University of Wisconsin Medical School; 135-4435, Project 170709, University of Wisconsin Graduate School; R01-MH-25546-03, K01-MH-70903-03, National Institutes of Mental Health; and the Wisconsin Psychiatric Research Institute.

Reference Notes

1. Jankowski, K. *Effects of psycho-, kinesi, and pharmacotherapy in emotionally disturbed adolescents as evaluated with physiological and psychological methods.* Final Reports.
2. Brown, R. Personal communication, 1977.
3. Kavanaugh, T. Personal communication, 1976.
4. National Institute of Mental Health Clinical Research Branch Collaborative Program on Psychobiology of Depression (Drs. Robert Spitzer, Jean Endicott & Eli Robins).

References

Akiskal, H.S., & McKinney, W.T., Jr. Overview of recent research in depression: Integration of ten conceptual models into a comprehensive clinical frame. *Archives of General Psychiatry,* 1975, **32,** 285-305.

Baekeland, F. *Practical running psychology.* Mountain View, CA: World Publishers, 1972.

Bonniwell, H. *The effects of participation in physical development clinic on the body-image of neuromuscularly disorganized children.* Unpublished master's thesis, University of Maryland, 1962.

Buccola, V.A., & Stone, W.J. Effects of jogging and cycling programs on physiological and personality variables in aged men. *Research Quarterly,* 1975, **46,** 134-139.

Dodson, L.C., & Mullens, W.R. Some effects of jogging on psychiatric hospital patients. *American Corrective Therapy Journal,* 1969, **23**(5), 130-134.

Driscoll, R. Anxiety reduction using physical exertion and positive images. *Psychological Record,* 1976, **26,** 87-94.

Folkins, C.H., Lynch, S., & Gardner, M.M. Psychological fitness as a function of physical fitness. *Archives of Physical Medicine and Rehabilitation,* 1972, **53,** 503-508.

Glasser, W. *Positive addiction.* New York: Harper & Row, 1976.

Guthrie, D., & Gary, V. The effect of jogging on physical fitness and self-concept in hospitalized alcoholics. *Quarterly Journal of Studies on Alcohol,* 1972, **33,** 1073-1078.

Gutin, B. Effect of increase in physical fitness on mental ability following physical and mental stress. *Research Quarterly,* 1966, **37,** 211-220.

Holden, R.H. Changes in body image of physically handicapped children due to summer camp experience. *Merill-Palmer Quarterly of Behavioral Development,* 1962, **8**(1), 19-26.

Ismail, A.H., & Trachtman, L.E. Jogging the imagination. *Psychology Today,* 1973, **6,** 79-82.

Johnson, W.R. Some psychological aspects of physical rehabilitation: Toward an organismic theory. *Journal of the Association for Physiological* and *Mental Rehabilitation*, 1962, **16**, 165-168.

Kasch, F. The effects of exercise on the aging process. *The Physician and Sportsmedicine*, 1976, **4**, 64-68.

Kavanaugh, T., Shephard, R.J., & Tuck, J.A. Depression after myocardial infarction. *Canadian Medical Association Journal*, 1975, **113**, 23-27.

Kostrubala, T. *The joy of running*. New York: J. B. Lippincott, 1976.

Linton, J.M., Harelink, M.H., & Hoskins, R.G. Cardiovascular system in schizophrenia studied by the Schneider Method. *Archives of Neurology and Psychiatry*, 1934, **32**, 712-722.

McFarland, R.A., & Huddleson, J.H. Neurocirculatory reactions in the psychoneuroses studied by the Schneider Method. *American Journal of Psychiatry*, 1936, **93**, 567-599.

Morgan, W.P. Selected physiological and psychomotor correlates of depression in psychiatric patients. *Research Quarterly*, 1968, **39**, 1037-1043.

Morgan, W.P. A pilot investigation of physical working capacity in depressed and non-depressed psychiatric males. *Research Quarterly*, 1969, **40**, 849-861.

Morgan, W.P. Physical working capacity in depressed and non-depressed females: A preliminary study. *American Corrective Therapy Journal*, 1970, **24**, 14-16.

Morgan, W.P. Influence of acute physical activity on state anxiety. *NCPEAM Proceedings*, 1973, 113-121.

Morgan, W.P. *Psychological consequences of vigorous physical activity and sport in introduction to sport psychology*. St. Louis, MO: C. V. Mosby, 1976.

Morgan, W.P. Involvement in vigorous physical activity with special reference to adherence. *Proceedings NCPEAM/NAPECW National Conference*, Orlando, 1977.

Morgan, W.P., Roberts, J.A., Brand, F.R., et al. Psychological effects of chronic physical activity. *Medicine and Science in Sports*, 1970, **2**, 213-217.

Muller, B., & Armstrong, H.E. A further note on the "running treatment" for anxiety. *Psychotherapy: Theory, Research, and Practice*, 1975, **12**(4), 385-387.

Orwin, A. The running treatment: A preliminary communication of a new use for an old therapy (physical activity) in the agoraphobic syndrome. *British Journal of Psychiatry*, 1973, **122**, 175-179.

Orwin, A. Treatment of a situational phobia—A case for running. *British Journal of Psychiatry*, 1974, **125**, 95-98.

Paolone, A.M., Lewis, R.R., Lonigan, W.T. et al. Results of two years of exercise training in middle-aged men. *The Physician and Sportsmedicine*, 1976, **4**, 72-77.

Petrushevski, I.I. Increase in work proficiency of operators by means of physical training. *Psychological Abstracts*, 1966, **40**, 767. In *Psikhologii*, 1966, No. 2, 57-67.

Plato. *Timeaus and Cortias* (H.D.P. Lee, trans.). New York: Penguin Books, 1971.

Pollock, M.L., Gettman, L.R., Milesis, C.A. et al. Effects of frequency and duration of training on attrition and incidence of injury. *Medicine and Science in Sports*, 1977, **9**(1), 31-36.

Post, R., Kotin, J., Goodwin, F., et al. Psychomotor activity and cerebrospinal fluid amine metabolites in affective illness. *American Journal of Psychiatry*, 1973, **130**, 67-72.

Powell, R.R. Psychological effects of exercise therapy upon institutionalized geriatric mental patients. *Journal of Gerontology*, 1974, **29**(2), 157-161.

Raab, W., & Gilman, S.B. Insurance sponsored preventive cardiac reconditioning centers in West Germany. *American Journal of Cardiology*, 1964, **13**, 670-673.

Schultz, L.E. *Relationships between body image and physical performance in adolescent girls.* Unpublished master's thesis, 1961.

Sheehan, G. *Dr. Sheehan on running.* Mountain View, CA: World Publishers, 1975.

Stamford, B.A., Hambacher, W., & Fallica, A. Effects of daily physical exercise on the psychiatric state of institutionalized geriatric mental patients. *Research Quarterly*, 1974, **45**, 34-41.

Tillman, K. Relationship between physical fitness and selected personality traits. *Research Quarterly*, 1965, **36**, 483-489.

Valliant, G.E. Natural history of male psychological health. *Archives of General Psychiatry*, 1976, **33**(5), 535-545.

Weissman, M.M. et al. The efficacy of psychotherapy in depression: Symptom remission and response to treatment. In R. L. Spitzer & D. F. Klein (Eds.), *Evaluation of psychological therapies—Psychotherapies, behavior therapies, drug therapies and their interactions.* Baltimore, MD: Johns Hopkins University Press, 1976.

Addendum To
Running Through Your Mind

John H. Greist, Roger R. Eischens,
Marjorie H. Klein, and Daria Linn

Interim History

To the extent that a field only 5 years old can have a history, the scientific study of exercise and its effects on mental health represents a fast-moving and fascinating study. Precursors of this recent scientific work are found in literature dating to antiquity, in personal testimonials to the virtues of "recreational activity" and the penalties associated with more supine and sedentary positions and dispositions, in case reports by alert clinicians, and in analog studies which found that exercise produced mood elevation in individuals who were not clinically depressed.

Our own interest arose as a result of an informal survey of more than 20 joggers who, with very few exceptions, reported mood elevation after exercise. An on-going study of the effects of two kinds of psychotherapy on moderate depression and the ready availability of pilot study money from the Wisconsin Alumni Research Foundation permitted us to study the effect of exercise on mood with acceptable scientific rigor in actual psychiatric patients. Entry and exclusion criteria were carefully defined in an attempt to obtain a homogenous population, patients were randomly assigned to different treatments, reliable measures were used to assess patient change, and systematic follow-up was conducted. There were, however, several compromises in the study design selected: Treatment time was not evenly balanced across treatments, and only one "running therapist" was used. Most critically, sample sizes were quite small.

Still, a beginning was made in January 1976, in the midst of a typically harsh Wisconsin winter. The results of that research are described in the preceding paper and in several others (Greist et al., 1978a, 1978b, 1978c, 1979a, 1979b, 1979c, 1979d) dealing with various aspects of the research and the exercise technique employed (Eischens, Greist, McInvaille, 1979). We were acutely aware that these results required replication and elaboration with larger sample sizes and better research designs. Thus, we were fortunate to obtain support for one study from the National Institutes of Mental Health and for another study of possible chemical mechanisms underlying the effects of exercise from the Wisconsin Psychiatric Research Institute. More importantly, a substantial number of workers in other settings have begun work in this area. The breadth and depth of this work is indicated in a recent bibliography (Sachs, Buffone, & Pargman, Note 1) and in three updates (Sachs & Buffone, 1980). Representative of careful work now appearing is a study of the relative contributions of exercise and psychotherapy to the reduction of depression (Rindskopf & Gratch, Note 2). Small numbers of mildly to moderately depressed college students were randomly assigned to running alone (three times a week on their own and once as a group) or to a similar regimen plus an hour and a half of group psychotherapy immediately after the collective run. After 6 weeks of treatment, both groups showed a significant decline in depression and anxiety. Improvement in interpersonal sensitivity also occurred in both groups but was significant only for the "running/therapy" group. At a 5 month follow-up, however, the running-only group continued to improve on all three measures whereas the running/therapy group had returned to baseline. This interesting result emphasizes the importance of follow-up evaluations and suggested to these researchers that the group therapy experience may promote greater early improvement in interpersonal sensitivity at the expense of overdependence on the group which may lead to a subsequent erosion of gains. It appears that in their study, running without psychotherapy may have provided subjects with a self-treatment technique which both initiated improvement at an acceptable level and provided a foundation for long-term gains in all areas measured.

Results of Second Wisconsin Study

Based on the results of our initial study reported earlier, we believed that it was important to demonstrate constancy of the effect of exercise on depression with larger sample sizes, using more than one running therapist and attempting to equalize treatment time and other treatment conditions as much as possible. Sixty subjects in three groups of 20 were recruited by means of a newspaper advertisement soliciting volunteers for a study of depression. Subjects meeting criteria based on SCL-90 depression scores greater than 23 for males, 28 for females and RDC criteria for minor depression were randomly assigned to either group psychotherapy, group meditation, or group running. It was difficult to begin therapy for groups of 10 subjects promptly because of the time required to recruit, screen, and actually initiate therapy at a workable time for all. This delay was in marked contrast to our earlier study in which subjects often entered treatment the same day they were screened and scheduled for treatment at their convenience. Thus, drop-out rates far exceeded those experienced in the first study: in the first group of 30, nine runners, four meditators, and six group therapy patients dropped out during the 12-week course of treatment (see Table 1). We learned that depressed volunteer patients find it difficult to simultaneously face other individuals in a group, schedule sessions at the convenience of the group or therapist, and undertake a novice treatment. This led to modifications in our procedure for the second group of 30 subjects. We continued to hold group treatments in meditation and psychotherapy while returning to our individual technique for running therapy. This time two runners, 10 meditators, and seven group therapy subjects terminated during the 12-week treatment. The group *therapist* terminated the group when only three subjects remained because the subjects were considered too ill for group therapy and too small in number to actually represent the group process.

Shown in Table 1 are the SCL-90 depression scores at beginning and end of treatment for all subjects who remained in treatment for 12 weeks. These sparse data warranted few conclusions, and thus, another study with 60 subjects and additional measures to reduce attrition was begun in August 1980.

Table 1

**SCL-90 Depression Scores For Depressed Subjects
At Beginning and End of a 12-Week Treatment Course**

	N	Drop-outs	Initial SCL-90	End of Rx SCL-90	Pa
Study 1					
Exercise	10	2	2.66	1.00	.01
Time limited	8	1	2.44	1.01	.025
Time unlimited	12	3	2.58	1.44	.025
Study 2					
First wave					
Exercise	12	9	2.04	1.42	b
Meditation	8	4	3.19	1.13	.062
Group psych Rx	10	4	2.40	1.42	.025
Second wave					
Exercise	10	2	2.00	1.11	.005
Meditation	10	10	2.29	—	—
Group psych Rx	10	7	2.56	—	—

aResults of Wilcox on matched pairs signed ranks test (Seigel, 1956)
bN to small to analyze

Underlying Mechanisms

Speculations about biochemical mechanisms underlying exercise effects on emotions are easily made but difficult to study. Daria Linn, a graduate student at the University of Wisconsin in the Departments of Psychology and Physical Education sought to define the effects of exercise on brain amine metabolism in Sprague Dawley rats in a carefully controlled study. She first found that there are "high" and "low" mileage rats and controlled for that difference. Rats were placed in a cage, some with treadmills and others without, and were permitted to exercise ad lib. After 12 weeks, the animals were sacrificed, their brains rapidly dissected and sent away for both catecholamine and indoleamine analyses. Because treadmills were in short supply, a split sample study (two successive groups) was required. Results from the first group indicated that animals who exercised more had increased levels of catecholamines. Unhappily, the second group's results were far weaker (although indicating a similar trend), and one rat's data were so deviant that the strong trend from the first group failed to reach conventional statistical significance. Eight rats were used in each cell, and Daria has proposed an expansion of Zinser's dictum that "two mice are no mice at all" to "eight rats are little better than two mice."

Conclusion

Undoubtedly, exercise has pronounced effects upon emotional state and functioning. Great confusion, however, remains about the nature of these effects and whether they can be manipulated to therapeutic advantage. The limited evidence from controlled studies presently available permits cautious optimism in this regard. The tasks for researchers are the same as with any therapy: To define with increasing accuracy the areas of utility and limitations of this technique, the course of effects of different patterns of exercise, interactions with other treatments and disorders, and, when possible, mechanisms underlying the several effects observed.

Acknowledgement

This research was supported in part by a research grant from NIMH MH 30084-02, Dr. Greist's research scientist development award MH 70903-07, a grant from Rosch Drug Company, and grants from the Wisconsin Alumni Research Foundation, Medical School and Psychiatric Research Institute.

Reference Notes

1. Sachs, M. L. Buffone, G.W., & Pargman, D. *Bibliography on psychological considerations in exercise* (Vol. 2). Personal com-

munication, 1979.
2. Rindskopf, K.D., & Gratch, S.E. *The synergy of running and psychotherapy.* Personal communication, 1980.

References

Eischens, R.R., Greist, J.H., & McInvaille, T. *Run to reality.* Madison, WI: Madison Running Press, 1977.

Eischens, R.R., Kane, P.M., Wilcox, J.M., & Greist, J.H. A new precise guide to running. *Behavioral Medicine,* June 1979, pp. 14-17.

Greist, J.H., Eischens, R.R., Klein, M.H., & Faris, J.W. Antidepressant running. *Psychiatric Annals,* 1979, **9,** 23-33.

Greist, J.H., & Greist, T.H. *Antidepressant treatment: The essentials.* Baltimore: Williams & Wilkins, 1979.

Greist, J.H., Klein, M.H., Eischens, R.R., & Faris, J.T. Running out of depression. *The Physician and Sports Medicine,* 1978, **6,** 49-56.

Greist, J.H., Klein, M.H., Eischens, R.R., Faris, J.W., & Gurman, A.S. Running as a treatment of nonpsychotic depression. *Behavioral Medicine,* June 1978, pp. 19-24.

Greist, J.H., Klein, M.H., Eischens, R.R., Faris, J., Gurman, A.S., & Morgan, W.P. Running through your mind. *Journal of Psychosomatic Research,* 1978, **22,** 259-294.

Greist, J.H., Klein, M.H., Eischens, R.R., Faris, J., Gurman, A.S., & Morgan, W.P. Running as treatment of depression. *Comprehensive Psychiatry,* 1979, **20,** 41-54.

Sachs, M.L., & Buffone, G.W. Updates to the bibliography on psychological considerations. *The Running Psychologist,* 1980.

Seigel, S. *Nonparametric statistics for the behavioral sciences.* New York: McGraw-Hill, 1956.

CHAPTER 2

"The Running Treatment": A Preliminary Communication on a New Use for an Old Therapy (Physical Activity) in the Agoraphobic Syndrome

Arnold Orwin

Agoraphobia was the name given by Westphal (1871) to the fear of walking through streets and public places. The agoraphobic syndrome, which covers much else and includes fear of confined spaces, crowds, travelling, and shopping, was carefully defined by Marks (1969). His full description and review revealed, perhaps surprisingly, that although the desire to escape rapidly from a feared situation has been clearly recognized in the literature, no detailed observation seems to have been made of the rate of locomotion in this condition.

The present author, who had been involved in the treatment of over a hundred mainly chronic cases by graded performance, desensitization and hypnotic techniques, had been casually aware that patients tended to walk either relatively slowly or rapidly, but attached no particular significance to this. Its possible importance became manifest when an attempt was made to treat these patients by voluntary control of respiration.

Respiratory relief (RR) (Orwin, 1971) was found to be of limited value in agoraphobia, and augmented respiratory relief (Orwin, 1972) was tried in the hope that the accentuation of the respiratory response induced by a CO_2/O_2 mixture would prove more effective. Briefly, in this technique CO_2/O_2 cylinders were taken along with the patients till a point was reached beyond which further walking would provoke anxiety. They were then given an inhalation of a previously determined CO_2/O_2 mixture and following maximum voluntary respiratory arrest were told to proceed as far as possible while respiration was labored and anxiety minimal. Although more successful, the procedure was cumbersome, and presented technical difficulties in the transport of cylinders. Moreover, inhalation of high concentrations of CO_2 in an upright position often caused dizziness which was antitherapeutic. At this point the need to obtain a simpler means of inducing breathlessness led to the introduction of running and drew attention to the patients' usual rate of locomotion.

It is a matter of common experience that animals and men, when panic-stricken, tend to remove themselves as rapidly as possible from the provoking situation, and satisfaction of the need to escape lowers their anxiety level. In agoraphobia rapid locomotion has been described as an anticipated necessity before, or as a result of, the anxiety reaction (Marks, 1969, pp. 132-134), and patients when questioned usually confirmed this. It appeared that in the main they walked rapidly once out of doors in order to cut down the journey time. If their anxiety level rose when immobilized for social reasons, for example waiting in a queue, they usually left as quickly as possible. However, some did move slowly, deliberately restraining the urge to hurry. These patients had become aware that speed might precipitate sensations which they had come to regard as components of the feared panic response, e.g., palpitations. They could not see the relationship of their internal sensations to the state of physical activity, but assumed that the external environment, the known and expected provoker of anxiety, was causal.

Thus, apart from the use of RR, treatment by running in agoraphobia would seem to be logical. Firstly, in that an instinctive response, i.e., rapid movement would be utilized to overcome the induced panic reaction. Secondly, the unusually vigorous and self-induced physical activity would give at a cognitive level a clearly perceptible cause for physiological responses. Finally it was presumed that, as well as breathlessness, the general increase in autonomic activity would compete with and inhibit the phobic anxiety provoked by the external environment, as simple RR appeared to do following presentation of a feared object.

Method

In simple phobias treated by RR, anxiety is inhibited at the moment of its development, and a similar approach was attempted in agoraphobia. After determining a situation in which an anxiety response would occur, the patients were made to reach it breathless from running, and then had to exhibit the anxiety-provoking behavior. For example, if the problem was walking in a certain street, arriving breathless they would walk until anxiety supervened. They then withdrew and again ran so as to reach this last point breathless, and so on. This assumed that patients extended their distance from the home base in a linear fashion, but generally and for practical reasons this was not the case. Usually patients advanced by running in a linear fashion away from the base until they entered an "anxiety zone," and were then made to travel as near as possible circumferentially, bearing in mind topographical features, so that they remained a fixed distance (and time) from base. The relationship of time to distance away from the home base may be important, but has not been fully explored. A variant was to make patients run up to and through a previously provoking environment without walking—and then to repeat this, gradually reducing the pace.

Application

Following routine physical examination, the patients who were considered to be not very fit physically because of their restricted activities were given sessions of physical training by physiotherapists and took part in fairly vigorous activities. They were then made to run measured distances, usually 50 yards and multiples, within or just outside the Unit as appropriate. This was in order to bring on marked breathlessness, which would last minutes rather than seconds.

Assessment was made of distances or situations which produced anxiety, as for treatment with desensitization and re-education, and a tentative schedule of hierarchical stages was drawn up, which might be varied as treatment progressed. The patients were then made to run (later in therapy walking rapidly might suffice) according to the previously determined distances to a scheduled anxiety-provoking situation. There they had to walk (while still panting for breath) to a known objective, and if anxiety supervened they could return, either walking or running as they felt necessary. Gains were consolidated by normal walking within the newly acquired anxiety-free areas.

Results

Table 1 gives an indication of the intensity of symptoms and the amount of treatment required for eight cases in the clinic setting. The patients' condition was described as "severe" where even if accompanied they would be unable to leave home (Case 1, 3, and 4) or similarly, unable to wait in street, shop, etc. (Case 2) unless heavily sedated. They were classed as "moderate" if, although unable to approach a feared situation alone, they would usually suffer only minor anxiety when accompanied, but this did not preclude occasional panic attacks. "Mild" signified occasional panic feelings, but mainly apprehension, always present if alone, and absent when accompanied.

Eight patients were successfully treated in a hospital setting, with a minimum of therapeutic time involvement by the psychiatrist; with one ex-

Table 1

Table of Results

No.	Sex	Age	Intensity of symptoms	Duration of symptoms (yrs)	Attendance days	Sessions Running	Sessions Walking	Total	Remarks	Result
1.	F	45	Severe	13	I.P. D.P. } 49	15	75	90	See text	No symptoms
2.	F	26	Severe	3	D.P. 51	60	10	70	See text. On Phenelzine for three years	No symptoms—finally—after treatment of frigidity
3.	F	30	Severe	1½	I.P. 25	10	50	60	Controlled anxiety by half bottle of sherry per day	No symptoms and overcame concurrent frigidity
4.	M	29	Severe	3	D.P. 28	14	20	34	Drank heavily—treated for alcoholism before therapy started	No symptoms—tended to become dependent on staff and complained of general lack of confidence
5.	F	23	Moderate	20	O.P. 7	21	0	21		No symptoms
6.	F	38	Moderate	2	D.P. 20	8	20	28		No symptoms—reluctant to leave—enjoyed her visit
7.	M	23	Moderate	3	D.P. 15	11	5	16	See text	No symptoms
8.	F	43	Mild	32	D.P. 7	4	8	12	Fluctuating symptoms—two major breakdowns. Drug treatment many years	No symptoms—all apprehension gone without drugs

I.P. = In-patient }
D.P. = Day-patient } Showing days on Unit.
O.P. = Out-patient. Figure showing attendances.

ception all actual treatment was by nurses. Three of these patients were also treated from home, by nursing staff and a welfare officer, to overcome specific environmental situations, e.g., one particular road (maximum number of sessions was four). Two other patients with symptoms of mild intensity were not included in the series as they did not require clinic treatment. But instead of the usual relaxation-desensitization therapy practised at home through tape recordings, they treated themselves with the assistance of their spouses by running, and with minimal psychotherapeutic support—and they reported success. Follow-up periods have so far been only a few months, but the procedure could easily be repeated by the patient in case of relapse, and a near relative could, after instruction, supervise "treatment."

Case Examples

Case I

A housebound woman aged 45 with a 13-year history had had previous treatment elsewhere by behavioral methods, including hypnosis, graded performance and a course of methohexitone desensitization (Friedman, 1966) with only moderate effect and with rapid relapse. Therapy was commenced with CO_2/O_2, and she was soon able to walk in the hospital grounds but she disliked the inhalations. Treatment was then switched to the usual graded performance programs bolstered by running or rapid walking (she initially weighed 14 st. 5 lb., at first from the Unit and later, as she improved, from home through the agency of a social worker being trained in behavioral methods.

She had 7 weeks in-patient therapy, and then attended 2 days per week for 7 weeks. She was also seen at home 4 times, at which time she was free of all symptoms except one which was reality based, i.e., she had minimal anxiety on pedestrian crossings in heavy traffic (fear of crossing a busy main road near her home was her original symptom). She was made to run about 600 yards to such a crossing (weight was now 13 st. 61 lb. [sic]) and crossed repeatedly with no anxiety. Not only was she completely free from all symptoms but she was very confident because she felt that by her own effort she would have the ability to overcome any tendency to relapse.

Case 7

A man aged 23 had had for 3 years a dread of walking more than 1½ miles from his own rural area. He was terrified of walking through strange building estates, up hills or in cities. He attended once a week for 15 weeks as a day patient, starting with two assessment sessions to survey the ground. On the third visit he managed to run (jog-trot) to a council housing estate 300 yards from the Unit, where he was met by nursing staff. He was asked to continue running by himself and to go as far as possible into the estate but to return as soon as he felt anxious. Unintentionally, he ran right through the area, reached a main road about half a mile away and found that he could walk back with minimal anxiety. It was the first time he had done anything like this in 3 years. Later he ran, and then walked, through other urban areas and up hills, and with his wife's assistance, he was made to complete the most difficult task of all, i.e., to walk around a city center block, which he achieved after a series of short runs.

The usual note of warning with respect to all behavioral treatment of agoraphobia must be sounded. Removal of these symptoms does not necessarily mean that they will not recur; and where the condition was being used as a means of social manipulation, for example, of the marital situation, this did happen. One patient (Case 2), who had had a 3-years dependency on phenelzine removed during treatment, "recovered" three times. After her initial improvement she relapsed within one week because of what she described as "flu"; she quickly made up the lost ground only to deteriorate more rapidly following a serious marital disagreement. She then confessed to previously concealed difficulties in her marriage, in particular frigidity. Following minimal therapy for her agoraphobia, which was soon resolved, her frigidity and other problems were treated and she and her husband declared that she had not been so well for years. She remained symptom free 3 months afterwards.

Discussion

In the agoraphobic syndrome the patients suffer from anxiety which arises, as with all phobias, in an incongruous setting, in this case in an environment not normally conceived of as hostile. The intense autonomic excitation may not be matched by an appropriate behavioral response, i.e., rapid, forceful action, because the environment is not recognized as demanding this. If it is recognized, action may be repressed because of cognitive factors (e.g., it appears illogical) or social circumstances. On the other hand, if the impulse is acted upon the resultant internal changes may be relatively violent and are usually exaggerated because of the patient's lack of physical fitness. They are then misinterpreted and identified with the original sensation of anxiety, for, as Schachter (1964) has shown, if the source of physiological arousal cannot be clearly defined it may be labelled at a cognitive level as the emotional state most in keeping with external influences.

No matter how provoked, cognitive examination of the extremely unpleasant somatic sensations are acknowledged as irrational, and result in feelings varying from generalized loss of confidence to fear of impending insanity which leads to an increase in anxiety level. It would appear that appropriate physiological action to dissipate the autonomic excitation and break down this circle of events should be of value.

It has long been realized that physical activity can be beneficial in neurosis, and this has often been used to diminish neurotic anxiety, being dispensed nonspecifically in the form of sport and exercise. Some experimental evidence of autonomic inhibition by motor responses was mentioned by Wolpe (1958), but there is little in the literature to suggest that vigorous physical exertion has been directly applied in agoraphobia, although intense rage has been noted to overcome agoraphobic fear (Shapiro, Marks, & Fox, 1963).

In the running treatment the anxiety response may be inhibited at a physiological level by competition from an already activated autonomic system coping with the urgent metabolic needs of vigorous physical activity. Moreover, the internal excitation is matched by appropriate external behavior, established before the anxiety can be produced. The patient only enters an "anxiety zone" when in urgent need of breath and with rational external cause for the obvious inner activity, so that cognitive labelling is now appropriate. If an anxiety response is produced it may not be recognized, being overshadowed by other needs, e.g., to breathe. Presumably the inhibition or lack of awareness of anxiety in relation to the external environment leads to realization that this situation is no longer anxiety-provoking, and this gives rise to expectations of a similar response in the future. This is in keeping with Valins and Ray's work (1967) which indicated that avoidance behavior can be altered by information concerning internal reactions.

The technique has the merit of being simple in application, and was easily understood by patients, so that motivation was, superficially at least, high. Moreover, it could be used by nursing and social welfare staff, and relatives could also assist in practice. The need to run or walk very fast in public did not present any serious difficulty—patients being coached in the grounds or other areas of the hospital as necessary and then graduating to quiet residential streets before trying crowded areas. The results will have to be confirmed by a much longer series with adequate follow-up and with controls; however, its very simplicity makes it worthy of consideration in agoraphobia.

Summary

Eight patients suffering from agoraphobia were successfully treated by a new method involving running. The method was derived from Respiratory Relief treatments of simple phobia, where the relief on breathing after prolonged breath-holding is temporally associated with the phobic anxiety, causing inhibition of the latter.

Patients were treated almost exclusively by nursing staff. Having developed marked breathlessness through running they entered an area or approached a situation ("anxiety zone") in which anxiety was normally aroused and were then required to walk until anxiety was manifest, when they withdrew and repeated the procedure up to that point. A variant was to make them run right through an "anxiety zone," and then to repeat this at gradually reducing pace.

Their anxiety was successfully inhibited, and it was assumed that this occurred because:

1. An instinctive response to anxiety, that is rapid, forceful action, was used to control it.

2. The ongoing autonomic excitation caused by vigorous physical exertion competed with and inhibited the anxiety reaction, allowing appreciation of the environment without awareness of fear.

3. If any autonomic component of the anxiety reaction could be detected it would be cognitively labelled as part of the body's response to physical exercise.

The technique was simple to use and allowed deployment of nursing staff, a welfare officer, and spouses. It did not prevent relapse from on-going emotional problems, for example, marital difficulties.

Further experience and controlled trials are necessary to establish its full value.

Acknowledgement

The author gratefully acknowledges the support of the nursing staff at the Regional Behaviour Research Unit in the treatment of these patients.

References

Friedman, D. A new technique for the systematic desensitisation of phobic symptoms. *Behaviour Research and Therapy*, 1966, **4**, 139-140.

Marks, I.M. *Fears and phobias*. London: Heinemann, 1969.

Orwin, A. Respiratory relief. A new and rapid method for the treatment of phobic states. *British Journal of Psychiatry*, 1971, **119**, 635-637.

Orwin, A. Augmented respiratory relief. *British Journal of Psychiatry*, 1972.

Schachter, S. The interaction of cognitive and physiological determinants of emotional state. In L. Berkowitz (Ed.), *Advances in experimental social psychology* (Vol. 1). New York: Academic Press, 1964.

Shapiro, M.B., Marks, I.M., & Fox, B. A therapeutic experiment on phobic and affective symptoms in an individual psychiatric patient. *British Journal of Social and Clinical Psychology*, 1963, **2**, 81-93.

Valins, S., & Ray, A.A. Effects of cognitive desensitization on avoidance behaviour. *Journal of Personality and Social Psychology*, 1967, **7**, 345-350.

Westphal, C. Die Agoraphobie: Eine neuropathische Erscheinung. *Archiv. für Psychiatrie und Nervenkrankheiten*, 1871, **3**, 138-171.

Wolpe, J. *Psychotherapy by reciprocal inhibition*. Stanford, CA: Stanford University Press, 1958.

CHAPTER 3

The Running Meditation Response: An Adjunct to Psychotherapy

Earl G. Solomon and Ann K. Bumpus

The Running Meditation Response is a new method for inducing a relaxation response, employing slow, long-distance running combined with transcendental meditation. Specifically, it utilizes practical meditation, as distinguished from spiritual or religious meditation (Carrington, 1977). Although the technique and effects of the Running Meditation Response are similar to those of meditation, there are several significantly different features experienced or practiced by the runner: (a) addiction, usually in two to four months; (b) physical as well as emotional benefits; (c) alertness and attentiveness with his or her eyes remain [sic] open most of the time; (d) vigorous and rhythmic contraction and relaxation of the large muscles of the arms, trunk and legs; and (e) a special breathing technique.

We examined reports by slow, long-distance runners that the physiologic changes produced by running result in an altered state of consciousness (ASC) and reports on studies of transcendental meditators that demonstrated the physiologic changes produced by meditation result in an ASC. We hypothesized that if the physical technique of running and the mental technique of meditation are both methods for activating an ASC, then a combination of the two techniques could not help but be beneficial as a psychotherapeutic adjunct. In addition, we hypothesized that the ASC in running (as well as in meditation) is a form of autohypnosis (Frankel, 1976, p. 18; Wallace, 1970). Based on this assumption, we suggested that the effects of running could be further enhanced in selected patients through the use of hypnosis, specifically by Spiegel's "Eye-roll" induction technique (1975, p. 1845) before running, for the purpose of facilitating and accelerating psychotherapeutic intervention and measuring trance capacity.

The hypothesis was confirmed. In each of the 50 cases where the Running Meditation Response was utilized, it proved to be an important factor in the course of treatment. In certain cases. it was clearly identifiable as the primary factor in the success of the treatment. In short, we concluded that the Running Meditation Response should be seriously considered as a psychotherapeutic adjunct.

In researching this subject, we found that in recent years considerable literature has been devoted to the phenomenon of running. Testimonials of many slow, long-distance runners, such as Henderson (1976), Rohe (1974), Kostrubala (1976), and Fixx (1977, pp. 13-35) reveal that the physiologic effects of running apparently produce a healthy body and a feeling of well-being popularly known as a "runner's high," or what we and Maslow (see Shor, 1969) call "peak experience (PE)," which essentially is an altered state of consciousness. Spiegel suggested to us, in a letter, the possibility that the high scorers on the Hypnotic Induction Profile probably feel the PE without difficulty, while the low scorers need more instruction to achieve their level of PE.

Similarly, many studies have been conducted to evaluate the effects of transcendental meditation (TM). Research by Benson (1975), Wallace (1970), Glueck and Stroebel (1975), Smith (1975), Carrington (1977), among others, has drawn attention to the value of meditation as a psychotherapeutic adjunct.

The examination of the reports of running and meditation showed that both methods produced a relaxation response, and that each possessed certain psychotherapeutic advantages. However, in the case of running, it was our belief that the enthusiasm of the writers led to somewhat extravagant and scientifically unsubstantiated claims. Similarly, we approached the subject of meditation with some caution, noting that none of the studies have been thoroughly conclusive of its therapeutic value. By carefully divesting running and TM of any elements of faddism or cultism (West, 1975, p. 2561) we devised what we consider to be a workable method for combining the best features of both techniques. The result is the Running Meditation Response.

Technique

Basically, the Running Meditation Response is activated by simultaneously practicing two techniques, or "centering devices," (Carrington, 1977) one physical and the other mental, which together elicit the ASC or PE.

The physical technique consists of slow, long distance running for a period of 1 hour, 3 to 5 days a week. We recommend a 1-hour run because the runner does not reach the PE state until about 45 minutes into the run. Axiomatically, running should not be prescribed until a preparation work-up has been conducted; in patients over 40 years old or with a history of heart disease, a stress EKG and a complete physical examination are prerequisites.

Ideally, the patient should run continuously for the full hour. Usually, this requires a training period of several weeks in which the neophyte can build up his stamina. When he first starts his running regime, he may be obliged to walk the entire hour, and in the course of other runs, gradually alternate walking with running. After many runs, as he increases his endurance capacity, he will be able to run constantly without undue strain. A gentle lope is generally best. The pace should be slow enough to enable the patient to speak; this means he is getting enough oxygen to produce the amount of energy needed to sustain his pace for an hour. Sudden bursts of speed rapidly deplete the body of oxygen, so the runner feels "winded" after only a short time. The patient should be instructed not to be concerned with how fast he is running, nor with how long a distance he is running. His concern should be only with the length of time he runs.

To illustrate our point, we refer to Rohe, who captures the spirit of slow, long distance running in his advice to beginning runners.

> How fast should you run? "You should run fast enough to make yourself breathe hard and sweat freely."[11] How far should you run? . . . "You should run far enough to make yourself feel dandy and if you don't you've probably run too far." How often should you run? . . . run often enough, whether daily or four times a week, to increase and maintain strength and endurance but not often enough to turn it into drudgery." (Rohe, 1974)

The patient may run at any time of day, although it is not advisable to run until 2 hours following a meal. For this reason, early morning is an especially good time for a run. In addition, a morning run permits the effects of the run to stay with the patient throughout the day. However, the effects of running are not cumulative. The patient cannot run 2 hours in one day to make up for a day missed; the effects cannot be stored.

We emphasize running 3 to 5 days a week simply because regularity leads to addiction, a key factor in the success of this method. The more frequently the patient runs, the more he will experience the pleasurable and desirable effects of running and, consequently, the more quickly he will become addicted. Addiction usually occurs in 2 to 4 months. Once the patient is "hooked," he will feel a compulsion to run. If he does not, he will experience withdrawal symptoms, such as anxiety, not feeling well, or insomnia.

The mental technique utilized is a slightly modified version of Benson's (1975) meditative technique for activating the relaxation response. The proper running pace encourages the passive, mellow attitude necessary for practicing the mental technique of the Running Meditation Response. We instruct the patient to run at a gentle, regular pace, effortlessly, almost mechanically. We say: "Deeply relax all your muscles; relax your feet and work up to your face; keep your muscles relaxed. Now, breathe in long through your nose; breathe out short and sharp through your mouth; say the word, ONE, or repeat the mantra, OM, silently to yourself each time you exhale. Breathe in . . . out, ONE, in . . . out, ONE, etc. Continue to breathe easily and naturally. Don't worry about whether you are becoming deeply relaxed. Maintain a passive attitude and permit relaxation to occur at its own pace. Just let it happen. If distracting thoughts intrude, try to ignore them by simply not thinking about them and return to repeating, ONE, or, OM." We caution our patients, however, to remain vigilant and normally attentive to any external danger, such as automobiles, while permitting body and mind to flow freely.

Physiologic and Psychologic Effects

What happens when the patient runs? Well, running is a form of aerobic exercise, which Cooper (1972) defines as the type of exercise that demands great amounts of oxygen and forces the body to process and deliver it to the tissue cells, where it combines with food to produce energy. It strengthens the cardiovascular system so that the runner can sustain his pace over a long period of time without building oxygen debt in his body.

Furthermore, Cooper (1972) claims running is the quickest and most beneficial aerobic exercise. He has devised a "point system" for measuring the value of various aerobic exercises, based on the amount of oxygen (and hence, energy) required to perform each exercise. The amount of oxygen is translated into points, the more vigorous exercises requiring more oxygen being awarded more points. In effect, points are earned according to the type of exercise, the duration, and the effort put into the exercise. Running earns more points in a shorter amount of time than any other aerobic exercise, Cooper concludes.

Cooper's (1972) studies show that if a runner runs long enough and hard enough, he is getting enough endurance exercise to produce certain beneficial physiologic changes which Cooper calls "training effect." Specifically, he claims, training effect: (a) increases the efficiency of the lungs, so they process more air with less effort; (b) conditions the heart, so it pumps more blood at a lower rate; (c) increases the size and number of blood vessels, and increases collateral circulation; (d) increases total blood volume; (e) improves muscle tone, and changes fat weight to lean weight; (f) causes the rhythmic contraction and relaxation of muscles; (g) induces sweating and raises body temperature; and (h) enhances cerebral oxygenation.

Running produces other physiologic changes that appear to protect the runner against heart disease and hypertension. Cooper's studies indicate that a runner's heart rate at rest is lower than an unconditioned man's heart rate, yet is capable of accelerating to much higher work loads without undue fatigue or strain. Some studies show that a runner's blood pressure is reduced and his blood chemistry altered. The levels of triglycerides, blood or serum cholesterol, and low-density lipoproteins can be lowered by vigorous exercise, while levels of high-density lipoproteins can be raised. In individuals highly immune to heart disease, the level of high-density lipoproteins is higher and the level of low-density lipoproteins lower than in the rest of the general population. Therefore, these studies suggest that vigorous exercise is probably an immunizing activity against heart disease. Further studies conclude that regular, vigorous exercise can result in substantial and permanent weight loss, often a factor in heart disease. Evidence of some studies suggests that running may fend-off premature mental and physical aging in some cases (Sheehan, 1975, p. 91).

All these physiologic changes are undoubtedly beneficial, helping the runner to increase his physical fitness; to reduce chronic fatigue (*President's Program*, p. 6); to sleep better; and generally feel more relaxed and refreshed. In short, it is advantageous to activate training effect. However, while respecting Cooper's point system for evaluating the effects of running, we find the competitive aspect of his system unsuitable for our psychiatric purposes. If the runner follows the specifications of time and distance established by Cooper's point system as the method for achieving training effect, he is apt to feel a sense of pressure or competitiveness as he races against time to reach a preestablished goal. This could be very detrimental to our method, which requires a spontaneous, relaxed, contemplative attitude to be effective.

We take, therefore, a nonperformance, nonspectatoring stance, much as we do when conducting psychotherapy of sexual dysfunctions. It is desirable, from our viewpoint, that the patient who is running neither develop performance anxieties, nor that he be concerned with how well he is doing. We tell the patient that the more he runs and the longer he does it, the more addicted he will become and the better he will do it.

The type of running we have been describing—slow, long-distance, meditative running—does produce, as previously mentioned a "runner's high." To paraphrase Ludwig (1966), an altered state of consciousness is any mental state induced by a maneuver, in this case running, that can be recognized by the individual himself as representing a deviation in subjective experience or psychologic functioning from his or her norms during waking consciousness.

Furthermore, the ASC, or what we call PE, is a healthful, subjectively pleasant phenomenon, instigated and terminated by design and under executive control, as opposed to spontaneous ASCs, such as fugues or depersonalization, which are apt to seem strange, poorly understood and fearsome, and not under cognitive control. The running PE helps the individual get his head together, or as Henderson (1976) says, it clears "gummed up thinking." Subjective experiences do vary, since this state is of a nonspecific nature, so that "Every time you run you create the quality of your own experience" (Rohe, 1974). But, generally speaking, the individual experiences a beneficial catharsis of anger, tension, stress, and frustration. He feels well, is relaxed and refreshed, and possesses a new sense of vitality. His mind feels clearer and is free of restraint. Barriers to the subconscious and unconscious loosen, permitting the free emergence of data, during which resistance to insight therapy frequently diminishes. Also, a treatment alliance is frequently strengthened and rapport is increased, so that more definitive psychotherapy can proceed.

Psychotherapeutic Applications

According to Wallace (1970), TM is another method for achieving autohypnosis. We'd like to carry that statement one step further and suggest that the PE in running reported by slow, long distance runners is a phenomenon akin to autohypnosis.

For example, during an anxiety attack, a patient experiences cardiorespiratory concomitants—pounding of the heart, breathlessness, sweating, a swimming sensation in his head, and a subjective feeling of impending disaster. When such an attack hits out of the blue, a person feels abject, dull, and out of control, further perpetuating the expectations and the anticipatory anxiety of wondering when this terror is going to strike again.

Running, by giving the patient a feeling of being in charge over functions such as heart rate, breathing, and muscles, automatically gives him a sense of mastery. This is a therapeutic maneuver frequently employed in behavior therapy and in the course of biofeedback treatment.

Similar techniques are used by hypnotic therapists. They may put the patient in charge by using imaginal images and linking other anxiety-provoking situations and phobic responses (for example, of elevators) in the mind's eye with a feeling of general muscle relaxation. The net result then is the same as would be achieved by behavior therapy and systematic desensitization. The patient can be programmed so that each time he ran, he would become not only more generally relaxed, but also more completely immunized against his phobia.

This imaginal aspect—time distortion and the sensory modalities— can be keenly orchestrated by the therapist experienced in hypnotic techniques by first inducing hypnosis with Spiegel's "Eye-roll" technique (1975). Once the trance is affected, the therapist suggests to the patient that he will see himself in his mind's eye as being very keenly alert and at the same time effortlessly floating over the ground as he puts one foot in front of the other in a slow, long distance running pace, and that each time he does this, it will be easier and it will be better. The therapist further suggests that the runner will see more clearly, think with crystal clarity, be more creative and imaginative, more relaxed, and all his sensory experiences (sight, hearing, taste, touch, smell) will be sharper. Readers interested in more specific standardized images should consult Kroger (Kroger & Fezler, 1976).

Hypnosis also allows the therapist to enhance the running PE to make it "take" more quickly and to speedily induce addiction to running. It can train hypnotizable people how to discipline their natural capacity to dissociate in the context of the running experience. In certain selected individuals we have been successful in hastening the addiction to running by first inducing a trance with Spiegel's "Eye-roll" technique, and then giving the same suggestions specified in the paragraph above. Also, we have enhanced each sensory modality through hypnosis and suggested to the patient that while he was running he would have thoughts which could greatly catalyze his treatment, and that at the next session, whether in the group or as an individual, he would report his associations and dreams which bear either consciously or subconsciously on his problem. We have been able to make this series of suggestions happen during and combined with running, with beneficial domino and "ripple" enhancement to traditional psychotherapy.

In essence, the therapist is creating a situation where the patient is waiting for the therapist to tell him what to experience and to program him so that he will experience it. The therapist is, in a manner of speaking, putting the patient on a simulated running "trip" in which everything is enhanced. The patient will see very deep green grass, hear very vividly the rustling of bushes, feel the light breeze, savor the smell of freshly mown grass, and taste the saltiness of his sweat. The therapist is thereby inducing a running PE enhanced by a trance "trip."

It should be noted, however, that patients should be diagnostically screened with respect not only to clinical diagnosis, but also dynamic diagnosis, genetic diagnosis, treatment possibilities and an assessment of transference and countertransference (Levine, 1952, p. 307). Psychotic and borderline patients usually should not be hypnotized.

Running can also be used in ego enhancement and supportive therapy, such as for some hyperkinetic adults without brain damage and some hyperactive children with minimal brain damage. Running reduces the general stress syndrome, allows them to work off excess energy, and sublimates dependent, sexual, and aggressive energy. Furthermore, it promotes a self-controlled, temporary, healthful regression in the service of the ego. It allows the child ego-state to "hang out" and temporarily be more "playful" and also dependent without shame or guilt. For example, patients with poor impulse control, assaultiveness or explosive personality are able to directly burn off much pent-up energy and therefore feel less need to act out self-destructive and destructive urges and impulses. Part of the function of running in patients with fragile personality organization, borderline or psychotic characters is to purposefully support their defenses. This is also true in individuals poorly motivated for exploratory psychotherapy.

In addition, running is one of the best forms of warm-up before group therapy. We have used group running as an "alternative group session" (Wolf, 1949), in which the patients run together as a group without the group leader, but do report back to the group leader at a regular group session. Some therapists, such as Kostrubala (1976), have described running with their patients. Although we do not do this, those who do would certainly realize that this is a supportive type of psychotherapeutic alliance, as opposed to the minimum type of self-revelation that one does in exploratory psychotherapy.

As a warm-up activity, we found that running reduced the disquietude of psychotic individuals at their confinement and produced significant feedback. This is also true with neurotic patients, for frequently their running together causes a beneficial abreaction. Running aids insight treatment by stimulating the patients' thinking, permitting the emergence of subconscious material, and facilitating their associations so they can report them at the group session with the group leader, or with their individual psychotherapist.

As a nonspecific adjunct, running has been used for the treatment of other psychiatric and psychosomatic syndromes, such as vascular or muscle contraction headaches which have been neurologically worked-up. Patients with psychophysiologic muscular-skeletal reactions, such as sciatic neuritis (where disc surgery is not indicated), patients with idiopathic epilepsy, or mild angina pectoris, or mild heart disease who have a superimposed cardiac neurosis, have benefited from running. Also, it has been used, with modest success, in drug addiction (Anderson, 1977), to reduce dosages of neuroleptic medications, and in alcoholism. It can be used in selected depressed patients (with or without antidepressant medication) and in cigarette smokers, to modify smoking behavior.

Indications and Contraindications

The Running Meditation Response is not a substitute for definitive professional psychotherapy, nor is it a universal panacea. Its effects will vary: (a) from individual to individual; (b) depending on the patient's needs; (c) according to the psychotherapist's experience and style.

It should be carefully explained to the patient when and if this technique is being used as a resistance to definitive psychiatric treatment. Many uninformed laymen, as well as cultists with little or no experience or training as psychotherapists, could try to tout running meditation as a panacea when actually definitive therapy is needed. We concur with West (1975) that nonprofessional approaches to psychologic self-improvement, "represent a potential hazard if pursued as a substitute for professional care because of the danger that serious psychiatric symptoms will be misunderstood, ignored, or even temporarily relieved but to the neglect of progressive underlying pathology, organic or functional." For example, it might be very detrimental to a schizoid, psychotic, withdrawn, or borderline individual to spend many hours alone or withdrawn while running and/or meditating.

By demonstrating how we have successfully treated specific psychiatric syndromes through the supplemental use of the Running Meditation Response, we seek to call the attention of professionals to it as a psychotherapeutic adjunct. We further believe that it is a subject worthy of continuing study. For example, one such study might be a control study comparing the effects of (a) regular, slow, long-distance meditative running with hypnotic enhancement, and (b) regular, slow, long-distance meditative running without hypnotic enhancement. The study also might include grading by means of the Hypnotic Induction Profile a larger series of meditators and running meditators who report a PE.

The recent position statement of the American Psychiatric Association ("Position Statement," 1977) correctly suggests, "the time has come for psychiatrists and behavioral scientists to examine and carefully evaluate the possible therapeutic effects of meditative techniques that have long existed in both Eastern and Western cultures." The Running Meditation Response is one of these modalities that we should utilize and study further.

Summary

An altered state of consciousness or peak experience is activated by simultaneously practicing the physical technique of slow, long-distance running and the mental technique of practical meditation. Hypnosis is used in selected cases to further enhance and accelerate addiction to this new modality. Indications and contraindications are discussed, as well as physiologic and psychologic effects. Specific uses in various psychiatric, psychosomatic, and somatic syndromes are outlined, and suggestions are included for incorporating this modality into the framework of individual and/or group psychotherapy.

References

Anderson, D. T.M. as an alternative to heroin abuse in servicemen. *American Journal of Psychiatry*, 1977, **134**, 11.

Benson, H. *The relaxation response*. New York: William Morrow, 1975.

Carrington, P. *Freedom in meditation*. New York: Doubleday, 1977.

Cooper, K.H. *Aerobics*. New York: Bantam Books, 1972.

Fixx, J.F. *The complete book of running*. New York: Random House, 1977.

Frankel, F.H. *Hypnosis: Trance as a coping mechanism*. New York: Plenum Medical Book Co., 1976.

Glueck, B.C., & Stroebel, C.F. Biofeedback and meditation in the treatment of psychiatric illnesses. *Comprehensive Psychiatry*, 1975, **16**, 303.

Henderson, J. *The long run solution*. Mountain View, CA: World Publications, 1976.

Kostrubala, T. *The joy of running*. New York: J. B. Lippincott, 1976.

Kroger, W.S., & Fezler, W.D. *Hypnosis and behavior modification: Imagery conditioning.* New York: J. B. Lippincott, 1976.

Levine, M. Principles of psychiatric treatment. In F. Alexander & H. Ross (Eds.), *Dynamic psychiatry.* Chicago: University of Chicago Press, 1952.

Ludwig, A.M. Altered states of consciousness. *Archives of General Psychiatry,* 1966, **15,** 225.

Position statement on meditation. *American Journal of Psychiatry,* 1977, **134,** 6.

President's program on adult physical fitness. Washington, DC: Government Printing Office.

Rohe, F. *The zen of running.* New York: Random House, 1974.

Sheehan, G.A. *Dr. Sheehan on running.* Mountain View, CA: World Publications, 1975.

Shor, R.E. Hypnosis and the concept of the generalized reality orientation. In C. T. Tart (Ed.), *Altered states of consciousness.* New York: Wiley, 1969.

Smith, J.C. Meditation as psychotherapy: A review of the literature. *Psychological Bulletin,* 1975, **82,** 558.

Spiegel, H. Hypnosis: An adjunct to psychotherapy. In A. Freedman, H. I. Kaplan, & B. J. Saddock (Eds.), *Comprehensive textbook of psychiatry* (Vol. 2). Baltimore: Williams & Wilkins, 1975.

Wallace, R.K. Physiologic effects of transcendental meditation. *Science,* 1970, **167,** 1751.

West, L.J. Transcendental meditation and other nonprofessional psychotherapies. In A. Freedman, H. I. Kaplan, & B. J. Saddock (Eds.), *Comprehensive textbook of psychiatry* (Vol. 2). Baltimore: Williams & Wilkins, 1975.

Wolf, A. The psychoanalysis of groups. *American Journal of Psychotherapy,* 1949, **3,** 529.

CHAPTER 4

Should We Advise Our Depressed Patients to Run?

Victor A. Altshul

The question posed by my title is so ingenuously contrived that at first blush it might appear to have been asked by an internist. This is not to belittle the contribution of internists to the mental health of their patients, but merely to recognize that their interventions, while valuable, are rarely influenced by psychodynamic understanding and tend to have unidimensional implications. An appropriate question for the internist is often a fatuous one for the psychiatrist and vice versa. As a psychiatrist who is hopelessly oriented in the psychodynamic tradition, let me hasten to state that I seldom advise my depressed patients to do anything at all; whatever modest therapeutic success I may have attained I attribute to this and other forms of self-restraint.

Nevertheless, it seems pertinent for the moment not to refine or deepen the question, not because it can be sensibly answered in its present form, but because asking it in this form brings more sharply into focus the assertion that depression and running are somehow interrelated. To assert this is not necessarily to assert that running cures or even alleviates depression. As I hope to show, a relationship between the two appears to exist, but it is far too complex to convey in a simple, declarative sentence. It is too complex in fact to base a viable therapeutic strategy on it.

First of all, I am both a runner and a depressive. As to the latter, readers will have to take my word for it. With regard to the former, I have been running daily for 7 years and am the veteran of 70 races and 19 marathons. Like many runners, I can't not run; I have in truth reached the point of no return. But *unlike* some runners, I try not to justify my running by claiming that it has helped me emotionally. Others tell me it is so, but I remain skeptical. I run not because running makes me feel better, but because not running makes me feel worse. It is, in fact, little more than a compulsion, sometimes pleasurable, sometimes joyless, but most often neutral with respect to mood. As such it seems to me to belong in the same category as bridge, tennis, the opera, wood-carving, and philandering: early, mid-, and late life enthusiams that lend piquancy to our lives and distract us from the specific, unconscious conflicts that consume us.

And yet running is also different from these other activities in that it is devoid of intrinsic content; it is inherently less structured. In an earlier communication (Altshul, 1978) I ascribed the psychologically helpful effect of running to the fact that it fosters the formation and organization of fantasy. I assumed the specific content of the fantasy to be a function of the runner's specific defensive needs and, to some extent, of his or her pace. But I attributed much of the value of running as a stimulator of fantasy to its automatic, contentless character. As such—as facilitator and organizer of fantasy—the multiplicity of meanings and motivations it is capable of generating on all levels of psychic development seemed to me to be crucial to an understanding of the psychological importance it has, of the depths it seems to reach in the everyday lives of almost all runners.

Running may be set apart from bridge, tennis, and philandering, not because it has any intrinsically superior therapeutic properties, but rather because it is so automatic that one does not have to think about it while doing it or in order to do it. The moment structured thought becomes necessary, the range of potential available meanings becomes constricted. Although sexual conquest may clearly have oral and anal components, its manifest content will bias the Don Juan's perception of his activities toward a phallic organization and render the earlier meanings less available.

Not so with running. The primitive transcendental bliss and blurring of boundaries that may occur at slower rates of speed are as available to the imaginative runner as are the phallic-narcissistic fantasies of the same runner when he or she is racing. The contentless nature of the manifest act of running lends it to the experiencing, simultaneously or seriatim, of fantasy-derivatives from multiple levels of development. The psychoanalytic situation, like running, is minimally intrusive and minimally structured, wonderfully suited to be experienced almost entirely projectively. The analogy fits so well that it may explain why so many runners like to attribute therapeutic powers to running—itself a projective fantasy.

This does not mean that running—or psychoanalysis, for that matter—is superior therapy. It does mean that running is a superior blank screen, available for projections. And it does mean that running is likely to be experienced as therapy by those who feel an intense inner need for therapy. In this connection, there is an ubiquity among runners of claims that running dissipates their tensions, discharges their anger, raises their spirits, and cures their depression. Where else is a group of people so ready to acknowledge their instability, their despair, their need for therapeutic help? They are not claiming that running really *cures* them of any of these things; they are merely asserting that it helps them deal with them, over and over and over again. My impression—and I wish someone would study this issue statistically—is that if, in this day and age, a lean, athletic man is consciously or unconsciously contemplating divorce, there is at least a 75% chance that he is, or will be, a compulsive runner. Thus, I would claim not that running causes divorce, but rather that divorce, among other forms of human misery, causes running.

This is not to say that running alleviates depression, but merely that runners think it does. Among the runner's favorite fantasies is that running lifts depression. It is an oversimplification, a form of mental shorthand, designed to shield runners from a more detailed knowledge of the content of the conflicts that lead to their depression and of the defensive purposes to which their running is put. Running should not be mistaken for a truly antidepressant activity merely because it has occasional transitory, euphoriant properties. It is, in fact, eagerly snatched up by depressed people and incorporated into their psychic economy in far more complex ways.

For example, a 33-year-old architect, a gifted and successful man, came to me for chronic, moderately severe feelings of depression and hopelessness. He was at a loss to understand why he should so frequently feel this way. He had, after all, everything in life that ought to make him happy: a successful career, job security, popularity with both sexes, and a happy family.

Yet he could not fit aspects of his life into this rosy picture. For example, he still could not understand why, while on a business trip 6 months earlier, he had involved himself in a passionate affair; moreover, given his conviction that his wife was all a man could ask for, he was still puzzled about why he was still obsessed with, and in contact with, his woman friend. His strict Lutheran upbringing as a boy in Minnesota and his 2 years of study for the ministry had not prepared him for such excesses of the flesh and, in fact, had left him with deep feelings of ineradicable guilt. In spite of the guilt, and much to his amazement, he responded to the beginning of his twice-weekly psychotherapy by quickly involving himself in three more short-term affairs. Whether this was out of defiance toward me as an external representation of an obviously harsh superego, or a feeling of license engendered by my permissive and accepting style, or out of a simple interest in testing the limits of my tolerance, I could not, at the time, have said. Perhaps it was all of these. At any rate, things had come to such a pass that he was seriously thinking of separating from his wife. He could think of no other way to bring his lifestyle in line with his manifest behavior, which he still did not understand. Although he felt he loved his wife very much and would miss her terribly, he also had begun to feel that only by leaving her could he relieve the pain of guilt and despair that was nudging him inexorably toward suicide.

Little by little, a very different picture of his interior life began to emerge. As therapy progressed, the patient became, for the first time, increasingly aware that he perceived his wife as cold and depriving. The details of their interaction were slow in coming, but eventually they coalesced into a composite image that was forbidding and a bit scary. Because he had been taught to blame himself for other people's mistreatment of him, he had simply ignored the possibility that his wife had problems of her own and instead concentrated solely on the question of what he had done to embitter her. Raised to a fine art, this process of self-blame had led him to consider himself a selfish and faithless hedonist—which had been, incidentally, his role in his nuclear family—and had protected him against the experience of rage he would have felt had he let himself view her as a shrew.

In spite of his undeniable assets and potential, he was dimly aware that his current adjustment rested on rather shaky foundations. For most of his life, his mother had been both seriously alcoholic and depressed while bearing seven children (of whom he was second). Her emotional unavailability to him had caused him to turn for support and nurturance toward his father, who was hardly fit to give them. A giant of a man at 6'5" and 250 pounds, he had a booming bass voice and a swaggering, frightening style. He spoke derisively of "skinny shits" who couldn't "screw" or drink and told his son that real men didn't yearn for closeness with or long to be comforted by their fathers. As might be expected from these transference paradigms, the patient's attitude toward me in the therapy alternated among a longing to be close, disappointment and anger at my supposed indifference, joyful camaraderie, and intense competitiveness.

All these aspects of the transference came sharply into focus when each of us became aware that the other was a dedicated runner. I do not recall how the subject first came up; I do remember that early in the treatment he began an hour by proudly announcing that he had run his first race, a 5-miler at a 6:05 pace. I also clearly remember the sharp pang of envy I felt at his announcement. But whether this was the first reference to running I am not now sure. He may have spied an issue of *Runner's World* in my office earlier, or I may have been even more directly exhibitionistic than this. When it comes to running, I seem temperamentally unable to keep my mouth shut, even though I am usually able to maintain some sort of therapeutic anonymity when I am talking about most other things. In any event, it was not long before the two of us were spending some of our time swapping training tips, injury stories, and racing times.

Evidently the thrust of this therapeutic development was too powerful to be contained within the confines of my office. It burst into flame in Hopkinton,

Massachusetts. Five minutes before the start of a Boston Marathon, he tapped me on the shoulder, chatted with me briefly, and wished me well. He told me he expected to come in about a half hour behind me. En route, I recall musing that he might be having trouble with the thought that he was so much faster than I. In fact, his marathon times were disproportionately slower than would have been predicted from his 5-mile times, in large measure because he had difficulty maintaining a lean racing weight—a legacy of his father's attitudes.

A few months later, as I was pounding exhaustedly toward the finish of a 10-kilometer race, he went streaking by me to nip me at the line by 5 seconds. Without my knowing it, he had been running 10 feet behind me the whole way, and had premeditated my humiliation. Afterward, he did not bother to disguise his pleasure. In a subsequent hour he himself suggested that, having done his penance at Boston, he could not feel free to run me into the ground. Could he have been whistling in the dark? Within weeks he had injured himself and had to postpone the third round of our competition for some time.

While he was injured, he spent one Thanksgiving morning traveling an hour and a half to watch a race in which he knew I would be running. He was aghast, and I quite pleased, to note that my 5-mile pace had picked up and was now beginning to rival his own. It turned out, however, that his appearance at the race had a deeper meaning. Earlier that morning he had attempted to engage his father in a serious conversation, to review troubled aspects of their past relationship, and to try to put it on a new footing. His father had been unable to follow step; he had misinterpreted his son's communications as an attack and had obviously felt hurt and defensive. After this, the patient impulsively decided to drive to the race. In a later hour he reconstructed that after the conversation he had felt a "deep, yawning hole" and had experienced an intense need to see me, a more accepting and understanding man. While in the car he had evidently suppressed this longing and concentrated instead on the race and on memories of his own running.

Some analysts would shudder at such an undisciplined departure from standard psychotherapeutic practice. Langs (1978), for example, would doubtless consider it a "bastion," an instance of a massive therapeutic misalliance. But I think it can be argued that in contrast with the usual bastion, our involvement in running was invariably turned to therapeutic advantage. Such was the patient's commitment to self-understanding that every encounter on the road, indeed every conversation about running was explored in therapy with regard to context, motivation, and function—even when I was more willing than he to continue to bask in the warmth of mutual resistance. I would prefer to think of the running issue not as a bastion but rather as a sweeping metaphor. Such disparate affects and motivations as competitiveness and longing to be close could be expressed in the language—not to mention the activity—of running. Perhaps, given the interlocking pathology of this particular patient and therapist, no other language could have been better suited to the purpose. Indeed, it was my impression that a good many steps had to be run and talked about before the major medium of affective exchange would move, as it eventually did, toward conventional therapeutic discourse.

The patient relied heavily on hypomanic defenses to combat the combined forces of guilt and object loss; he clearly felt that his running, when it was going well, lifted his spirits immeasurably. But it was not an altogether reliable device. When guilt or despair exceeded a certain level, he found he could barely run at all. Either he would injure himself, or he would be unable to summon the necessary discipline to get himself on the road. In the latter case, he would look on himself with self-loathing as he watched himself slowly lose conditioning and gain weight. Then, when the pain of despair and self-hate became too intense, he would force himself back on a diet and running regimen, which he would experience as a kind of mortification of the flesh. Slowly, his self-esteem would start to rise again.

In exploring this pattern, we came to understand that running and not running each had important derived meanings. Not running was equivalent to the shame of uncontrolled instinctual gratification, specifically that of infantile and adolescent masturbation; whereas running—the mortification of the flesh—was the self-punishment for these inadmissible urges. On the other hand, not running was often accompanied by a rueful sense of compulsive vengeance enacted upon the body, whereas running was sometimes experienced as a kind of bodily self-indulgence that had to be paid for with future lapses in training. Getting into shape was variously, or simultaneously, experienced as a selfish indulgence that took time away from the family, a hardening of the body with fantasies of increased potency and masculinity, and a loss of masculinity in association with the fantasy of being a "skinny shit." Getting out of shape was experienced as an externalization of his self-loathing, in which he took grim satisfaction, as a refuge from guilt, as a retreat from competition with me, and as a consolidation of his identification as a hard-drinking, brawling "real man."

The story of this therapy could have been told to illustrate the therapeutic value of running in depressed patients. In fact, it does and it doesn't. The patient certainly used many devices to attempt to relieve depression, running among them. But it did not strike me that running was a particularly effective device with this man. Although the depression was still mild, he would run well for a while and experience a transient euphoria and hopefulness. Eventually, however, the depression would deepen, and the attempt to relieve it through running would give out, only to be replaced by the even less effective mechanism of not running.

The story better exemplifies the multiple intrapsychic uses to which running may be put—defensive, adaptive, instinct-gratifying, and metaphorical. It also illustrates a highly condensed language with which a particular patient and therapist were able to organize their perceptions of each other. Finally, it demonstrates the difficulty of making valid objective observations on the psychological functions of running when the therapist-observer is as neurotically involved with it as the patient. The best we can presently hope for is a more thorough appreciation of the complexity of the problem.

I do not advise my depressed patients to run. But I don't exactly discourage them either. If running helps me more than it helps them, that is probably because, in general, I am not quite so depressed to begin with.

References

Altshul, V.A. The ego-integrative (and disintegrative) aspects of long-distance running. *Current Concepts in Psychiatry*, 1978, **4**,(4).

Langs, R. *The listening process*. New York: Jason Aronson, 1978.

CHAPTER 5

Anxiety Reduction Following Exercise and Meditation

Michael S. Bahrke and William P. Morgan

Psychological problems involving anxiety states have been estimated to be from 2 to 4% in the general population and from 16 to 25% in psychiatric patient samples (Lader, 1972; Pitts, 1969; Wilkinson & Latif, 1974). Furthermore, it has been estimated that 30 to 70% of all patients currently being treated by physicians in general practice are suffering from conditions which have their origins in unrelieved stress (Pitts, 1969). The prevalence of anxiety states makes it readily apparent that anxiety represents one of contemporary society's major health problems.

Therapies of various types, including autogenic training, biofeedback, drugs, hypnosis, exercise, meditation, and various relaxation techniques have been employed as a means of reducing anxiety. In this context it is noteworthy that acute physical activity (Byrd, 1965; de Vries, 1968; de Vries & Adams, 1972; Morgan, 1973, 1978) and meditation or relaxation techniques (Benson, 1975; Benson, Steinert, Greenwood, Klemchuk, & Peterson, 1975; Benson & Wallace, 1972; Ferguson & Gowan, 1975; Wallace, 1970; Wallace & Benson, 1972), two seemingly divergent therapies, are both capable of reducing tension and improving psychological states. This becomes an important theoretical point when one considers that meditation and relaxation techniques produce quiescence, whereas exercise produces the converse, arousal. Hence, two procedures representing opposite ends of the quiescence-arousal continuum produce a similar effect—anxiety reduction. The assumption made, however, that peripheral neurophysical and biochemical changes reflect central alterations, is debatable and certainly not proven. In other words, it is possible that changes occurring centrally are not reflected peripherally. Also while both of these techniques produce a decrement in tension state there has been no direct comparison of these two divergent therapies heretofore.

The primary purpose of this investigation was to compare the effects of acute physical activity and noncultic meditation on state anxiety. The secondary purpose was to assess the influence of differential anxiety states on the anxiety response.

Method

Subjects

The subjects consisted of 75 regularly exercising adult male volunteers. Subjects' ages ranged between 22 and 71 years with a mean of 51.9 years. The mean height and weight of this sample were 177.6 cm $(SD = 6.5)$ and 78.4 kg $(SD = 9.7)$, respectively.

Procedure

The experimental protocol was described to each subject with the understanding that random assignment to one of the following three groups would follow: (a) exercise, (b) meditation, or (c) quiet rest (control). Subjects were asked to sign an informed consent document and complete a 24-hour history dealing with consummatory behavior and activity during the previous day as well as their general state of health. Prior to being randomly assigned to a group, anxiety was assessed by completion of the STAI X-1 (State) and STAI X-2 (Trait) (Spielberger, Gorsuch, & Lushene, 1970). State anxiety (STAI X-1) was also measured immediately following and 10 minutes following each experimental session. Electrodes for monitoring and recording cardiac frequency were placed in a C-5 position.

Treatment Conditions

Subjects in the exercise group $(N = 25)$ walked for 20 minutes on a motor-driven treadmill at 70% of their self-imposed maximal heart rate (MHR) following 3 minutes of warm-up. Seventy percent of MHR was calculated from each subject's most recent modified Balke Treadmill Test (Balke & Ware, 1959). Subjects rated their perceived exertion at 5 minute intervals during exercise according to Borg's revised psychophysical scale (Borg, 1973). A 3-minute "warm-down" followed each exercise walk. Heart rate was recorded during the final 15 seconds of each minute using a Gilson Recorder. Postexercise state anxiety was obtained immediately and 10 minutes following exercise. Systolic and diastolic blood pressure were also measured 10 minutes after cessation of exercise.

Subjects in the meditation group ($N = 25$) received tape-recorded instructions describing the Relaxation Response (Benson, 1975), and they practiced the technique while seated in a standard "Lazyboy" recliner. Resting metabolism (oxygen consumption) was continuously monitored by means of a Webb Metabolic Rate Monitor (MRM), and skin temperature was measured throughout meditation with a United Systems Digitec digital thermometer. Electrode placement for skin temperature was 1 inch proximal to the right wrist on the dorsal side, and skin temperature was recorded at 2-minute intervals. Heart rate was continuously recorded on a Gilson polygraph recorder with the final 15 seconds of each minute used to determine cardiac frequency. As in the exercise session state anxiety was measured immediately following and again 10 minutes following the session. Blood pressure was obtained at the completion of the 10 minute time interval as well.

The control group ($N = 25$) rested quietly for 20 minutes in the recliner and subjects were provided a current issue of the *Reader's Digest* to read during this period if they so desired. The magazine contained no articles relating to relaxation, exercise, or cardiovascular health. Oxygen consumption, heart rate, and skin temperature were monitored and recorded as described earlier for the meditation procedure. State anxiety levels were assessed immediately and 10 minutes following this session by means of the STAI (Spielberger et al., 1970).

Means, standard deviations, and standard errors were computed for each variable. A series of two-way repeated measures ANOVAs for blood pressure, state anxiety, skin temperature, heart rate, and oxygen consumption was performed. In cases where significant F ratios ($p < .05$) were observed, a probe of the means was carried out utilizing the Newman-Keuls procedure (Winer, 1971).

The results of the primary analysis are summarized in Figure 1. State anxiety decreased across time for the exercise, meditation, and control groups. A two-way repeated measures analysis of variance (Winer, 1971) demonstrated a significant decrease ($p < .05$) in state anxiety across time ($F = 48.94$). No significant differences ($p < .05$) were demonstrated between groups ($F = 1.82$) or for the interaction between time and group ($F = .32$).

When the three groups were combined and subjects were divided into high- ($N = 10$) and low- ($N = 10$) anxious categories based upon their initial level of trait anxiety, mean state anxiety values decreased significantly ($p < .05$) in both the high trait anxious (41.7 to 31.8) and in the low trait anxious subjects (27.4 to 22.0) across trials ($F = 27.02$). An additional analysis was carried out in which the *state* anxiety response of four high *trait* anxious sub-

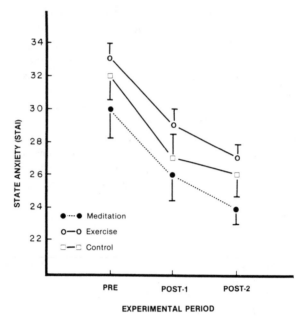

Figure 1. State anxiety before and following exercise, meditation, and control treatments.

jects from each group was evaluated. A significant ($p < .05$) decrement in state anxiety was observed for the three groups across trials ($F = 9.79$), but the group ($F = 1.20$) and group by trials interaction ($F = .29$) effects were not significant. An evaluation of state anxiety responsivity in high ($N = 11$) and low ($N = 11$) state anxious subjects revealed that state anxiety decreased significantly ($p < .05$) for the high-anxious (44.7 to 32.1) but remained virtually unchanged for the low-anxious subjects. This resulted in significant F ratios for groups ($F = 102.53$), trials ($F = 16.80$), and groups by trials interaction ($F = 14.72$). The nature of this interaction rules out statistical regression since the high-anxious decreased substantially, whereas the low-anxious did not change.

A small increase in skin temperatures occurred for both the control and meditation groups. A two-way repeated measures ANOVA (25) demonstrated a significant difference ($p < .05$) across time within groups ($F = 6.73$) but no significant differences between groups ($F = .71$), nor interaction for time and group ($F = 1.28$). The temperature of the test room was stable, having a standard error of .99°C across the 20 minutes for the control session and a standard error of .73°C for the meditation session. The increased skin temperature can be taken to reflect a state of relaxation, and as such offers physiologic support for the self-report or state anxiety data. However, it should be emphasized that the meditation and control groups did not differ in this respect.

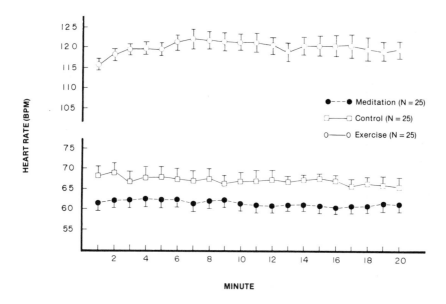

Figure 2. Heart rate in beats per minute during exercise, meditation, and control treatments.

The response of heart rate to the three sessions is illustrated in Figure 2. A relatively constant heart rate occurred in each session. Initial values for the meditation group were lower than those of the control and exercise groups and remained lower throughout the sessions. Final values were also lower in the meditation group than those of the control and exercise groups. A two-way repeated measures ANOVA demonstrated a significant difference ($p <$ .05) between the three groups ($F = 261.77$), and the Newman-Keuls procedure showed the meditation and control groups to differ significantly ($p <$ .05) from the exercise group. However, no significant difference was demonstrated between the control and meditation groups. No significant difference ($p < .05$) was demonstrated across time for the groups ($F = 1.74$), but the interaction of time and group was significant ($p < .05$). This interaction was due to the increase in heart rate of approximately 5 bpm across the first 6 minutes for the exercise group. It will be noted in Figure 2, however, that the exercise group achieved a virtual steady state after the fifth minute of exercise. The failure of heart rate to decrease following the meditation or control period can be explained by the observation that cardiac frequency was quite low in the two groups from the very outset (61-67 bpm). While heart rate is often employed in psychophysiology as a somatic indicant of anxiety, it often proves to be an inappropriate measure. The present case is an example.

The consumption of oxygen across the 20 minute period for the control and meditation groups is illustrated in Figure 3. Data are presented for only

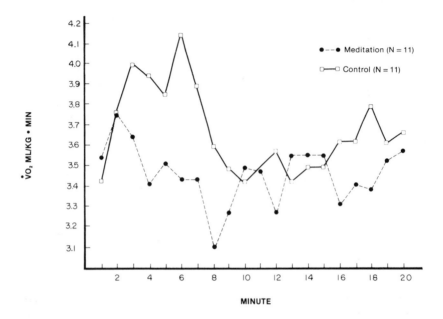

Figure 3. Oxygen consumption during meditation and control treatments.

11 subjects in each of these groups owing to equipment malfunction during the testing of 14 subjects from each group. Following a moderate increase in oxygen consumption, a decrease and then a plateau occurred for each group. The subjects in the meditation group, however, initially consumed less oxygen than did subjects in the control group, but after approximately 10 minutes the oxygen consumption values of both groups were very similar. A two-way repeated measures ANOVA (Winer, 1971) demonstrated no significant differences ($P > .05$) between groups ($F = .01$), across time for each group ($F = 1.00$), nor for the interaction of time and group ($F = .86$).

Discussion

The results of the present inquiry support the expectation that acute physical activity can reduce state anxiety. This study further corroborates the existing literature which presents evidence that decreases in state anxiety follow acute physical activity of a vigorous nature (Morgan, 1973; Morgan & Horstman, 1976).

It is important to note that in the present investigation state anxiety was also reduced in those subjects judged to be either high trait or high state anxious. This result is in agreement with the anxiety reduction reported by Morgan (1973) in that those subjects falling within the normal range on anxiety, as well as those classified as high-anxious, experienced decrements. In contrast, Sime (1977) was unable to demonstrate a significant decrease in anxiety following acute exercise. However, previous research has shown that light or moderate exercise does not have an influence on state anxiety (Morgan, Roberts, & Feinerman, 1971) and, therefore, decrements in state anxiety would not have been predicted in Sime's study. The exercise stimulus used in the present study required a strenuous level of activity (70% self-imposed MHR).

The present data support the earlier work of Ferguson and Gowan (1975) and Lazar, Farwell, and Farrow (1975), who reported that meditation (TM) resulted in reduced anxiety. These data, however, are in disagreement with the recent report by Sime (1977), who failed to observe a decrement in state anxiety following the same form of "noncultic" meditation (Benson, 1975) employed in the present investigation. The apparent disagreement may be due to the fact that Sime (1977) employed meditation within a stress paradigm involving test-induced anxiety, whereas the present study was presumably devoid of pretreatment stress.

Physiological response to the meditation treatment does not support the findings of Wallace (1970), Wallace and Benson (1972), Benson and Wallace (1972), and Benson (1975). These investigators have reported decreases in oxygen consumption and heart rate following both Transcendental Meditation (TM) (Wallace, 1970; Wallace & Benson, 1972) and "noncultic" meditation (Benson et al., 1975), which has been labeled the relaxation response (RR) by Benson (1975). In the present investigation a decrease in oxygen consumption occurred during the meditation period, but the decrease was small and nonsignificant. It will also be recalled that heart rate was quite constant throughout the 20 minutes of meditation in this study. It should be pointed out that every effort was made in the present investigation to obtain *accurate* as opposed to *pseudo* baselines from the outset. In other words, the subjects rested quietly for a period of 20 minutes *before* the meditation or control procedure began. Had the experimental period begun as soon as they assumed a resting position in the chair it is likely that a substantial decrease in metabolism and heart rate would have occurred.

Perhaps the most important observation in this investigation, and a truly serendipitous finding in our view, was the decrement in state anxiety which accompanied the control treatment. The psychophysiologic responsivity of the control subjects was identical with that of the meditation group. Earlier research has demonstrated that both acute physical activity (Morgan, 1973; Morgan & Horstman, 1976) and meditation (Ferguson & Gowan, 1975; Lazar et al., 1975) are capable of reducing anxiety. The primary purpose of the present investigation was to evaluate the comparative efficacy of vigorous exercise (70% self-imposed MHR) and a popular meditation procedure known as the relaxation response (Benson, 1975) in their ability to reduce state anxiety. In other words, two seemingly different procedures, one designed to provoke arousal (e.g., physical activity), and the other quiescence (e.g., meditation), are commonly used to reduce tension states. A rather basic and important question in our view related to the comparative effectiveness of the two procedures. The use of a control or placebo[1] group was simply employed in order to quantify the extent to which the Hawthorne effect, or any *treatment* vs. *no treatment* (Morgan, 1972), was operative.

The present results and the recent reports by Michaels, Huber, and McCann (1976) and de Vries, Burke, Hopper, and Sloan (1977) suggest that simply taking "time out" is just as effective as exercise, biofeedback, or meditation (cultic or noncultic) in reducing anxiety. Furthermore, this appears to be the case whether anxiety is operationalized in a traditional psychometric sense (present study), biochemically (Michaels et al., 1976), or neurophysiologically (de Vries et al., 1977).

In many respects the present findings, along with those of Michaels et al. (1976) and de Vries et al. (1977), raise far more questions about anxiety states than they provide answers. First of all, these investigations support the widely held beliefs that exercise, biofeedback, and meditation are capable of reducing anxiety, but these studies finally, in a compelling fashion, force the basic and fundamental issue of *why*. If these procedures reduce anxiety, and they are clearly *associated* with anxiety decrements, is there evidence of *causality?* In other words, do these treatments *cause* the tension reduction to occur, or are they simply *associated* with the lowered anxiety? While the assumption appears to be one of a causal function in both the exercise and meditation literature, there has surprisingly been no apparent evidence advanced in support of causality.

The question of causality has major theoretical, as well as applied implications. The basis of beneficence, for example, resulting from exercise and meditation may not rest in the physiologic changes provoked by such procedures, but rather in the *diversional* aspects of such activities. It is conceivable that "time-out" therapy, whether in the form of exercise, meditation, biofeedback, or simple rest breaks, may represent the effective ingredient in therapies designed to reduce anxiety. There are, of course, many questions which should be addressed prior to adopting the view that "time-out" therapy is just as effective as more traditional therapies. The time course or decay of the response following various treatments must certainly be explored. It is possible, for example, that while "time-out" is just as effective as exercise in reducing anxiety, the decrement following exercise may be sustained for a longer period. In other words, the quantity of the shift may be similar, whereas the quality may differ. In addition, the long-term or chronic effects of

---

[1] In view of the fact that subjects in the "control" group were treated exactly the same as subjects in the meditation group, with the exception that they were not introduced to the meditation procedure, it might be more appropriate to regard the "control" group as a "placebo" group. The "control" subjects were also seated in a sound-filtered room for a 20-minute period in a comfortable reclining chair while oxygen consumption, heart rate, and skin temperature were monitored.

such acute changes may differ owing to the additive nature of such divergent therapies. Finally, another important consideration relates to the target population; that is, "time-out," meditation, and exercise may differentially influence individuals who have adopted various lifestyles.

The present evidence suggests that acute physical activity, noncultic meditation, and a quiet rest are equally effective in reducing state anxiety. The finding that no difference exists between physical activity, meditation, and control treatments in terms of anxiety reduction has implications for therapeutic practice. For those unable or unwilling to exercise, meditation or a quiet rest could be effective therapy in reducing tension. Conversely, individuals opposed to meditation feel that physical activity possesses inherent physiological advantages not found in sedentary methods. The underlying cause for the reduction of anxiety following exercise, noncultic meditation, and quiet rest is open to speculation. There may be common internal or central mechanisms operating during exercise, meditation, and quiet rest. These mechanisms may go undetected by tools presently employed to assess tension levels. Perhaps taking "time-out" from the daily activities is in itself sufficient in reducing anxiety. It is concluded that vigorous physical activity of an acute nature, noncultic meditation, and quiet rest periods are equally effective in reducing state anxiety, and this holds for individuals who fall within the normal range on anxiety, as well as those who are elevated on state and/or trait anxiety.

References

Balke, B., & Ware, R.W. An experimental study of physical fitness of Air Force personnel. *U.S. Armed Forces Medical Journal,* 1959, **10,** 675-688.

Benson, H. *The relaxation response.* New York: William Morrow, 1975.

Benson, H., Steinert, R.F., Greenwood, M.M., Klemchuck, H.M., & Peterson, N.H. Continuous measurement of oxygen consumption and carbon dioxide elimination during a wakeful hypometabolic state. *Journal of Human Stress,* 1975, **1,** 37-44.

Benson, H., & Wallace, R.K. Decreased blood pressure in hypertensive subjects who practice meditation. Supplement II to *Circulation 45* and *46,* 1972.

Borg, G. Perceived exertion: A note on "history and methods." *Medicine and Science in Sports,* 1973, **5,** 90-93.

Byrd, O.E. The relief of tension by exercise: A survey of medical viewpoints and practices. *Journal of School Health,* 1965, **43,** 239-240.

de Vries, H.A. Immediate and long-term effects of exercise upon resting muscle action potential level. *Journal of Sports Medicine and Physical Fitness,* 1968, **8,** 1-11.

de Vries, H.A., & Adams, G.M. Electromyographic comparison of single dose of exercise and meprobamate as to effect on muscular relaxation.

American Journal of Physical Medicine, 1972, **51**, 130-141.

de Vries, H.A., Burke, R.K., Hopper, R.T., & Sloan, J.H. Efficacy of EMG biofeedback in relaxation training. *American Journal of Physical Medicine*, 1977, **56**, 75-81.

Ferguson, P.C., & Gowan, J.C. Psychological findings on transcendental meditation. *Scientific Research on the Transcendental Meditation Program*, Switzerland, MERU Press Publication, 1975. (1, Number S 180)

Lader, M. The nature of anxiety. *British Journal of Psychiatry*, 1972, **121**, 481-491.

Lazar, Z., Farwell, W., & Farrow, J. The effects of the transcendental meditation program on anxiety, drug abuse, cigarette smoking, and alcohol consumption. *Scientific Research on the Transcendental Meditation Program*, Switzerland, MERU Press Publication, 1975. (1, Number S 180)

Michaels, R.R., Huber, M.J., & McCann, D.S. Evaluation of transcendental meditation as a method of reducing stress. *Science*, 1976, **192**, 1242-1244.

Morgan, W.P. Basic considerations. In W. P. Morgan (Ed.), *Ergogenic aids and muscular performance*. New York: Academic Press, 1972.

Morgan, W.P. Influence of acute physical activity on state anxiety. *Proceedings of the National College Physical Education Association for Men*, January 1973, pp. 114-121.

Morgan, W.P. Sport personology: The credulous-skeptical argument in perspective. In A.H. Ismail (Ed.), *Psycho-social behavior of sport and play*. Indianapolis: Indiana State Board of Health, 1978.

Morgan, W.P., & Horstman, D.H. Anxiety reduction following acute physical activity. *Medicine and Science in Sports*, 1976, **8**, 62.

Morgan, W.P., Roberts, J.A., & Feinerman, A.D. Psychologic effect of acute physical activity. *Archives of Physical Medicine and Rehabilitation*, 1971, **52**, 422-425.

Pitts, F.N. The biochemistry of anxiety. *Scientific American*, 1969, **220**, 69-75.

Sime, W.E. A comparison of exercise and meditation in reducing physiological response to stress. *Medicine and Science in Sports*, 1977, **9**, 55.

Spielberger, C.D., Gorsuch, R.L., & Lushene, R.E. *Manual for the State-Trait Anxiety Inventory (STAI)*. Palo Alto, CA: Consulting Psychologists Press, 1970.

Wallace, R.K. Physiological effects of transcendental meditation. *Science*, 1970, **167**, 1751-1754.

Wallace, R.K., & Benson, H. The physiology of meditation. *Scientific American*, 1972, **226**, 84-90.

Wilkinson, J.C.M., & Latif, K. *Common neuroses in general practice*. Bristol, England: John Wright and Sons, 1974.

Winer, B.J. *Statistical principles in experimental design*. New York: McGraw-Hill, 1971.

SECTION TWO

Psychodynamics of Running

The papers in this section focus on the psychodynamic aspects of running and analyze various motivations that may lead people to run and sustain them at it. For these authors, running is not simply running—it is a complex intrapsychic drama that includes figures from the past, idealized images of the self and others, and past triumphs and humiliations. Although the runner is dramatist, director, and actor in this drama, he or she may be aware of only a small part of it. Much of runners' mental activity may be outside of their consciousness and only vaguely perceived in fleeting sensations and thoughts derived from the unconscious fantasy-drama. For the contributors in this section, running is similar to dreaming, in which the richness of past and present gratifications and frustrations are elaborated into a story the dreamer may only partially recall on awakening.

In Chapter 6, Perry and Sacks, in their examination of the running syndrome of Dr. S. P., emphasize the play aspects of running. Utilizing a psychodynamic approach, they emphasize that the critical factor in play is its unreality: It doesn't count because it is "only a game." This unreal or "not counting" quality of running frees runners to experience a wide range of fantasies which might otherwise be unacceptable to their conscience and to society. In addition to providing an opportunity for playful symbolic activity, Perry and Sacks find in running a remembrance of the early experiences of toddlers excitedly taking their first steps. This provides running with a unique quality not found in other forms of play, active or sedentary, such as swimming or card playing.

John Sours, in Chapter 7, draws attention to the remarkable resemblance between many long-distance runners and individuals with anorexia nervosa. Fear of being fat, a tense preoccupation with thinness, and a pleasure in constant motoric activity provide intriguing similarities. Sours speculates that the runner, like the anorectic, is attempting to flee from feelings of isolation, worthlessness, and inadequacy by striving to attain a perfect physical image. To Sours, it is an imperfect solution for both the runner and the anorectic.

Thaddeus Kostrubala, the author of Chapter 8, is one of the earliest clinicians to have described the therapeutic aspects of running. In his book, *The Joy of Running*, he drew attention to the antidepressant and antianxiety aspects of running and proposed it as a new and important therapeutic modality. In his contribution to this book, Dr. Kostrubala views running as a special kind of delusion that enables one to surmount intrapsychic and intrapersonal pain. It is a delusion, however, that may be necessary as well as beneficial. Kostrubala claims that we all need to believe in something magical and ultimate, and running is the currently fashionable "ultimate," one which has much to recommend it because it contributes to health and mental well-being.

In the last article in this section, Berger and Mackenzie present the complexity of the psychodynamic meanings of running in a detailed examination of a female runner. They show how the meaning of her running shifts from the present to the past and back, and how it relates to a special relationship with the woman's father. The authors discuss how running has within it the entire drama of the woman's family in her childhood and its relevance to her present life.

An overview of these four articles from a psychodynamic perspective suggests that running can lend itself to any meaning or significance the runner wishes to project into it. This concept is very much in keeping with psychodynamic theory and its emphasis on the plasticity of behavior in representing conflicts and fantasies. Certainly this could explain the immense popularity of the sport among so many different people, each of them finding in their running a meaning special to their own history and character. Still, one cannot help but wonder if there is something specific to running, a question which needs comparative study. For example, how does the search for perfection by runners who are preoccupied with being as thin as possible compare with the fantasies of body builders who search for perfection by carefully sculpting their body? Whether there is something specific in the physiology and chemistry of running that differentiates it from other physical activities is a problem addressed further in other sections (particularly Section 5) in this volume.

CHAPTER 6

Psychodynamics of Running

Samuel W. Perry and Michael H. Sacks

We have all been told by now the many reasons why we should run—to stay fit, live longer, reduce tension, and prevent or cure heart attacks, headaches, depression, constipation, marital discord, varicose veins, or any number of problems. It seems as though every time someone with a problem puts on a pair of running shoes, the list of running cures becomes longer. This paper will not add to that list. We do not plan to discuss why people *should* run, rather, we will discuss why people *do* run—which is quite a different matter.

As psychoanalysts, we suspect that many people run for reasons outside of their awareness, that are unconscious. A person may say that he runs to lose weight or she runs to meet guys, but that may not be the whole story. For example, a runner one of us recently saw in his office illustrates in the brightest of colors how running for many people goes beyond being something one should do and becomes an activity one *must* do. We will use his Runner's Syndrome as a starting point and then take off from there for a misty-morning jaunt through the psychodynamics of running.

The Case of Dr. P.

Dr. S. P., a 37-year-old physician, was first admitted into the runner's world 2 years ago. At that time, Dr. P. considered himself in good health, suffering no more than the miseries of everyday life. He did have occasional twinges of neurotic pain, but he thought of these quirks as no more than nostalgic reminders of all he had accomplished during his many years of psychoanalysis. Having accumulated a rewarding private practice, acquired a respectful academic position, and settled with his loving wife and children into a pleasurable suburban life, Dr. P. had reason to be satisfied with who he was and where he was going.

And then it happened: One day Dr. P. decided to take a jog . . . a couple of days later, another jog . . . then another . . . well, perhaps you know the rest. Why did he start? He's not sure. A friend's suggestion? To get in shape? To stop smoking? To join the fad? He gave these and other answers at different times, but no answer ever seemed completely satisfactory. He couldn't explain why he ran any more than he could explain why he caught a cold. It just happened—not all at once, but gradually out of nowhere, like a wave taking form far out at sea. We will not describe for you the insidious progression of his Runner's Syndrome (although Dr. P. himself would be more than willing to provide a mile-by-mile account in boring detail). We will only say that whereas the first jogs seemed to Dr. P. painful interruptions in his busy day, a year later life itself seemed a painful interruption eclipsed between his daily runs.

As his conditioning improved and his runs extended into one suburban town and then another, his expectations extended as well. After a few months, the 3-hour marathon became for him an illusive white whale. Like Ahab consumed with the quest, Dr. P. spent hour after hour planning his runs, charting the courses, gluing his shoes, stretching his body; meanwhile his job, family, and friends became tolerable intrusions in this more meaningful pursuit. Medical journals were left unopened, but running literature—even advertisements and results of races in areas unknown—were read, then reread thoroughly. Aspects of medicine he had considered previously with either indifference or contempt began to fascinate him: nutrition, podiatry, lipid metabolism, muscle physiology, respiratory function, and so on. This knowledge was not acquired in the abstract. On the contrary, Dr. P. applied every tidbit of information to himself; his body became a laboratory for unsystematic experiments with vitamins, body fat percentage, aspirin, electrolytes, glycogen storage, and so on. His training schedule took on the logistical considerations of the Normandy Invasion with calculations of intervals, fartlek, distance, hills, surfaces . . . and on it went.

Of course, Dr. P.'s behavior aroused the concern of his professional colleagues. They worried if his loss of weight, social withdrawal, and mystical gaze were signs of a dreadful illness or heralded an imminent breakdown. When asked what in God's name was going on, Dr. P. could only shrug and say, "I run." The reply left friends bewildered and frustrated. Their pleas for him "to grow up" were simply ignored.

This distress of colleagues and friends was nothing compared with the distress of Dr. P. himself. Whatever his original reasons for jogging, they now had faded from view. It was not that running made him feel so good; it was that not running made him feel so bad. He now ran because he had to run. Like a junkie, he craved his daily run at a cost to family, job, and other parts of his life. Without it, he became despondent, irritable, and preoccupied with the run that had been withheld. Also like a junkie, he hated the very thing he craved: those first hundred yards on stiff limbs in the bitter cold of a winter morning, the cooked calf muscles in the scorching sun of a summer's run, and the constantly crippling injuries—a sore hip, a swollen knee, a torn Achilles. Yet, afraid he would rot if he stopped, determined to continue on his quest without a conquest, Dr. P. wandered into the office for some advice. Because he was not interested in getting treatment for his Runner's Syndrome, but only wanted to find out why people run, he was advised to find a colleague and write a paper on the psychodynamics of running.

Running as Play

Where can we begin in trying to understand psychodynamically this perplexing behavior of Dr. P.? For openers, we can say that there is something childlike about his dedication to running. We can understand how his friends would urge him "to grow up," and we can appreciate how the word sport actually comes from *disport,* which means to carry away from work. There is a contrast between Dr. P.'s adult work and his "child's play," a contrast Dr. Sheehan eloquently describes:

> Like most distance runners, I am still a child. And never more so than when I run. I take that play more seriously than anything else I do. And in that play I retire into a fantasy land of my imagination anytime I please. Like most children, I think I control my life. I believe myself to be independent. I am certain I have been placed on this earth to enjoy myself, the best of all possible worlds, a world made for running and racing, where nothing but good can happen. And, like most children, I am oblivious to all of the work done by the other people to make it that way. (Sheehan, 1978, p. 211)

Along with saying that Dr. P. engaged in some form of play, we can also say that running has become especially meaningful for him. He appears driven by inner forces he cannot fully explain. Physical fitness may have been the reason he started to jog—that's unclear—but, at this point, to say he runs to stay in shape would be like saying Michelangelo sculptured to build up his forearms. Running has a meaning for him which goes beyond simply moving fast down a road. And we can say running itself has something which has caused this change in Dr. P.'s life. Although he has had some fun in the past swinging a golf club or a tennis racquet, no other sport had ever got hold of him the way running has.

Let us now explore these opening points in more detail: because we stated that Dr. P. is "at play," we will take a closer look at what play really is; and because we noted that Dr. P.'s play is especially meaningful for him, we will speculate about what that special meaning may be; and finally, because we saw that running captured him in a way no other sport ever did, we will try to understand what is unique about running that got Dr. P. into such a state.

What Play Is

Defining play is not so simple as it first appears. Asked what play is, many quickly answer that it is just having fun, but then they think for a moment and realize their answer isn't really adequate. After all, people can put a lot of intense strain and pain into play and look like they're having anything but fun. And the opposite is true as well; people who are not playing a game have fun in many other ways: watching movies, working, going to dinner parties, having sex, making jokes, raking leaves. Clearly, there is more to play than fun.

Searching for a more thoughtful answer, Johan Huizinga (1950) studied many different cultures to find the essential ingredients of play. He concluded that above all else the primary requirement of play was that it produced nothing in the real world. Certainly, play can have goals—a score in rugby, soccer, or hockey is called a goal—but the goals represent nothing off the field. Mark Twain conveyed this same idea in his glib remark that play is an activity full of meaning but with no purpose. In fact, once the attainment of a goal becomes the central reason for the activity—making a buck or cleaning out the coronaries—it is no longer play; it is a task and more related to work than play. The concept sounds simple enough, but on reflection, it becomes clear that play is the one thing no one can ever make another do; once it's not voluntary, once it is for something or someone else, it is not play.

Closely related to the apparent absence of any utility to play is the separation from the real world. This is why play is the traditional activity of children, who are not yet expected to participate and shoulder the burdens of reality. It is also why play requires its own special space and time—the playground—a make believe world with its own boundaries, time, rules, and order. Whether it be a backgammon board or a baseball field, all play has an ideal "magical circle" removed from the imperfect and confusing "real" world.

Huizinga also appreciated a third requirement of play. Although it is a purposeless activity in a make-believe world, the feelings expressed in play can be very real and very intense. On this playground, "the thrill of victory and the agony of defeat" are felt as intensely if not more so than anywhere else. Play can be a fun activity, but it also can be quite serious, hard work, and filled with the range of emotions which characterize the human experience. These emotions don't count, however, because they are part of the game. You can "murder" your opponent, but when the game is over you both go home together looking forward to the next match. The opposite of play is therefore not seriousness; the opposite of play is reality.

Why We Play

Although Huizinga descriptively characterized the main features of play, he did not explain why we do it. In fact, those interested in why people behave in the way they do—philosophers, psychologists, biologists, and ethologists—have largely ignored the issue because play seemed so frivolous an activity. A few, however, became intrigued for this very reason; if play is not useful, why do we do it? Darwin was intrigued by the apparent unrelatedness of play to the survival of the species. Carl Gross offered one solution to this problem, proposing that play offered a chance to practice important instincts, such as fighting or courting rituals which enabled the player to prepare for adult survival. Other attempts to find a meaning in play are too numerous to enumerate. They have included relaxation for the purpose of recuperation, a discharge of surplus energy, a method for learning new cognitive skills, a way of insuring socialization, a mechanism for maintaining psychological arousal, and an activity which fosters a sense of competence. These and other theories are excellently summarized by M. J. Ellis (1973) in *Why People Play*. The model which seems to us to be the most satisfactory explanation of human behavior is psychoanalytic with its insights regarding the significant influence of unconscious factors on human behavior. It is the model which we will use to further explore the significance of play.

The earliest effort by psychoanalysis to understand play made reference to "instinct theory." In this early formation, human beings are seen as trying to keep sexual and aggressive drives under control. If the lid is kept on too tightly, however, the result is anxiety or the partial discharge of the drives transformed into symptoms like obsessive neatness, or physical problems like headaches and weakness.

Using this instinct model, analysts thought play provided an acceptable way to let off steam. The idea is not so farfetched. Many teenagers, as hormones start to surge, are advised to take up sports as a distraction from sex; and many games have a foreplay tension and rise to a climax, followed by release and relaxation. As for giving us a channel to discharge anger, play is often invested with this capacity. An illustration of this concept is a comment made by one incredulous runner to another: "Can you imagine, the guy runs 10 miles a day and he's *still* a bastard!"

Although the instinct theory helps explain the tremendous energy put into sports, the explanation is not adequate. If nothing were involved besides the discharge of energy, one could simply pound a tree or do push-ups. Clearly, play involves more than that.

A second analytic theory—the "structural model"—states that not only do our egos have to contend with the push from unconscious forces (the id), we also must contend with our own consciences (superegos) which can come down on us hard. Applying this model, analysts argued play gave us a holiday from the prohibitions of our own consciences, what Erickson (1963) has called a "vacation from reality." Because play gives us an opportunity to express what is often inhibited in the real world, Dr. P. can run through suburbia with nothing but shorts and shoes, and he can talk openly and acceptably about wanting to kill a rival in the next race. Outside of the unreal world of play, these exhibitionistic and murderous feelings would have to be contained because of their social unacceptability. Murdering one's adversary in a distance race does not result in the consequences it would at work or love. After all, the race is just a "game" even though the murderous feeling was quite real in its intensity.

A more recent analytic theory—the "object relations model"—emphasizes the importance of childhood experiences and especially the relationship to early caretakers in influencing the way we see the world and ourselves as adults. Because these theorists focus on very early experiences—before words and before more rational thinking—one has to be willing to imagine and speculate, but they do have some interesting notions about the meaning of play. For instance, Winnicott—a pediatrician turned psychiatrist—watched children at play and thought about how and why they did it. He realized that as infants develop neurologically and psychologically and become more aware of what's happening, they are confronted with an awesome truth: The real world just isn't what they wish it to be. The gratifying mother may not be there the instant they want her, pain may be around every sharp corner, and wishing or crying doesn't always bring comfort and relief. At some point, infants have to appreciate the limitations of the world and of themselves. The blissful, all-providing infant-mother oneness must inevitably come to an end.

According to Winnicott, when children come to this recognition—and it happens gradually—they *pretend* to make the going a bit easier (Winnicott, 1953, 1967). Pretending helps make the transition from the world we want to the world that is. The earliest kinds of pretending are, of course, not very sophisticated. Take a teddy bear or a blanket, for example; a 3-year-old knows that the little doll is not magically going to make everything come out perfectly, keep away monsters, and make sure mother is always around. The child is saying, "Look, that real world out there is tough, too tough for me right now. So give me a break, let me play my silly games and make-believe." This capacity to make-believe in order to soften the harshness of the real world continues into the adult world in play. Play provides the adult, like the child, with a temporary suspension of reality. It gives adults the opportunity to gratify wishes and fantasies which might not be acceptable in the real world because of personal limitation or societal constraints. Where else can you escape the inevitable decline of age by a run on a summer day that in fantasy finishes in the Olympic Stadium where millions cheer your victory and the setting of a new world record?

Like children, we pretend because we never can completely accept reality for what it is. Pretending is make-believe, an illusion. In fact, the word illusion means "in play," but it's an illusion we need to create. Our surburban runner,

Dr. P., despite his satisfying job, friends, wife, and kids, would readily admit his life is far from perfect. He must constantly struggle to accept limitations—the world's and his own. To seek temporary relief from that strain, he heads for the open road where he can make believe, where he can enter the "magic circle" and pretend the world is quite different than it really is, pretend that life is played by the rules, that time and space can be controlled, and that all things are possible and no record cannot be broken. Picasso said, "Art is the lie that tells the truth." For Dr. P., running is a similar lie, a created activity that seeks perfection while realizing it is impossible. George Sheehan plays the same game to contend with unavoidable limitations as he describes coming to a steep hill:

> I am fighting God. Fighting the limitations He gave me. Fighting the pain, fighting the unfairness. Fighting all the evil in me and the world. And I will not give in. I will conquer this hill and I will conquer it alone. (Sheehan, 1978, p. 247)

Why We Run

Having looked at what the requirements of play are and at some of the reasons we do it, we are left with the third question raised by Dr. P.: What is there about running that can make it particularly meaningful? Certainly no one would suggest running is meaningful and other games are not. Any form of play—chess to curling—can capture an illusion. But for Dr. P., running had an uncanny way of becoming invested with special meaning. Why?

Jim Fixx has proposed that running provides a relatedness to our evolutionary past: After our biological ancestors crawled out from the sea, we were shaped by evolution to catch or escape from prey by running; this basic movement thereby connects us to our earliest heritage (Fixx, 1977). Although we do not advocate that a new pair of Nikes puts us in touch with our prehistoric ancestors, we do agree that running does recapture the primal experience of our most distant past—the past not of our species, but of the individual. Again, we must look at our earliest experiences.

Developmentally, at the same time children are separating from that grand "oceanic" oneness with mother and are acquiring the mental equipment to figure out what reality is and is not, they are also acquiring the muscular ability to sit, stand, walk and, by basic movements, assert themselves against the world. Margaret Mahler (1966), a renowned child psychoanalyst, has studied young children and described the immense elation and feelings of invulnerability and power in those first few steps. Mahler notes that during this period children feel no pain when they fall. They rapidly get up and continue excitedly to push ahead, much to the joyful acclaim of their parents. This excitement is short-lived. They rapidly feel the constraints of gravity, the pain of a bruised knee and learn that they are not invulnerable. The initial inflated mastery of the world is deflated by a recognition of gravity.

We outlined earlier Winnicott's ideas about how a child—how all of us—must struggle to accept the limitations of reality and of ourselves, and how play is a way of separating from the real world and devising a make-believe, perfect world instead. We now can see how that struggle to accept what is possible and what is not becomes for children more than just a cognitive struggle, more than just a struggle going on between their ears. This struggle is occurring motorically as well. Before words and even before memory, moving upright reveals to children that same tension in life between mastery and limitations. But—and this point is crucial—more than just reveal-ing this tension, movement allows children to play out this struggle by asser-ting themselves against the world. Their early steps are usually away from the parents. Although it is important that parents be there—and children will fre-quently check this—children are now able to explore the world in a way they previously could not. They have indeed become all powerful. In this way, upright movement—walking or running—becomes a sort of primitive game, a way of pretending to be on top of the world as we once were when as toddlers we experienced the excitement of those first steps. Simultaneously, however, we vaguely recognize that this belief is an illusion and that "in reality" we are quite limited and very subject to stumbling.

What does this have to do with our established middle-aged physician, Dr. P.? Well, imagine that after only a few weeks of aerobic conditioning, Dr. P. found that if he ran slowly enough, if he did not press and just let it flow, he could feel—at least momentarily—as though he could run forever. In fact, he may have felt as though he were not running at all, as though his legs were ef-fortlessly carrying him, and for an instant or so, Dr. P. became impervious to the restraints of his body and of the world. At times he may have had only a hint of this sensation, a possibility; at other times, more carried away, Dr. P. may have reached a point where, like the youngest infant, he felt that the world was his to explore under the delighted and approving eyes of his proud parents.

But also like the young child, Dr. P.'s blissful feelings of elation and mastery could not last. As he went a little further or pushed a little harder, Dr. P. found this sensation of floating was replaced by the all-too-painful awareness of what his limitations really were: his heart pounded, his lungs gasped, his legs tired, and he struggled against the world rather than excitedly exploring it. He was no longer able to pretend, to make believe he could run forever. Gravity, not he, was the master. And with this intensified awareness of his body's aches and pains and of every little incline on the road, his illusionary sense of omnipotence collided with the harshness of the real world. As though awakening from a pleasant dream, a tiring Dr. P. discovered that his limitations could no longer be disavowed.

We have already described how this same collision between bliss and reality occurs in the very young child's first steps and how play provides a make-believe world to relieve this tension. We also stressed from the very start that other games can capture this same tension and be intensely invested with meaning. A perfect 2-iron shot 4 feet from the pin, a 70-yard pass completion, parallel skis clicking down an expert's slope, all can provide a momentary—though illusionary—sense of being master of the world. The love of sport, the endless hours of practice or vicarious spectating, are in part attempts to repeat these fantastic experiences and to gain mastery over them. However, one unique feature of running is that only a minimum of aerobic conditioning is required to recapture the early experience of pretending to be in control. Most other sports require inherent skill or hours of practice to simulate this childlike "prehistoric" experience. Running is different. Without inherited hand-eye coordination and without years of practice, someone like Dr. P. can become attached to running the way a young toddler becomes fascinated and later frustrated by those intriguing first few steps. Like those steps and like a teddy bear, running provides an accessible make-believe world, an opportunity to play with the tension between the magical bliss that was and the harsh reality that is.

Of course, these psychoanalytic expeditions into our deepest past do not totally explain why we run—and why others do not. There are less fanciful reasons as well, not the least of which is individual temperament. But before we simply leave it at that, let's go back to an earlier point about how play must be free and voluntary and about how the moment one is forced to play for something or someone else it is no longer play, but a task. Parents who have tried to make a child love a new, clean teddy bear instead of the dirty, old one he or she has come to cherish will appreciate how the make-believe cannot be enforced by another person. With this in mind, we can see how running can become invested with so much meaning: by its very nature, running has the potential to become one's personal, private creation. True, runners can train beside each other, compete against each other, race distances set by another, and share all these experiences with each other, but more than most other forms of play, running has the capacity to remain a private playground, an empty canvas on which runners can paint their personal illusionary view of the world and of self. How can 15,000 people crowded together on the Verrazano Bridge in numbered underwear before the New York Marathon be thought of as playing a private game? Four reasons come to mind.

First and foremost, because running is a basic and simple movement acquired in childhood, a runner doesn't have the sense of acquiring a new skill. The sensation is more of *remembering* how to run rather than *learning* how to run. After all, our species was genetically designed to run and not to bowl a ball or finesse a queen. Because running has already become a part of the self, the runner does not struggle to master some new-fangled, involved motion invented by another. Even after some modification of running technique takes place as time goes on, runners still have a general feeling of doing what is innately part of themselves—and as we have pointed out, the more personal the experience and the less influenced by others, the more meaningful it becomes.

A second reason runners feel they are creating their own private game is that they set the goals. In most other sports, a goal or a score or a point is determined by the structure of the game. In running, the goal is set by the runner. The term PB—personal best—becomes the most meaningful score of all. And in what other sport would one be proud to finish 12,486?

Another reason running feels like a personal creation is that the boundary lines of the field are drawn by runners. They decide how far and where they will run. For track runners, distance and pace are played with constantly; for road runners, boundaries are even more self-determined because they decide where they will go on a given day. And after repeated runs over the same course, many runners feel they personally have carved out a portion of the real world and made it their playground, that it is now theirs.

Finally, runners create their own game clock. Time is at their command. Not only can runners play the game anytime, night or day, they can determine to the second how long the game will last. At any instant they can call "time out"—for a moment, for a day, or forever. Certainly, other sports offer a chance to get out of the game temporally as well as spatially, but running provides that opportunity at every second—and most importantly, the opportunity comes not from a referee's whistle, it comes from within. To have that illusion of controlling time is as close to magic as we ever get.

We have pointed out four reasons why running—like a work of art—can be experienced as one's personal creation. The game's movements, the goals, the space, and the time come from within. Just as young children are alone as they create a make-believe world, runners are also alone as they create a similar intermediate world in order to play with reality and struggle with limitations. This aloneness of the long-distance runner helps make the running experience a more private creation, and therefore, more personally meaningful.

Conclusion

In closing, we realize that we have not discussed large areas about Dr. P.'s psychodynamics. In emphasizing why he needs to run, we have left out why he hates to run and why the child puts the teddy bear back on the shelf and says, "Enough, enough. Time out. Let me back into the real world." We have also left out the interpersonal experiences of running—the camaraderie, the competition—but in our view these aspects are layered onto the more fundamental meaning of the running experience.

Let's conclude by taking one last look at the mysterious case of Dr. P. There he was, at one moment contemplating what appeared the most outlandish feats, as though he were some kind of superman capable of anything, capable of starvation diets, racing up mountains, and running 100 miles a week—or even 100 miles at once! And secretly tucked away in a corner of his mind was the notion that with a little more training and just a little more time he could run with the best of them. Rodgers and Shorter could be caught. But we also know that after reading in *Runner's World* about someone racing to the foothills of Mount Everest with nothing but teabags and a change of socks, he would turn the page and see the other side, confront the inevitable limitations, the effects of harsh weather, too much mileage too fast, and the need to respect the moans and groans of the body. And when he failed to listen, he turned to the running literature, which was filled with advice about how to treat the crippling injuries that took their toll on neck, back, groin, quads, knee, calf, heel, foot—took their toll tip to toe.

So, Dr. P.'s feelings of invulnerability collided with the recognition of his body's limitations. We now understand the force of this collision and its meaning. Playing with what is possible and what is not is the essence of play, the grand illusion. The runner sets out to create a magic world, while realizing at the same time that it is only make-believe.

References

Ellis, M.J. *Why people play*. Englewood Cliffs, NJ: Prentice-Hall, 1973.

Erikson, E. *Childhood and society*. New York: W. W. Norton, 1963.

Fixx, J. *The complete book of running*. New York: Random House, 1977.

Huizinga, J. *Homo Ludens: A study of the play element in culture*. Boston: Beacon Press, 1950.

Mahler, M. Notes on the development of basic moods: the depressive affect. In R.M. Loewenstein, L. M. Neuman, M. Schur, & A. J. Solnit (Eds.), *Psychoanalysis—A general psychology: Essays in honor of Heinz Hartmann*. New York: International Universities Press, 1966.

Sheehan, G. *Running and being*. New York: Simon & Schuster, 1978.

Winnicott, D.W. Transitional objects and transitional phenomena. *International Journal of Psycho-Analysis*, 1953, **34,** 89-97.

Winnicott, D.W. The location of cultural experience. *International Journal of Psycho-Analysis*, 1967, **48,** 368-372.

CHAPTER 7

Running, Anorexia Nervosa, and Perfection *

John A. Sours

All the new thinking is about loss. In
this it resembles all the old thinking.

Robert Hass

On First Avenue

He uses superballs for squash and takes Linus
Pauling's Vitamin C's. He carries a capsule of
Humphrey Bogart in his pocket and brings it out
at night when his lover comes to wash his dishes.
. . . he belongs to nobody.
He spends his days running in Central Park.

It is difficult to assess all the factors
responsible for the increase in running
and anorexia nervosa. Indubitably, societal emphasis on slimness and beauty, as well as the
female role, cannot wholly explain the
phenomenon. Nor can our society's increase in
discretionary income explain it. What are the
responsible cultural and societal forces? From the
standpoint of preventive medicine and primary
prophylaxis, we must understand these causative
factors.

---

*Parts of this paper appear in *Starving to Death in a Sea of
Objects: The Anorexia Nervosa Syndrome*. New York: Jason
Aronson, Inc., 1980.

In many respects, running has parallels with anorexia nervosa and the recent explosion of interest in physical fitness and survival (Sours, 1979). Both have captured the interest of the media, which one suspects may be responsible, in part, for the increased numbers in both the eating disorder and the sport. The anorectic is glorified in newspapers, magazines, TV, movies, and books (Broyard, 1980), as is the long-distance runner (Morgan, 1978; Rogers, 1980; Sheehan, 1975). And both draw their energies from our society and culture (Branch, Hardin, & Eurman, 1980).

Long Distance Running and the Running Culture

The popularity of running is symptomatic of the changes in our society and the emergence of a prominent ego-style. Approximately 25 million people run these days, from Alice Cooper to Ed Koch, on streets, in parks, along motel hallways and airport runways (Fixx, 1977, 1980; Rogers, 1980). Some run for health benefits and physical and mental alertness (Morgan, 1969, 1974, 1978), knowing very well that their life is really one of bedrest with bathroom privileges; others run for companionship, out of the need to relate to other people (Eischens, Greist, & McInvaille, 1976); some run to be part of the current fad (Bittker, 1977) while the merchants dash for the dollars. And many run for a sense of survival, self-realization, and autonomy.

The rhythm of strenuous, repetitive activity indicates, for these runners, a metaphoric journey to independence or a chance to "be born again," to overcome alienation (Bell, 1971). Rejection of this certified self-help nostrum, some say, shows a yearning for the grave, or an indication of intractable lassitude and terminal mental flabbiness. Like a teenager, runners think they are supposed to endure agony without asking themselves why they should; furthermore, they believe that running must dominate their life. At any time, they may preach the running gospel with annoying hyperboles, stretch against a tree or wall, or "prop up" a building. If these runners are not gaunt—, they are out of shape, indeed, fat, not moved by the drive for the "body-perfect," or the desire for unending strength and endurance. For them, running is part of life's survival course, a test of body, mind, and self. The run is essential to their sense of security and well-being, as well as an anodyne to their pain of everydayness and their feelings of futility and purposelessness (Coles, 1978). As a runner once put it, "Without the run, [we] become engulfed in an extreme sense of guilt and shame and exhibit tension and strange outbursts of tension because of excessive energies." We are told that running becomes a habit (Glasser, 1967), a daily event that requires no planning. "Automatically, at a certain hour the body starts changing its clothes and tells the mind it's going running. I have no control over the process."

Although the "running high" is ill-defined, it is supposedly an experience of every runner who has surpassed the initial release of tensions. Skeptics call it hypoxia; those in the drug culture hope it is a release of morphine-like substances from the brain. Those more spiritual call it a mystical unity with the surroundings, a transcendental peak of great pleasure with feelings of boundless endurance and mental acuity (Kostrubala, 1976; Sheehan, 1978). The body becomes the object of its own sensuality, and aggression forgets its object and is dissipated in solipsistic, repetitive activity. Others prefer to refer to the "high" as a Zen experience, in which visual perception changes, colors run together, and thought patterns shift into a fluid, more free-form, creative style resembling the approach, they hope, to primary-process thinking and the promise of creativity. "It was like I'd just gotten a jolt of morphine, a warm rush all over," the runner reported. "I felt I could run forever."

According to many runners, a mystical self-awareness and heightened self-direction occur (Shainberg, Note 1). Some report a religious experience and view it as essential to the new life of the "new me." As one runner described it: "For humanity to survive, it will have to invent a new religion. A religion has been invented. It is the religion of the runner." But for the more ambitious and self-directed, running is an indulgence of the self and what it can become. It can never, for them, be a religion, for religion implies a belief in a force bigger and better than any person can be. Nevertheless, for some, running is a cult that draws them together, but without the malignant magnetism of a cult leader.

For many runners, running is a kind of psychotherapy (Altshul, 1978; Bahrke & Morgan, 1978; Kostrubala, Note 2), a cleansing experience through the psychic pores, or a cosmic laxative, a natural psychotherapy which, "unjams the time locks on the past," heightens both inner and outer sensory experiences, evokes memory, and plays out fantasy; it makes one more accessible to deeper emotions. The self is transformed into a new consciousness (Peretz, Note 3; Perry & Sacks, Note 4).

The popularity of running has astounded even professional runners (Milvy, 1977). There has been an "Americanization" of running, with all the energy and drive the obsessional character can bring to an activity and purpose. We can also attribute the popularity to the self-centered mood of the nation, the unabashedly narcissistic attitudes that now permeate our culture and provide a life-style for people (Glick, 1979; Lasch, 1978). This contemporary narcissistic wave is attested to by self-help manuals, like *Looking Out for Number One* and *Pulling Your Own Strings,* documents obvious enough in their encouragement toward self-assertion, self-fulfillment, and sexual gratification, without guilt or shame.

From Individualism to Narcissism

The preoccupation with death in our society is everywhere—not just in the free verse of contemporary poetry. Human beings, as self-conscious beings, are preoccupied with being and existence and their perpetuation. And in the last decade, interest has shifted from being to becoming. Physical hunger is secondary to a narcissistic appetite for recognition. love and immortality

Human rage against order reflects the awareness that there is no order. Individuals look for a guarantee of self-continuity in a new life-style. Whatever threatens their "cosmic heroism" must be placated, if not vanquished. Their self-consciousness, separating them from the subhuman primates, is, in many respects, their vulnerability. Narcissistic self-consciousness has taken primitive human beings from nature and has shifted them to rituals which provide an uncertain feeling of permanance, making them sing their narcissistic blues. Behind the religion and immortality rites is the need for power, which people try to metamorphosize into culture and society (Warren, 1975). Their quest for power makes them delegate it more and more to intermediaries, whereby they lose some freedom and then barter anything for it. They wonder about their immortality, but have no notion of its source. They struggle for eternity with a sense of shattered afterlife. Missile-destroying ray weapons threaten to upset the world balance of power and change the strategy of war; mutually assured destruction is no longer a deterrence. Nuclear death seems more likely. People forge ahead in the attempt to usurp power while seeing the ecological disruption it has brought to their environment. They shudder when they learn of India's underground nuclear explosions, knowing full well that control systems for atomic energy do not limit the potential for world destruction. They know that the prevailing attitude of nations—"If we don't go nuclear, our enemies might"—is a danger ever-present in a world of uncontrolled nationalism and nuclear weaponry. Although people are aware that all nations must seek alternate sources of energy, they know the dangers from nuclear power plant "melt downs." And now technologists are capable of producing nuclear power for a nation of any size, as long as it can pay the bill.

Our literature is filled with the imagery of death (Gardner, 1978). A common metaphor for the tragic passions of our time is terminal leukemia. Wolitzer's *Ending* (1974)—Liebestod in Rego Park—is the story of death through the eyes of a soon-to-be young widow. She struggles with her vulnerability and susceptibility to pain. People want to be oblivious of social evils and the transient nature of their existence. One self-indulgent middle-class diversion is to anesthetize the sensibilities and obliterate the self. Nevertheless, despair and pervasive ambivalence drive people to "new solutions" (Handke, 1976). Those who can break through middle-class repression, think "beyond depression," to "prophets" like Alvin Toffler (1974), who predicts not inflation, stagflation, recession or bust, but eco-spasm. Economists forecast a catastrophic breakdown of the international monetary system, a major capital crisis which could wreck any economy and forward-moving social program. Thinking about sociopolitical likelihood of work disillusionment and collapse, people mutter that the "old rules do not work any longer." They talk about the crisis in industrialism. Their *Weltschmertz* forecasts the collapse of the industrial civilization, its gradual fragmentation and ensuing chaos.

At the same time, "the 'me' decade," in response to these threats promises an alchemical dream, a hope of personal transcendence, leading to a new personal metaphysics (Coles, 1978). The infinitude and omnipotence of the self are given homage (Warren, 1975). New narcissistic therapies offer quick relief from depression, guilt, and responsibility; they encourage the search for experience in a frenzy of greed. The development of the self has become the main object of life, with many trends in therapy promising certification of the diminished self. Culture and character structure are to be mirror-images. The self is the tombstone of originality. Commitment to societal, group ego-ideals are passé; they are now viewed as remnants of 19th century neuroticism. A sense of omnipotence sedates a tugging pull of vulnerability and worthlessness. A new lover is idealized and then discarded for the promises of a new persona. Anger, resentment, and bitterness have become the everyday emotions, giving way momentarily to undisguised feelings of envy. Distinguishing the self from the outside world seems to have become more difficult, leading the modernists to narcissistic exploitation and manipulation of others in the quest for admiration and fame. The new humanism promised communion with the universe, but this led only to more isolation. In the midst of personal affluence, a diminished sense of individual power and hints of impending catastrophe ensue. Politicians and government are no longer to be trusted. The disenchanted in the narcissistic society become more fascinated with charismatic, fascistic leaders who promise relief from uncertainty and the threat of chaos. These leaders promise delivery from wants while ignoring the necessity of needs.

Relinquishing responsibility and commitment, people continue in their egocentric search for experience. The "Slocum's" of Joseph Heller's *Something Happened* (1974) feel sorry for their wives who "drink during the day and flirt or try to at parties they go to in the evening." They are frightened of the boredom that inundates their life as they head toward the mid-life crisis in their "domestic torture chamber" in Connecticut.

Father has become the dominant "myth of the middle-class," the veteran who came home from Korea and Vietnam to be the head of the nuclear family (Reiss, 1971). He took jobs more than slightly dishonorable in the hope of making as much money as he could to support his family in the mythologies of the 1970s. Meanwhile, he discovered his inability to form human relationships and to appreciate and share other people's feelings. The gulf between himself and others widened. In his race for money, achievement, and fame, his work associates and family have become mere accessories to self-aggrandizing efforts. Much to his dismay, he has found that bureaucratic institutions support his new style of living and leadership and, in fact, often showcase him as an object to be emulated. The shallowness of and exploitations in his relationships add to his sense of emptiness and malaise, which he wards off by psychosomatic symptoms, frenetic activity, and drugs. He knows deep within himself that he should have postponed marriage and child rearing in order to bid for validation of his self-esteem. Now he wonders if it is too late to gain a heightened consciousness and growth of the self. Survival is now the leitmotif in a society whose future is questionable and where hope seems to be mainly in "transcendental-attention." Experience is the important activity which often makes more than one object the center of attention. Seldom is one article read from start to finish. With a reduced attention span, being is the act of doing.

Therapy has replaced religion in a nonstop celebration of the self. To realize one's full potential for self-gratification is autinomian. Smorgasbord displays of the means toward transcendence and survival are found everywhere. The conviction that to love oneself is better than to love another is public knowledge. Growing up and becoming a responsible adult are no longer appealing. Old age is not discussed, except for those people in their 50s, who make early reservations at nursing homes. Personality is now largely buttressed by defenses against rage and deprivation. Fantasies of omnipotence guard against helplessness. A grandiose concept of the self is constructed with fantasies of beauty, wealth, and omnipotence. The new religion of narcissism tries to find in therapeutic relationships verifiable support for the fantasies of omnipotence, power, and beauty. In the flight from aging, the new narcissist finds no comfort in any identification with continuities in history. Pansexuality, especially oral sex, and panhedonism allow little relief from fears of annihilation. Soon the individual experiences low sexual interest and response after repeated sexual disappointments and joins the "chastity underground."

Believing that their society has no future, the new narcissists tend to ignore the needs of their children and the hopes of the next generation (Keniston, 1977). They convey to them a profound sense of historical discontinuity; they view their children and the generation to succeed them as intruders into their short-lived future and right for self-fulfillment. On the one hand, they maintain a cool detachment from their children and, on the other hand, they narcissistically lose themselves in their children, trying to convince themselves of their own entitlement and favored position in the family. They pander, manipulate, deceive, and lay themselves open to further corruption.

Parents who have emerged from the middle-class give their children many of the problems of the very poor; namely, material deprivation, a shadow-father, and a feeling of discrimination as a "special group." The third generation rich founders in the uncertainties created by their parents, or they turn to hard work, living on the edge of leisure. Imitating the machinery they have built and maintained, they let work consume their lives and take them from their spouses and children (Jacques, 1970).

The structured, neurotic symptomatologies, described by Freud, seem less frequent; instead, character disorders reflected in the areas of relationships, love, ideals, and work are more prominent with the concomitant shift on psychoanalytic theory to separation—individuation and narcissism. The arts reflect many of the same cultural trends (Broyard, 1980; Edel, 1975). The theatre has become an extension of advertising. Second puberty rites occur daily for some artists who are disillusioned with disillusionment. They find themselves unable to discover any sense of surprise and pleasure. The self is seen as a work of art in a Dionysian frenzy. An amnesia in art cuts off the self from the past. The dialectic of identity is the need for novel experience, contrasting with a need for continuity. Identity and intimacy become separate. Self-actualization is part of the Eriksonian moratorium, a sanctuary from which adolescents are reluctant to leave. Teenagers now feel like blank art, trying to explore space and stretch time into emptiness. They seek a new "objective aesthetic," a simpler set of ideas and forms. John Cage's music encourages randomness and embellishes silence as a meditative approach to life. Satie-esque styles are now the evening's entertainment, broken only by the "Esperanto" of rock and the punk-rock of the Ramones, with its triple-chorded, monochromatic primitivism. The musical, choreographic, and visual inspirations from the avante-gardists provide youth with a blank aesthetic, mixed with an anti-intellectualism and nonverbalism.

The family finds itself in transition with a challenge from within (DeBurger, 1977; Goode, 1971; Verloff & Feld, 1970). The divorce rate has now doubled, and women are convinced of the wisdom of putting off children until the biological last minute. A burgeoning instability of the family, according to some observers, now threatens democratic institutions. With ideals and values changing, young people do not know what to tell themselves and one another, much less the children they may have in the future. They cannot identify their lineaments. Households headed by women have increased by more than one-third in the last 10 years. Two out of every five children, born in this decade, now live in single-parent homes. Half of all the others of school-age children work outside of the home. One out of every three school children lives in a home with only one parent in authority. Day care centers have sprung up with unpredictable services and questionable qualifications. The "latchkey child" is commonplace. Mothers who want to be with their young children are forced into the labor market because of dwindling family finances. More women now try to develop careers before facing the pain of children going off to college and husbands seeking relationships with younger women, often emotional and characterological "clones" of the first wife. Divorce is not only more possible but more probable in a symmetrical family where there are two incomes and where the working woman has the financial capability of delegating the care of her children to someone outside the family.

Running, Anorexia Nervosa, and the Contemporary Ego Style

The psychological and physical characteristics of anorexia nervosa syndrome are well presented in the literature (Bruch, 1973; Cohen, 1980; Crisp, 1977; Palazzoli, 1974; Thomä, 1967). Variations in the syndrome are numerous (Dally & Gomez, 1979) and the occurrence of anorexia nervosa in athletes has been noted (Druss & Silverman, 1978; Sours, 1980).

Many long distance runners astoundingly resemble adolescents with anorexia nervosa. They are hyperactive, full of energy, and hardly ever tire.

They restrict their food intake, go on food fasts, and follow repetitive and routinized daily exercise programs with intense dedication. They annoy their lovers or spouses with their monomaniacal focus on running and fitness, often to the relative exclusion of instinctual interests. Women distance runners find that amenorrhea eventually occurs (Frisch, Wyshak, & Vincent, 1980) if body mass decreases below the critical point for menstrual function. In general, they maximize pain and minimize pleasure in their ascent to control and mastery. The functional pleasure of thinness and fitness exceeds and substitutes for oral gratification. The fear of fat is constantly with them. They can only freely eat if they first run long distances, the reverse of bulimic vomiters who eat first and then rid themselves of food. And like the anorectic, these athletes keep a record of calories, as well as miles. They make into a metaphysic the cliché: "You are what you eat." They know that running dulls the appetite and decreases hunger. They look forward to carbohydrate loading before a marathon, but yet still fear weight gain. George Sheehan reminds us of this enemy. "The struggle against the slowly advancing glacier of lard begins before we attain our maturity. It never ends. In this war against fat, you have to be a career person."

Distance runners, much like anorectics, regard their bodies as complicated machines which must be regularly used and serviced. They sleep like anorectics, waking up early full of energy and ambition. They start their physical routine often before sunrise. Fat is abhorred—it must be reduced to 12% of body mass—and the body is never really thin. Runners often examine their bodies, palpating fascial planes for lumps of fat. The top runner, who runs for perfection, is the idealized hero of the distance runner. Body image distortions are common. Even professional Boston marathoners marvel at their bodies when they see themselves reflected in Hansen's plate glass windows as they run toward the Newtons. Many runners cannot believe that they are thin, for they tend to overestimate their body size. They distrust their body perceptions, unless they are photographed along the course.

Also like anorectics, they do not trust their bodies to the medical profession, for they know an orthopedist will advise rest for an injury. As Fixx says, "Running is my doctor." At best, only a sports podiatrist, preferably one of their own, can be trusted.

The body must be perfect; it must be controlled and denied sensuous pleasures. Only by control and mastery can the anorectic runner get beyond pain and boredom to a transcendental state filled with the pleasure of closeness with an omnipotent ideal. These satisfactions take primacy over instinctual oral and genital pleasures and nullify the pain of intensive training, dieting, self-denial, and asceticism. These narcissistic satisfactions become habituating; the runners must strive for a better time before their pleasure begins to pall, just as the abstaining anorectic must repeatedly attempt to reduce calories. If these runners are forced to give up running, a sense of loss ensues with increasing tension and dissatisfaction with themselves, like the anorectic who must relinquish starvation and return to everyday eating and

the threat of a fat body out of control. Like anyone aspiring to perfection—be
it a composer, figure skater, ballerina, or anorectic—distance runners live for
their ego-ideal, for the moment when they might be "bathed in a column of
white light," and when the sense of passage of time and distance is lost and
they pass out of their body into a timelessness.

Running, like fasting and starvation, narrows the distance between what
runners are and what they can be, between the ideal-self and the actual-self,
between aspiration and reality (Greist, Klein, Eischens, & Faris, 1978). For
some, running is a means to divine perfection, a way whereby a transforma-
tion of self can occur, a means that will enable one to be left alone with the self
and experience the body and self as a separate, ultimate reality.

This spirit has bred a new elite (Morgan & Pollach, 1977), the long distance
runner and marathoner (Morgan, 1978). These are runners who are interested in more than being simply fit (Little, 1965, 1979). They want to be in
competitive shape—and totally sure of body and mind (Morgan & Costill,
1972). They search for perfection, try to project a physical self which fulfills
an ego-ideal. They run to be at the top of the game, where everything perfect
will fall into place. They long for days of perfection on the road. They must
feel special. As George Sheehan says, "We need that feeling if we are to go it
alone. We need the support of self-esteem, of a positive self-image, of feeling
ourselves worthy. We need some way of being special." If runners can maintain a sense of being special, they have a secret to support them in societal
isolation. As one runner said, "Without running life has no meaning, no purpose, no way to supremacy." Long-distance runners look to power and control, to be "a runner moving in a slow-motion universe in absolute control."
Competitively, they want to increase their speed, do a sub-three marathon
and perhaps someday the "perfect marathon." Their drive toward the inner
goal of perfection is private, something people often cannot understand. Only
professional dancers (Druss & Silverman, 1978), figure skaters, Olympic
swimmers—and anorectics—can understand this inner drive (Morgan et al.,
1970).

People must play out old childhood traumas and impairments in object
relations around which they have over the years organized their character
structure. Attempts at the realization of the "perfect image" is one "solution"
to childhood feelings of worthlessness and inadequacy. But regrettably a solution to an old trauma usually results in a repetition of the trauma—a frantic
and abortive try at "getting it right this time." As Solzhenitsyn reminds us,
those who are born to the cage return to the cage. The long-distance runner
cannot run it out. Perfection is no cure for pain—for either the runner, the
anorectic—or anybody else. Narcissistic restitution efforts are maladaptive;
they do not correct distortions in the sense of physical and mental well-being
when distorting defects occurred early in the formation of the self.

Reference Notes

1. Shainberg, D. *Long distance running as meditation.* Paper presented at the American Medical Joggers Association, Boston, 1976.
2. Kostrubala, T. *Depression and physical activity.* Paper presented at the Nebraska Symposium on Physical Activity and Mental Health, Lincoln, 1971.
3. Peretz, D. *Running: The alteration of fantasy in action.* Paper presented at The New York Hospital—Cornell Medical Center Running Conference, October 1978.
4. Perry, S., & Sacks, M. *The psychodynamics of running.* Paper presented at The New York Hospital—Cornell Medical Center Running Conference, October 1978.

References

Altshul, V. The ego-integrative (and disintegrative) effects of long distance running. *Current Concepts in Psychiatry,* July-August 1978.

Bahrke, M.S., & Morgan, W.P. Anxiety reduction following exercise and meditation. *Psychiatric Annals,* 1979, **9,** 34-48.

Bell, M. *The escape into you.* New York: Atheneum, 1971.

Bittker, T. Runner's gluttony. *Runner's World,* 1977, **12,** 10-11.

Branch, C.H., Hardin, & Eurman, L.J. Social attitudes toward patients with anorexia nervosa. *American Journal of Psychiatry,* 1980, **137,** 631-632.

Broyard, A. (Review of *Early Disorder* by Rebecca Joseph.) *The New York Times,* May 9, 1980, p. C25.

Bruch, H. *Eating disorders: Obesity, anorexia nervosa and the person within.* New York: Basic Books, 1973.

Cohen, P. An eating disorder in adolescence: A preliminary report. *Bulletin of the Hampstead Clinic,* 1980, **3,** 46-49.

Coles, R. *Walker Percy: An American search.* Boston: Atlantic Monthly Press, 1978.

Crisp, A.H. The differential diagnosis of anorexia nervosa. *Proceedings of the Royal Society of Medicine,* 1977, **70,** 686-688.

Dally, P., & Gomez, J. *Anorexia nervosa.* London: William Heinemann, 1979.

DeBurger, J.E. (Ed.). *Marriage today: Problems, issues and alternatives.* New York: John Wiley, 1977.

Druss, R.G., & Silverman, J.A. Body image and perfectionism of ballerinas. *General Hospital Psychiatry,* 1978, **10,** 115-121.

Edel, L. The madness of art. *American Journal of Psychiatry,* 1975, **32,** 1005-1012.

Eischens, R., Greist, J.H., & McInvaille, T. *Run to reality.* Madison, WI: Madison Running Press, 1976.

Fixx, J. *The complete book of running.* New York: Random House, 1977.

Fixx, J. *The second book of running.* New York: Random House, 1980.

Frisch, R.E., Wyshak, G., & Vincent, L. Delayed menarche and amenorrhea in ballet dancers. *New England Journal of Medicine,* 1980, **303,** 17-19.

Gardner, J. *On moral fiction.* New York: Basic Books, 1978.

Glasser, W. *Positive addiction.* New York: Harper & Row, 1967.

Glick, R.A. Individualism in our time: A report on the interdisciplinary symposium on narcissism. *Bulletin of the Association Psychoanalytic Medicine,* 1979, **18,** 33-40.

Goode, W.J. *The contemporary American family.* Chicago: Quadrangle Press, 1971.

Greist, J.H., Klein, M.H., Eischens, R.R., & Faris, J.W. Antidepressant running. *Behavioral Medicine,* June 1978, pp. 19-24.

Handke, P. *The left-handed woman.* New York: Farrar, Straus & Giroux, 1976.

Hass, R. Meditation at Lagunitas. *Antaeus,* 1979, **30/31,** 9-10.

Heller, J. *Something happened.* New York: Alfred A. Knopf, 1974.

Jacques, E. *Work, creativity, social justice.* London: William Heinemann Medical Publishers, 1970.

Keniston, K. *All our children: The American family under pressure.* New York: Harcourt Brace Janovich, 1977.

Kostrubala, T. *Joy of running.* New York: J. B. Lippincott, 1976.

Lasch, C. *The culture of narcissism.* New York: W. W. Norton, 1978.

Little, J.C. *Physical prowess and neurosis.* MD thesis, University of Boston, 1965.

Little, J.C. The athlete's neurosis: A deprivational crisis. *Acta Psychiatrica Scandinavica,* 1979, **45,** 187-197.

Milvy, P. (Ed.) *The marathon: Physiological, medical, epidemiological, and psychological studies* (Vol. 301). New York: New York Academy of Sciences, 1977.

Morgan, W.P. Physical fitness and emotional health: A review. *American Corrective Therapy Journal,* 1969, **23,** 124-127.

Morgan, W.P. Exercise and mental disorder. In A. J. Ryan & F. L. Allman, Jr. (Eds.), *Sports medicine.* New York: Academic Press, 1974.

Morgan, W.P. The mind of the marathoner. *Psychology Today,* 1978, **11,** 38-49.

Morgan, W.P., & Costill, D.C. Psychological characteristics of the marathon runner. *Journal of Sports Medicine and Physical Fitness,* 1972, **12,** 42-46.

Morgan, W.P., & Pollach, M.L. Psychological characterization of the elite distance runner. In P. Milvy (Ed.), *Annals of the New York Academy of Sciences,* 1977, **301,** 24-30.

Palazzoli, M.S. Emaciation as magic means for the removal of anguish in anorexia mentalis. *Acta Psychotherapica,* 1974, **9,** 37-45.

Reiss, I.L. *The family systems in America.* New York: Holt, Rinehart & Winston, 1971.

Rogers, B. *Marathoning.* New York: Simon & Schuster, 1980.

Sheehan, G.A. *Dr. Sheehan on running.* Mountain View, CA: World Publications, 1975.

Sheehan, G.A. *Running and being.* New York: Simon & Schuster, 1978.

Sours, J.A. Anorexia nervosa. In J.E. Noshpritz (Ed.), *Basic handbook of child psychiatry* (Vol. 2). New York: Basic Books, 1979.

Sours, J.A. *Starving to death in a sea of objects: The anorexia nervosa syndrome.* New York: Jason Aronson, 1980.

Thomä, H. *Anorexia nervosa.* New York: International Universities Press, 1967.

Toffler, A. Beyond depression. *Esquire,* February 1974, p. 53.

Verloff, J. & Feld, A. *Marriage and work in America.* New York: Van Nostrand-Reinhold, 1970.

Vigersky, R. (Ed.). *Anorexia nervosa.* New York: Raven Press, 1977.

Warren, R.P. *Democracy and poetry.* Cambridge: Harvard University Press, 1975.

Wolitzer, H. *Ending.* New York: William Morrow, 1974.

CHAPTER 8

Running: The Grand Delusion

Thaddeus Kostrubala

Webster's (1966) dictionary has the following definitions for the word delusion:

1. Act of deluding or state of being deluded; often a misleading of the mind . . . . an abnormal mental state characterized by occurrence of delusions.

2. Something that is falsely or delusively believed or propagated: false belief or a persistent error of perception occasioned by false belief or mental derangement: customary or fixed misconception . . . . : as, a): a false conception and persistent belief unconquerable by reason in something that has no existence in fact. b): a false belief regarding the self or persons or objects outside one self that persists despite the facts and is common in paranoia, schizophrenia and psychotic depressed states . . . . (p. 598)

It is apparent that many runners appear to view their own running, and the running of others, in a delusional manner. These belief systems vary across a wide spectrum and range from impassioned beliefs in particular diets, vitamins, and restorative liquids (i.e., beer, ERG, or special potions made by individuals) to shoes, clothing, and training patterns. Often, they appear to coagulate into quite specific organized delusional patterns that attach themselves to a kernel of "truth." Examples of these are individuals who firmly believe that running marathons provides cardiovascular immortality and those who believe that running and a process of active imagination will protect against carcinoma. Other examples are those who believe that running is a religion and/or a panacea for many interpersonal and culturally distressing situations. I intend to briefly examine these beliefs, focusing upon their underlying psychodynamic principles.

In "Psycho-analytic Notes on an Autobiographical Account of a Case of Paranoia," Freud, when discussing the mechanism of paranoia, stated that "The formation, which we take to be the pathological product, is in reality an attempt at recovery, a process of reconstruction" (Freud, 1911/1958, p. 71). Discussing delusions, he states "The attempt at recovery . . . , observers mistake for the disease itself" (p. 77).

These early statements by Freud indicate a position about delusions that differs from the dictionary's definition in which the delusional state is explicitly identified as a cultural value: a false belief. Freud thought the belief was not false in a deeper sense and, in his paper on Narcissism, he extended his concept of the function of a delusion.

> He [the patient] seems really to have withdrawn his libido from people and beings in the external world, without replacing them by others in phantasy. When he does so replace them, the process seems to be a secondary one and to be part of an attempt at recovery, designed to lead the libido back to objects. (Freud, 1911/1958, Vol. XIV, p. 74)

Freud expanded his (1911/1958) perception of the delusion as a process of recovery in a discussion of the delusions of litigous paranoia, the "grande nation" that was defeated in war, the alcoholic, and others. He concludes with the following statement:

> In every instance the delusional idea is maintained with the same energy with which another intolerably distressing idea [such as a fear of death or disability by coronary disease] is fended off from the ego. Thus, they love their delusions as they love themselves. That is the secret. (Vol. I, p. 211-212)

If the approach to the delusions of the runner is in keeping with Freud's dynamic interpretation, we will view the delusion as defined by the following statements: "process of reconstruction," "the attempt at recovery," "designed to lead the libido back to objects," and "they love their delusions as they love themselves."

Jules Masserman (1961) describes delusions as culturally relative. He posits that "our own common beliefs of today will be the residual superstitions of the ignorant tomorrow" (p. 79). Masserman then escapes this position in linking individual psychodynamics with the following three UR-Delusions:

Fifty or more thousands of years ago man already derived essential comfort from three fundamental faiths to which men externally cling and will eternally be available in psychotherapy. These faiths, which we may call ultimate or UR-fantasies, are:

First, a man's perennial trust in his capacity to control his milieu through various technologies, from chipped flints then to space satellites now.

Second, a wishful reliance on the collaboration of his fellow-man and,

Third, an arrogation of power to employ one or another form of Supreme Magic to serve his own purposes. (p. 182)

It is apparent that all three UR systems fail at one time or another in the life of an individual, or we perceive their failure in others. Nevertheless, in accord with the first UR-Delusion, the effects of exercise, especially properly conducted long-distance running which mechanically promotes improved cardiovascular and other physiologic factors, find constant support in the medical literature. Cautious and informed long-distance runners are convinced that they are technically improving their body and keeping at bay the hounds of disease and death.

The second UR-Delusion is visibly operant in the functions of all types of running groups, from the "neighborhood buddy" systems to group therapies that use running to marathon clinics. Many runners begin to experience being members of a unique group, a concept which can foster friendships, marriages, in-group mini-cults, and feelings of elitism. This is often expressed within the group and expressed as "What's your best PR?"

The reports of physical attacks on runners and the seeming criticism of runners appears to be a state in the cultural impact of the running movement. These cultural responses, both critical and affirmative, tend to aid in the process of the runner's social identification. For example, the sociocultural aspects of women runners are a case in point. Demonstrating their physiologic capacity by running, they directly confront cultural sexist patterns.

Under the rubric of the third UR-Delusion, runners "employ one or another form of Supreme Magic to serve their own purposes." The "Supreme Magic" of the runner takes a variety of forms. At one end of the spectrum is the logical-sceptical-atheistic runner who "only believes" in distance, speed, and effort, and at the other end is the theistic-believing-alogical runner who believes any one of a number of patterns from orthodox faiths, to meditation, to consciousness expansion (Andrews, 1979). Most runners, however, are somewhere in between these polarities.

It is common for running therapists to find in clinical practice all of the aspects of the three UR-Delusions. In the course of the runner's development from beginner to ultra-marathoner, the focus of the fantasies about running may shift emphasis from one UR-Delusion to another over a period of years. And the voluminous running literature (*Runner's World, Running Times, The Runner,* and so on) will support each aspect or all three at once.

The remarkable thing about each of these UR-Delusions, when carefully examined, is the aspect of "fact" inherent in each. Thus, it appears "true" that running, done properly, can improve technical control over one's internal physiologic milieu; for example, running improves cardiac performance. The camaraderie and support of running groups, the social aspect, is also clearly evident. And, finally, it is difficult to dispute the many transcendent experiences reported by many runners.

In examining delusions, Freud (1911/1958) discussed the neuroses of defense.

> The process (of failed defense in the return of the repressed) reaches its conclusion either in melancholia (a sense of the ego's littleness) which in a secondary manner, attached to the distortions the belief which has been withheld from the primary self-reproach, or what is more frequent and more serious—in protective delusions (megalomania), till the ego has been completely remodeled. (Vol. I, p. 227)

Freud's statement indicates the potential strength of the delusion in influencing and even shaping the ego. This potential may help us to understand the remarkable changes in behavior that runners report, especially those behaviors that, in the individual's past, had been ego syntonic. Such changes range from the apparently increased ability, or strength, of the ego to manage behavior patterns like cigarette smoking, destructive use of alcohol, obesity, and perhaps more significantly, the symptoms and behaviors associated with disease entities we currently identify as the schizophrenias and affective disorders. One model would be the powerful delusional system of the running movement influencing the ego of the individual or "Participation Mystique."

Runners who have undergone such transformations, which may be the result of a remodeled ego under the aegis and power of the protective delusions associated with running, often are aware of this personal change and are eager to share this experience with others. This latter reaction is often associated with the now familiar "show and tell" of the former fat person. Often, runners who have undergone this personal change will utilize all of the UR-Delusions as they demonstrate increased technologic control over themselves, claiming allegiances and alliances with running clubs, groups or geographic localities, and finally, organizing their personal experience into a belief system that they treat like a form of religion or supreme magic. For example, some runners "must run every day to make things go right." At times, runners may attempt to convert both runners and nonrunners alike to their "system."

Freud, in his "Constructions in Analysis" (1937/1958) states:

> If we consider mankind as a whole and substitute it for the single human individual, we discover that it too has developed delusions which are inaccessible to logical criticism and which contradict reality. If, in spite of this they are able to exert an extraordinary power over men, investigation leads us to the same explanation as in the case of the single individual. They owe their power to the ele-

ment of historical truth which they have brought up from the repression of the
forgotten and primeval past. (Vol. XXIII, p. 269)

These words would be seized upon by some theorists who would claim that
the 4,000,000-year heritage of Genus homo as our hunting-gathering mobile
ancestors is the "element of historical truth" leading to the "extraordinary
power over men" that is the hidden factor in the defense-fantasy-delusional
systems of the runner and the running movement. Evan Hadingham, in his
(1979) book, *Secrets of the Ice Age,* examines cave paintings with one goal:
"How, then, are we to understand and investigate the largest portion of our
existence? To what extent did the hunting past shape our faculties, our instincts, and our relationships in the modern world" (p. 1).

Of course, in order to accept such a concept, it is necessary to emphasize
and re-examine human beings in an expanded biologic, genetic, and
behavioral framework. For example, 40,000 years ago our ancestors buried
their dead and began painting. Common to both activities is the function of
memory reflected in the term "memorialize." The popular concept of
memory today is that it is chronological, functioning historically in linear progression. Instead, close examination of human memory demonstrates a more
global holographic function including the multidimensional effects of perception, emotion, and environmental factors which are all mediated by
neurophysiologic mechanisms. At this point memory, aesthetics, and biology
touch each other in the ceaseless dance between "inside" and "outside."

The biology of any species is linked to its behavior. This range of behaviors
is "released" by that species' specific environment which, for that species, is
considered optimal or normal. A major shift in the environment of a species
(from mobile-hunter-gatherer to sedentary-agriculture-urban in the human)
can produce "abnormal" behaviors in that species (cardiovascular and other
environmental diseases). Thus, zoos attempt to have the polar bear in a
white environment and often fast the carnivores 1 day a week. Both the color
of the environment and the usual pattern of the carnivore, with periodic food
deprivation, promote the well-being of those individuals within that species.

It is also apparent that other behaviors such as appropriate and successful
mating of many species will be "released" when other environmental factors
are made to conform with the genetically established patterns of that species.
As Gregory Bateson (1975) states:

> The information which is accumulated in organisms by evolutionary process is
> not usually any of the sorts described above. [Ostensive, Digital, Iconic Analogic
> and Casual and Correlative] It is rather *complementary* to those environmental
> phenomena to which the organism must adjust. The embryo shark does not have
> information about hydrodynamics but about how to grow to a shape which,
> though the creature does not—need not—know it, will *fit* with the surrounding
> hydrodynamics. (p. 7)

The environment to which we as a species had to adjust, then, was that of the mobile-hunter-gatherer and the information we have accumulated in that evolutionary process is patterned in our genetic matrix. Thus, we evolved in the "hydrodynamics" of the mobile-hunter-gatherer and are built to swim well in those waters.

Bipedalism is our species-dominant biologic behavior and, according to Johanson and Edy (1981), was well-established prior to the development of the human brain. Running may be a genetically preprogrammed releasing mechanism that has profound biologic (including neurohumoral) and psychologic effects. Thus, in considering the behavior of runners we should heed Masserman's (1955) advice, which states:

> Delusions are the denials and the substitutive or compensatory beliefs necessary to make each man's world seem a little more like the heaven he so ardently desires. We dare not, then, disregard the psychologic truism that such beliefs, in a deeply humanitarian sense, are indeed sacred, and that we tamper with them at our patient's—and our own—peril. (p. 484)

Conclusion

Runners do get ill and die, and they experience interpersonal pain (even from their fellow runners). Their own Supreme Magic, however well-constructed, will occasionally fail them. Nevertheless, viewed from the psychodynamic point of view, running currently qualifies as a serious contender in the on-going search for more effective delusional systems.

Running can offer individuals the physical, technical skills to directly improve their physiologic well-being and increase their consciousness. Social structures like marathon clinics and other running groups offer runners the opportunity of improving their interpersonal relationships. Finally, the apparently spontaneous emergence of religious, transcendent, or Supreme Magic desires in runners offers them the advantage of understanding that this development in themselves is only a welcome sign indicating another benefit from running.

Viewed in this fashion, the delusions associated with running are part of the running therapist's armantarium. It follows, and is confirmed by my clinical experience, that running, especially long distance running, is a powerful psychotherapeutic tool. In addition, psychological effects stimulated by running have been discovered and used by many runners without professional consultation. It is suspicious, however, that a single activity, as opposed to a wide spectrum of varied activities, should produce such startling results. In this sense, running may be a unifying activity for the individual.

Running is best conceived of as a "tool," just as Freud's use of the couch and free association was a tool. The tool often shapes the behavior of the tool user. It would appear, then, that this activity called running, with so much springing from it to assist ourselves and our patients, can be called "The Grand Delusion." Or perhaps we can return to Webster's and find that the word "delude" comes from the French, de-ludere, To Play. "We can be nothing without playing at being" (Sartre, 1956).

References

Andrews, V. *The psychic power of running.* New York: Rawlins, 1979.

Bateson, G. Reality and redundance. *Co-Evolution Quarterly,* Summer 1975, p. 7.

Freud, S. [*The complete psychological works of Sigmund Freud*] (J. Strachey, Ed. and Trans.). London: Hogarth, 1958.

Hadingham, E. *Secrets of the Ice Age.* New York: Walker, 1979.

Johanson, D., & Edy, M. *Lucy.* New York: Simon & Schuster, 1981.

Masserman, J. *The practice of dynamic psychiatry.* Philadelphia, PA: Saunders, 1955.

Masserman, J. *Principles of dynamic psychiatry* (2nd ed.). Philadelphia, PA: Saunders, 1961.

Sartre, J.P. [*Being and nothingness*] (H. Barnes, Trans.). New York: Philosophical Library, 1956.

Webster's third new international dictionary. Springfield, MA: G. & C. Merriam, 1966.

CHAPTER 9

A Case Study of a Woman Jogger:
A Psychodynamic Analysis

Bonnie G. Berger and Marlin M. Mackenzie

The present study represents a line of investigation which focuses on answering the general question, "Why do so many people participate in sports?" Imagine a woman wearing brief shorts and T-shirt, bounding along the pavement on the east side of Manhattan on a hot, summer day, dodging people, cars, trash cans, and litter. What is she thinking? Why does she feel compelled to run under these adverse conditions? Is she simply fulfilling her desire to be fit and trim, or is she satisfying some inner dynamic needs? Although the jogger may be aware of the reasons for her running, they probably are influenced by her needs and desires as well as by her personality and socio-cultural background.

"Why is sport meaningful to so many people?" Those who have sought answers to this question represent an enormous array of interests and scholarly expertise. Philosophers have explored the inherent values of sport (Novak, 1976; Shvartz, 1972; Weiss, 1969); physical educators have tried to understand the meaning of sport (Harris, 1973; Metheny, 1965; Slusher, 1967); psychologists and psychiatrists also have been intrigued by physical activity (Aigner, 1974; Beisser, 1967; Moore, 1966). Also included in the search for the meanings of sport were writers and sports writers (Furlong, 1976; Lipsyte, 1975; Michener, 1976; Smith, 1975). Athletes themselves have searched for meaning in their sport participation (Clarke & Harris, 1967; Huey, 1976; Neal, 1972; and others). In spite of the large amount of literature concerning the meanings of sport to participants, little concrete information is available.

The present investigators were interested in the insights which people of all ages can gain from participating in many forms of sport and physical activity without judging those meanings. In the present study, we used a different and unusual approach which focused on gaining a deep understanding of a woman jogger. We wish to share our procedures, tentative observations, and methodological problems despite the specificity of our findings. Eventually we will refine our mode of inquiry and expand it to include participants in other forms of physical activity.

This initial study focused on the insights which one woman acquired when she jogged. A clinical, case-study approach rather than an experimental research design was employed to generate hypotheses concerning the meaningfulness of jogging. The openended, naturalistic strategy of Mahler and associates (1975) influenced our choice of approach. Use of the experimental method to investigate human motivation in sport would be a stab-in-the-dark at the present time. Once potentially significant determinants of human behavior in sport have been illuminated, they may be subjected to controlled, experimental research paradigms.

The present report focused on an in-depth study of the feelings, emotions, and thoughts of one woman jogger over an extended period of time. This contrasts with the work of Glasser (1976) who surveyed a large number of joggers and Moore (1976) who studied a select group of highly skilled joggers.

Jogging was the sport selected for analysis because it is a relatively simple activity. Compared to many sports, jogging requires no implements nor do participants necessarily compete or interact. Physical contact, danger, or violence generally are absent. Consequently, the jogger is free to introspect and reminisce unhampered by attention to rules, opponents' performance, and environmental safety hazards.

Our selection of jogging was influenced also by the widespread interest in the activity at the present time. Not only is the number of recreational joggers increasing, but cardiologists (Lamb, 1974), physiologists (Ismail & Trachtman, 1973), and psychiatrists (Glasser, 1976; Spino, 1976) have been increasingly aware of the potential prophylactic and therapeutic value of jogging.

Method

Subjects

The volunteer subject was 35 years of age, married, a mother, and teacher of physical education. Both parents (ages 58 and 59 and still living) were college graduates and divorced when the subject was 15 years old. Her only sibling, a brother 4 years younger than she, was killed less than a year ago in a motorcycle accident. The jogger began psychotherapy 7 months prior to the study.

Swimming (a sport in which the subject participated and competed between the ages of 7 and 22) was one of her first and most intensive sport experiences. Other sport interests were tennis and basketball and skiing. She did not begin jogging until her pregnancy in 1973 but participated in the activity until the end of her eighth month. She did not pursue jogging again until March, 1976, when she was experiencing marital and professional problems.

Procedure

During a 4-month period between March and June, 1976, the subject completed 33 running sessions in which she averaged about three sessions per week. Each session contained three or four intervals of 0.6 mile which resulted in complete runs of 1.8 to 2.4 miles. The total distance covered during each session varied depending upon the subject's wishes. Running occurred in two different settings. The subject ran 30 times in a park located in her suburban home community. She ran three times on the East side of Manhattan between 74th Street and 89th Street so that she could be interviewed immediately after her run. The environment was somewhat similar to the suburban setting because the traffic was minimal in the city location which included Gracie Park.

Since we were interested in answering the broad question, "Why is sport meaningful to so many people?" our subject was asked directly what she had experienced while jogging. The procedures employed to collect her responses included psychiatric interviews and a personal diary. The diary prepared by the subject contained 32 dated entries maintained throughout the 4 month period. Three hour-long psychiatric interviews of more than an hour length were conducted by a trained clinician and were held weekly during June, 1976.

We did not ask the simple question, "Why do you run?" because our experience indicated that we could expect only culturally accepted answers such as "I like it," "It's fun," or "I want to keep in shape." The basic reasons for sports participation are often obscure because of unconscious needs, wishes, and feelings. Conscious answers are merely rationalizations, and the true reasons remain hidden by the use of defense mechanisms (Freud, 1966).

Psychiatric Interviews. The psychiatric interview was a useful procedure to break through defensive resistance and ultimately uncover the meanings associated with running. Three weekly interviews were conducted immediately following the subject's runs in Manhattan and each was approx-imately 50 minutes in length, audio-recorded, and later transcribed to facilitate analysis. The foci of each interview were the identification and ex-amination of the subject's reactions to both the external events which oc-curred during each run and to her private thoughts, feelings, and emotions which she had while running. Although thoughts were an important part of the interaction, feelings and emotions were the focus because they signified more accurately the authentic phenomenological experience.

During each interview, the subject was encouraged to freely associate the feelings, emotions, and thoughts she had during the run with past ex-periences of her life. She was also encouraged to fantasize the meaning of selected events and thoughts. Fantasy allowed us to uncover the inner world by bypassing her defenses. The interviewer's responsibilities were to elicit and reflect the feelings and meanings of the subject, to support her in whatever she revealed, and to seek confirmation or denial of his reflective interven-tions.

Personal Journal. The subject's journal consisted of 32 one-to-two page written reports of her stream-of-consciousness thoughts while jogging. Thought processes of one running session were not recorded. The subject at-tempted to record the sequence and content of her consciousness as ac-curately as possible. The first 12 reports were recorded immediately upon the subject's return home from jogging by automobile, a distance of ½ mile. Recognizing the difficulty of recalling her inner experiences in complete detail, the subject recorded her thoughts immediately following each 0.6 mile run-ning interval of each complete running session during the remaining 20 ses-sions instead of waiting until she returned home.

Results and Discussion

Analysis and interpretation of the large corpus of verbal material (more than 100 typewritten pages) was troublesome. The first task was to gather the data as systematically and reliably as possible and to complete the artistic stage of using the data to generate hypotheses. As our theoretical base becomes established, we will follow the "scientific" procedures of content analysis (Gerbner et al., 1969).

The analysis suggested four propositions which are intended to serve as guides for analyzing data collected from future subjects. These tentative pro-positions may be altered or expanded in number with new evidence. Data for one subject does not reveal the truth for everyone, however, the propositions are broad statements which are applicable to a wide variety of people. As data is collected on additional subjects, we anticipate discovering similar meanings common to other women and men.

A subjective analysis of interview and journal data produced evidence to the following propositions:

Proposition One. Participation in sports involves experiencing a wide spectrum of emotions ranging from agony to ecstasy.

Proposition Two. Sports such as jogging are conducive to introspection as well as to thinking in general.

Proposition Three. Engagement in sport satisfies inner psychodynamic needs.

Proposition Four. Awareness of private, phenomenological experiences associated with sport can be useful for gaining self-understanding.

Proposition One

Participation in sports involves experiencing a wide spectrum of emotions ranging from agony to ecstasy. Our subject clearly experienced more than 30 different kinds of feelings and emotions which included: fright, hostility, hopelessness, loneliness, pleasure, power, and resentment (Davitz, 1969). The following quotations reflect several more common emotions the subject experienced while she ran.

Aliveness. It was a privilege to run today. It was great. It was great to be alive. It was great to be in the City. I love running over there by the Park. I like the people; I like the water; I like Gracie Mansion . . . Oh, what a marvelous feeling; the park—dark, drizzling, with seagulls flying and squawking. It felt so good to be alive!

Anger. I can rub everybody out like Superwoman. Zap! Just stay out of my way. . . . It's my secret blowgun, just to wipe people . . . . Erasing them.

Competency. Good workout—could hardly breathe for the last ¼ of the run. When I started out, I really felt strong. Went fast and felt great. Seem to recover quickly from the ½ mile intervals. CAN DO IT!

Control. I was running around people . . . around cars. I was watching the lights. Timing everything. I was dodging traffic and I felt like cars couldn't hurt me which is a very dangerous feeling. (Interviewer: Maybe not. Maybe you were in supreme control.) I was . . . I feel great, energetic, alive, the master of my fate.

Fear of Death. My heart started hurting . . . the chest pains made me feel my chest and say, "Hey, is that my imagination or is that real?" My chest was really moving a lot . . . So I didn't know if it (her chest) was doing it too much or if it was customary, and I was concerned as to what the feeling meant . . . I was wondering, "Gee, what would happen if along here I had a heart attack . . . I would fall dead.

Guilt. I steal time from things that I should be doing to jog . . . What's happening at home? What else do I have to do? Dinner has to be on the table at five-thirty . . . . It's taking from him (her son) . . . . I do have some guilt there that I have not resolved . . . . I should learn not to have the guilt in some way.

Power. I felt very powerful. I guess you could call it in control . . . . It feels good . . . . I felt as though I could run forever . . . . I could jump over the top of buildings.

Proposition Two

Sports such as jogging are conducive to introspection as well as to thinking in general. In support of the introspective opportunities in jogging, the subject reported, "When I'm running, it seems like I'm dreaming and a lot of thoughts go through my mind very, very quickly. And you can get in touch with things quickly if you are aware of what you're doing and what the day has been like."

A major area of self-examination by the subject was her view of herself as a legitimate runner. Was she running fast enough? Did she run far enough? Should she enter a marathon? Is she too old for competition?

Often the subject contemplated the psychological benefits of running and her ever-present feeling of being inundated with obligations. In one of her journal entries, she said:

> Jogging is a real gift to oneself. It's a form of self-affirmation to say that one is important enough to devote an entire hour to oneself. Too often we are doing things that we "must." Things that we have allowed other people to dump on us—so many obligations, responsibilities. So little choice . . . Time to get out of that trap . . . I have had enough of that shit . . . of blaming self, self-criticism.

As for thinking in general, the subject reviewed conversations she had with members of her family and friends, planned her time to accomplish both family and professional tasks, entertained solutions to problems, and reflected on the people, scenery, and events that she encountered as she jogged. She seemed to give a great deal of thought to physical symptoms associated with running such as rapid heart and respiration rates, sore muscles, and tiredness. As reported in her journal, "The legs felt good . . . All I felt was my lower calf muscles working—like they are supposed to, I guess."

On other days, there was a complete absence of thoughts and introspections—a mediation or self-hypnotic form of experience. Our subject reported,

> Fun! Today, I was running *away* from it all. Originally I thought, "I'll really use this time to figure out my problems." Then a little way into my run, I decided, "This is nonsense. I need time for myself today. I want to get into my *space* and *float.*" No worries; no cares. I need to get away for a little while.

Proposition Three

Engagement in sport satisfied inner psychodynamic needs. Analysis of the subject's family history, her history of jogging, journal entries, and interview transcripts leads to the inference that two interrelated psychodynamic factors were working to ward off or contain her anxiety. One factor is her characteriological structure; the other factor is her relationships with her father and brother.

Similar to many successful, professional people, our subject exhibited an obsessive-compulsive constellation of behaviors. Obsessive-compulsive behavior is characterized, *in its most extreme form*, by intense, highly focused rigidity; driven preoccupation with technical detail; over-reliance on intellectuality with a shrinking of affective capacity; worry and marked self-criticism; over-concern for moral and professional responsibility with emphasis on what should be done; and constant routine activity performed with the use of a schedule and checklists (Shapiro, 1965, pp. 23-53).

The subject's obsessive-compulsive behaviors were manifested and reinforced by jogging and her professional life. She had a riveted concern for accomplishment and criticized herself when she didn't reach her goals. She was driven to "get things done" and "not waste time" at home, at work, and while jogging. For example, she set daily tasks for herself before she jogged. She reported in her journal, "I've been running late at night simply because . . . I have not gotten finished my daily list of things to do."

Our subject reports that she first started to jog during her pregnancy. She said she was "anxious and afraid of becoming obese and shapeless." Although we did not follow up on her concern for obesity, we speculate that it was unfounded because her ectomorphic body type hardly lends itself to obesity.

Following the birth of her son she stopped jogging for 2 years and took it up again when she was experiencing intense personal (marital) and professional problems. Similarly, the subject engaged in competitive swimming during adolescence while her parents experienced discord, separation, and divorce. She said it was a way to get away from it all.

The similarity between swimming and jogging is congruent with an obsessive-compulsive character. Both activities require the completion of repetitive routine laps, necessitate focusing on exact time and distance, are performed alone, and provide little variability in temporal and spatial factors. The obsessive-compulsive personality thrives on control, intense focus, and routine to ward off anxiety. The subject used swimming to ward off anxiety associated with her parents' marital discord and jogged to contain the anxiety related to her physical appearance when pregnant and her own marital and professional problems.

Our jogger's compulsive style also was evident in her repression of feelings—even over pleasant ones. During one interview she revealed how she avoided feeling at ease and relaxed after she jogged. When asked, "Does this kind of relaxed feeling occur frequently following jogging?", she replied,

> Generally not . . . because I'm not sitting and relaxing . . . . Generally, immediately after jogging, I go straight home and work at my desk and do a lot of writing or whatever the horrible things were that during the day I couldn't stand to do . . . . That's when I have my most productive spurts of work . . . . My usual days are that I'm locked into a time space—totally tight.

During another interview she avoided the experience of pain. The following interview exchange occurred immediately upon her return from a jogging session during which she had fallen on the pavement:

> *I* — Does that hurt? (pointing to her bleeding shin)
> *S* — No!
> *I* — That was a fast answer.
> *S* — Why should my shin hurt?
> *I* — It would if it was my shin. I know I'd be in agony.
> *S* — There? (pointing to shin) That doesn't hurt at all. It's a scratch. It doesn't hurt. No, I have a lot more hard knocks than that, Mac. You see, I'm Wonder Woman.

The following vignette, taken from several interviews, supported the proposition that the subject's approach to jogging was characteriologically determined. Throughout her journal entries and interviews, the subject expressed concern about wearing shorts; she was also extremely reluctant (certainly embarrassed) to examine sexuality and feminine seductiveness. It became clear that she was denying her sexual feelings and thoughts and was caught up in social sanctions. The following extended interview quotations illustrate this idea:

> *I* — Do you ever run in shorts?
> *S* — At home in the park, I feel fine . . . . If it's hot, I have an excuse.
> *I* — So you have an excuse. An excuse for what?
> *S* — For wearing my shorts. That I'm not an exhibitionist. I'm not wanting everyone to look at me as I run around and have people think, "Oh, look at that strange person."
> *I* — What's the matter with people looking at you?
> *S* — I don't like that at all. Oh, I don't (sic) mind it if I feel that they're thinking something funny about me like (pause)
> *I* — Like what?
> *S* — Look at that peculiar person. What's she running for? What's she trying to prove. OR (pause)
> *I* — Look at that sexy broad running down the . . . .
> *S* — Yes! No, I don't want them to think that. So I try to be very professional about my running and make everyone know that I am serious . . .

later in the interview

I — What are you excusing when you put on trousers?

S — I don't have to excuse myself when it's hot, do I? Excusing (pause) exposing my body.

I — O.K. Well, what's the matter with your legs?

S — Nothing. Then we get into sex. Then I might excite somebody, and I don't want to be responsible for that.

I — You take responsibility for somebody else's excitement?

S — Yes, yes. If I have on shorts (laughs anxiously). If I have a long dress or something, then whatever they do to themselves they have done it and I am the innocent person.

The subject did, however, strongly believe that her concern about running attire was socially, rather than personally based. Approaching the topic of shorts in a subsequent interview, the subject reacted defensively saying, "I would like to point out also that . . . when I was discussing running with a girl friend of mine who runs in the City, one of her first questions was not only "*Where* did you run?" but "*What* did you wear?" . . . Another female who runs at least has the same reaction."

Although jogging exacerbated the subject's behavioral style, it also had beneficial effects. While she jogged, she experienced a sense of power and control (see pp. 103-104) which offset her feelings of helplessness (Hogan, 1974) during the time of her parents' discord, when she was pregnant, and while she was having personal and professional problems. She reported after many jogging sessions, "I feel fantastic. That's the way I always feel when I run, and sometimes if I'm in a bad mood or feeling ineffective, the thought of getting ready to run makes me feel better."

When our subject recalled her early family history, it was illuminating to discover other important reasons for her interest in jogging. Two dynamics seemed to be at work. On the one hand, she may have been competing with her brother as a form of sibling rivalry. On the other, she was trying to assure herself of her father's love because he had recently been very critical of her. On one occasion during her run in Manhattan, our subject reported:

There's a Doctor's Hospital or some hospital along East End, in the 80s. And there's this tall, elderly man carrying what looked like a physician's bag. And I decided, "Well, I'm really going to show you what a female can do!" So I ran very fast to impress him. (Interviewer: So you have to prove something?) I had to show him that women aren't weak, and it's hot, and women can run very well. Because most doctors think women are weak.

In her inner world, the subject seemed to be trying to win her father's approval. During her adolescence, he claimed she was "wasting time" as a competitive swimmer and insisted that she stop. In an attempt to prove that her father's judgment was wrong, she continued to try to prove herself unconsciously while jogging. During one interview she said:

> I want to see how far I can go, how long I can go, how fast. I want to know what I can do if I try . . . . So I think I could do this and that but I don't test myself to find out. So you never know if you're kidding yourself or not. And I'd like to know what I could do.

Another journal entry supported the idea that a relationship existed between the subject's family and her interest in jogging. The "fellow jogger" in the following quotation fitted her brother's age, and she associated her father's anger with jogging.

> Passed another fellow jogger going in the opposite direction . . . . Typical athlete of 15 years ago . . . . He had run further than I in the same length of time. Always comparing. Always *SHOULD* do more. Upset that my father is angry. He is disappointed in me—very much. *STOP*. Must go on to other things.

During the final interview, the puzzle about why she ran began to fit together as evidenced by the following extended conversation:

I — You were trying to prove the thing (her legitimacy as a runner) to the doctor last week.

S — Right. Right. I did that again today. I do that.

I — What did you do again today?

S — There was this older man coming out of a building and walking across the street somewhere as I was coming back.

I — Hey, gramps! Look at me, gramps! Man, I'm a strong woman, gramps!

S — Right! . . . And he, and he was staring, you know, he really looked at me very peculiarly . . .

I — Well, if you could take his role, what do you think he was saying?

S — I don't have any idea. How's that . . . all about?

I — In your fantasy, what do you think he was saying?

S — He could have thought I was an idiot. How's that for a negative view? He could have thought I was an idiot. Or thought (pause) I don't know. I refuse to do that . . . .

I — O.K. So there's something there you don't want to look at. That's O.K.

S — But it's like whenever there are people around I definitely react to them. Last night as I was jogging, there were two other joggers behind me and one of them passed me.

I — Oh-Oh!

S — (laugh) And then I speeded up and the second one didn't pass me. But I don't want to speed up to make it look too obvious that I cared. So, I did it a little sneakily (laugh). I had to make it so that they couldn't notice I was speeding up. They just couldn't pass me, that's all.

I — Well, my guess is that those people—the old man, the doctor last week, the runner who didn't pass you—represent your own internal critic . . . .

later in the interview

S — . . . Because my brother was a very good runner and gave it up because he didn't want to do it after high school. And his . . . .

I — I'll show you, brother. I won't quit. You quit, but I'll never quit.

S — Right! That, disturbed me when he quit . . . . And then my father was a runner in high school and college . . . in college, the State Champion in Iowa.

I — At what distance?

S — At a mile (laugh). Fits, eh?

I — It sure does!

S — No, it's ridiculous. This really is. I'm just running because I want to run. (At this point, the subject was defensively annoyed and was obviously defending against the pain of her poor relationship with her father and the loss and grief related to her brother's recent death. Later in the interview she openly expressed her hurt and grief.)

I — Yeah, but both can be working. You can enjoy your running and want to run. But, then, you're after the question in your notes constantly, "How come I'm running?"

S — Right. That's what I want to know.

I — I think we're touching on that right now.

S — Probably. That when my father comes to visit me, if I'm running or jogging, he'll go out and jog with me.

Proposition Four

Awareness of private phenomenological experiences associated with sport can be useful for gaining self-understanding. Our subject was beginning to understand her need to jog and her intense competitiveness. She also gained insight into her drive to accomplish as she reflected on her family experiences.

The subject viewed herself as being very competitive both with herself and others. In reference to self-competition, she observed, "I just won't know how far I have gone (as a result of running in a new unmeasured setting). Being in great competition with myself, I find that greatly distracting. Why do I get caught in this race with myself? Can I tolerate not knowing how far I have gone?" Other joggers (all male) also made her aware of her competitiveness:

There was one other jogger out today—a male who had a lot more speed than I . . . . We met at one point on each cycle around . . . . I was wondering how much stamina he had—felt a little insecure since he was going faster than I. What a competitor! Is it good or bad? Interesting. Will have to test my reactions another time. Can I stop competing . . . ? I kept in the back of my mind, the other jogger. Where was he? What was he thinking about me?

Further analysis of the profuse amount of journal and interview data indicates how our subject expanded her self-awareness and self-understanding. She began to realize the depth of her hurt. She became aware of her self-criticism and self-punishment and how these attitudes contributed to a denial of her obvious capability to function adequately. She grew to realize that she worried compulsively about inconsequential details, and began to see how her personality was related to her father and brother. As a result of the findings of this study, it is responsible to postulate that analysis of experiences in sport can facilitate self-understanding.

The case study of a woman jogger revealed four propositions concerning the psychological meaning of jogging. It resulted in a wide spectrum of emotions ranging from agony to ecstasy. It was conducive to introspection as well as to thinking in general. It satisfied inner psychodynamic needs. Awareness of private, phenomenological experiences associated with jogging was useful for gaining self-understanding.

Several methodological needs for future studies are evident. First, the journal-keeping procedures should be formalized. That is, subjects should receive instructions as to how and when to record their thoughts and emotions, and a procedure for obtaining an explanation of unclear entries should be established. Second, each interview transcript must be reviewed carefully before the succeeding interview. It may be necessary to clarify or pursue an idea, and make connections between material uncovered in one interview and material revealed in subsequent interviews. This is particularly important since the number of interviews in future studies will be limited to three or four to make data collection manageable.

Lastly, it is important to systematize the analysis and interpretation of interview data. Content analysis of the data could provide a totally objective summary of the material. However, there is much more than verbal content that inheres in a psychiatric interview (Psathas, 1969). There are roles which the two participants assume, nonverbal content, vocal or sound content associated with words, idiosyncratic syntax, and hidden meanings revealed by surface structure of what is said (Bandler & Grinder, 1975). Combining the objective method of content analysis with an explicitly described subjective analysis probably will result in the most accurate and informative interpretation of the collected data.

We are aware that our research relies heavily on artful, intuitive interview techniques and inferential analysis of interview and journal entries. Nonetheless, we will undoubtedly obtain new kinds of data that will serve to illuminate the significance of sport to athletes. We believe that it is necessary to postpone and also forego absolute scientism for a nonreductionistic, humanistic understanding of human behavior in a compelling and obviously meaningful part of human experience.

References

Aigner, H. Why sports get you high: An interview with R. Ornstein. *Women Sports*, 1974, **1**(7), 53-54.

Bandler, R., & Grinder, J. *The structure of magic* (Vol. 1). Palo Alto: Science & Behavior Books, 1975.

Beisser, A. *Madness in sports*. New York: Appleton-Century-Crofts, 1967.

Clarke, R., & Harris, N. *The lonely breed.* London: Pelham Books, 1967.

Davitz, J. *The language of emotion.* New York: Academic Press, 1969.

Freud, A. *The writings of Anna Freud* (Vol. 2). New York: International Universities Press, 1966.

Furlong, W.B. The fun in fun. *Psychology Today,* 1976, **10**(1), 35-38; 80.

Gerbner, G. et al. (Eds.). *The analysis of communication content.* New York: John Wiley & Sons, 1969.

Glasser, W. *Positive addiction.* New York: Harper & Row, 1976.

Harris, D.V. *Involvement in sport: A somatopsychic rationale for physical activity.* Philadelphia: Lea & Febiger, 1973.

Hogan, P. Some aspects of my theory and practice of group therapy. In D. S. Milman & G. D. Goldman (Eds.), *Group process today.* Springfield: Charles C. Thomas, 1974.

Huey, L. *A running start: An athlete, a woman.* New York: Quadrangle Books, 1976.

Ismail, A.H., & Trachtman, L.E. Jogging the imagination. *Psychology Today,* 1973, **6**(10), 78-82.

Lamb, L.E. (Ed.). Jogging, exertion and sudden death. In *The health newsletter,* 1974, **4**(2).

Lipsyte, R. *Sports world: An American dreamland.* New York: Quadrangle Books, 1975.

Mahler, M., Pine, F., & Bergman, A. *The psychological birth of the human infant.* New York: Basic Books, 1975.

Metheny, E. *Connotations of movement in sport and dance.* Dubuque, IA: Wm. C. Brown Co., 1965.

Michener, J.A. *Sports in America.* New York: Random House, 1976.

Moore, K. Watching their steps. *Sports Illustrated,* 1976, **44**(18), 80-90.

Moore, R.A. *Sports and mental health.* Springfield: Charles C. Thomas, 1966.

Neal, P. *Sport and identity.* Philadelphia: Dorrance & Co., 1972.

Novak, M. *The joy of sports.* New York: Basic Books, 1976.

Psathas, G. Analyzing dyadic interaction. In G. Gerbner, et al. (Eds.), *The analysis of communication content.* New York: John Wiley & Sons, 1969.

Shapiro, D. *Neurotic styles.* New York: Basic Books, 1965.

Shvartz, E. Nietzsche: A philosopher of fitness. In E. Gerber (Ed.), *Sport and the body.* Philadelphia: Lea & Febiger, 1972.

Slusher, H.S. *Man, sport and existence: A critical analysis.* Philadelphia: Lea & Febiger, 1967.

Smith, A. Sport is a Western yoga. *Psychology Today,* 1975, **9**(5), 48-51; 74; 76.

Spino, M. *Beyond jogging.* Milbrae, CA: Celestial Arts, 1976.

Weiss, P. *Sport: A philosophic inquiry.* Carbondale, IL: Southern Illinois University Press, 1969.

SECTION THREE

Running Addiction

Although the term "addiction" has been used for decades in relation to drugs, alcohol, and other "negative" substances, Glasser (1976) introduced the concept of "positive addiction" to describe activities which the individual cannot do without, but which have beneficial psychological and physiological effects. This has stimulated much popular interest in the concept of running as a positive addiction.

In Chapter 10, Sachs presents an overview of addiction to running, incorporating work that he and David Pargman conducted at Florida State University. Of particular note are findings on psychological withdrawal symptoms associated with addiction to running. Runners emphasize the importance of responses such as guilt, irritability, anxiety, and tension during periods when they do not or cannot run. Although some physiological withdrawal symptoms are offered as reactions during these nonrunning periods, the preponderance of responses are psychological.

Sachs also differentiates between addiction and commitment to running. Addiction refers to the psychological relationship of the individual to running, whereas commitment represents the cognitive-intellectual aspects of this relationship. An individual may be committed to a running program because of a logical analysis of its benefits, such as attaining social contacts, health benefits, or monetary rewards, but he or she may in fact not enjoy running. These committed runners do not seem to suffer withdrawal symptoms if unable to participate, in contrast with the addicted runners, who run for psychological and physiological pleasures (Carmack & Martens, 1979; Jacobs, 1980; Sachs & Pargman, 1979).

Sacks, in Chapter 11, presents a clinical report on the syndrome of "running addiction." He considers this phenomenon as primarily a compulsive activity. The anxiety associated with the addicted runner being unable to run is viewed not as a morphine-like withdrawal, but as the irrational and peremptory anxiety of failure to complete the compulsive act. Addiction to running is for Sacks a symptom of an underlying conflict that has been symbolically expressed by compulsive running and which may require therapeutic intervention.

Joseph and Robbins also examine commitment/addiction to running. In Chapter 12, they examine the difference in work satisfaction between heavily committed runners who identify themselves primarily as runners, and those runners who do not similarly identify themselves. They found that heavily committed runners are more likely to be dissatisfied with their work as a source of creative possibilities and self-expression than the nonheavily committed runners. This difference is interpreted as part of a generally observed shift in our culture from work to leisure as a primary source in defining one's identity. The authors suggest that commitment/addiction to running may represent a symptomatic attempt to deal with such problems in being able to define a stable and satisfactory sense of self through work.

Whether addiction to running is a phenomenon or pseudophenomenon is still a subject of debate, and the issue may lie in the failure to adequately distinguish addiction from habit, commitment, or compulsion (Peele, 1979). The potential importance of neurochemical factors in addiction to running complicates the debate, as discussed by Mandell and Riggs, who in Section 5 examine neurophysiological and biochemical changes associated with distance running. Of special importance is the relationship of the opiate-like peptides known as the endorphins to the general state of addiction to running. The addicted runner may be biologically dependent on a self-induced chemical high. Other physical changes such as improved muscle tone, pleasurable sensations of fatigue, changes in hippocampal neuronal discharge activity, endocrine changes, and so on may also play an important role in the effects of and continued attraction to running. Although many questions remain to be answered, research in this area may prove to be of particular importance in providing a greater understanding of the intimate interrelation between psychological and biological components of running addiction.

References

Carmack, M.A., & Martens, R. Measuring commitment to running: A survey of runners' attitudes and mental states. *Journal of Sport Psychology*, 1979, **1**, 25-42.

Glasser, W. *Positive addiction*. New York: Harper & Row, 1976.

Jacobs, L.W. *Running as an addiction process.* Unpublished doctoral dissertation, University of Alberta, 1980.

Peele, S. Redefining addiction II. The meaning of addiction in our lives. *Journal of Psychedelic Drugs,* October-December 1979, **11,** 289-297.

Sachs, M.L., & Pargman, D. Running addiction: A depth interview examination. *Journal of Sport Behavior,* 1979, **2,** 143-155.

CHAPTER 10

Running Addiction

Michael L. Sachs

In 1979 more than 10,000 runners competed in, and completed, the 26 miles, 385 yards of the New York City marathon. Yet this large number of marathoners represents only a fraction of the millions who now jog or run regularly. Some of these regular runners and joggers will eventually drop out of running, turned off by injuries or nonattainment of goals, or bored by the repetitive nature of the activity which is unlike, for example, tennis or racquetball. But many millions will adhere to a regular program of running, will continue for months and years, through all kinds of injuries, weather, family turmoil, travels, or whatever. These runners are well on their way to becoming, if they have not already become, addicted.

This article will attempt to assess the phenomenon of addiction to running. Background on the topic of addiction in general and addiction to running in particular will first be provided. Then, recent developments and thinking in this area will be examined and thoughts for the future offered.

It would first be appropriate to define the context in which the term addiction will be used in this paper. Seventeen years ago the World Health Organization suggested dropping terms such as drug addiction and drug habituation in favor of the term drug dependence. This was due in part to the frequently inappropriate use of the term addiction. The same criticisms may be levied today. Although the term dependence may be preferable, addiction remains in extensive use and will be used herein.

Peele (1978) has provided a number of points to consider in discussing addiction. It is important to note that addiction is a process, rather than a condition. It is not an all-or-none state of being, unambiguously present or absent. Addiction is an extension of ordinary behavior, a pathological habit, dependence, or compulsion. It is not characteristic of drugs or activities per se, but of the involvement a person forms with these substances or events. When involvement eliminates choice in all areas of life, then an addiction has been formed. Given this view, it is reasonable to assume that addiction may become characteristic of participation in physical activity, including running, swimming, and playing tennis.

The concept of addiction used in relation to such salubrious experiences as exercise and meditation was first popularized by William Glasser (1976) in his book *Positive Addiction*. Glasser's work is essentially an examination of addictions which he views as supportive of the addict's psychology and physiology. Positive addictions, such as running and meditation, are thought to provide psychological strength and increase the satisfaction derived from life. This is in sharp contrast to common, or negative, addictions such as to alcohol or heroin, which weaken and often undermine the psychological and physiological integrity of an individual. The thesis of Glasser's work is that "Many people, weak and strong, can help themselves to be stronger; and an important new path to strength may be positive addiction" (p. 11).

Although Glasser's work is not scientifically based in the sense of rigorous experimental design and statistical analysis, useful clinical and psychiatric assessments are included. A general feeling of "high" or euphoria experienced by regular runners is reported. Classic descriptions of the positive addiction state include a loss of the sense of oneself, floating, euphoria, and a total integration with running. Glasser recommends running for anyone, both psychologically strong and weak, who desires a positively addicting activity.

The literature on addiction to exercise is relatively sparse. One major reason for this is that you cannot persuade addicted runners to stop running in order to study the effects of exercise deprivation on these individuals. The confounding effects of physical injury, often the only factor causing the addicted runner to stop running for a period of time, makes interpretation of psychological reactions during this deprivation state difficult.

A few studies, however, have examined psychological characteristics of the exercise addict. Sachs and Pargman (1979) examined runners at varying stages of addiction. Reasons for beginning participation were varied and included influences from other individuals, concerns of general health, improvement of cardiovascular fitness, and body weight reduction. These reasons continued to be present as the running programs of the participants were maintained and as addiction developed, but additional psychological considerations such as feeling better, relaxing, and getting away from things became manifest. Running developed into a significant part of the participants' lives.

A definition of running addiction was proposed: addiction, of a psychological and/or physiological nature, upon a regular regimen of running, characterized by withdrawal symptoms after 24-36 hours without participation. These withdrawal symptoms appear to be critical in the determination of the degree of addiction to running. Reported withdrawal symptoms include feelings of anxiety, restlessness, guilt, irritability, tension, bloatedness, muscle twitching, and discomfort. Glasser suggests that a period of 2 years may be required before positive addiction can be developed, but the runners in our studies and other reported research have indicated development of exercise addiction within 4 to 6 months.

Research by Carmack and Martens (1979) has examined what they term "Commitment to Running," which we view as synonymous with addiction to running. Runners scoring higher on a measure of commitment to running indicated experiencing greater discomfort when a run was missed, a higher level of perceived addiction, and ran for longer periods of time on their regular runs. In this study, as in those we have conducted, runners scoring high on commitment to running tend to give reasons of a psychological nature for adherence to participation.

Combinations of running and meditation have been used in programs to develop positive addiction and promote the psychological benefits resulting from participation in these activities. Solomon and Bumpus (1978) have proposed a "running meditation response" as a viable adjunct to psychotherapy. They indicate that running regularly leads to addiction:

> We emphasize running three to five days a week simply because regularity leads to addiction, a key factor in the success of this method. The more frequently the patient runs, the more he will experience the pleasurable and desirable effects of running and, consequently, the more quickly he will become addicted. Addiction usually occurs in two to four months. Once the patient is 'hooked,' he will feel a compulsion to run. If he does not, he will experience withdrawal symptoms, such as anxiety, not feeling well, or insomnia. (p. 585)

Investigations have also been conducted into the physiological components of addiction to exercise. The discovery of naturally occurring opiate-like peptides known as the endorphins has been the cause of speculation that these compounds may be related to altered states of consciousness experienced during running and the development of running addiction. Although this line of research holds promise, initial research efforts, by Glasser (1978, 1979), for example, have not produced results that support this suggested relationship, and we must await more sophisticated investigations before assessing the effects of the endorphins on the development of exercise addiction. Researchers such as Brown and Mandell are presently conducting research which may achieve such results in the near future.

One area receiving fairly strong interest has been the personality of the runner. Approximately 40 studies deal in some manner with personality and running, be it an examination of personality characteristics of runners or changes due to participation in an exercise program. This literature is characterized by use of a wide variety of personality inventories, by a predominance of studies examining changes in personality due to participation in an exercise program, by investigation of, for the most part, male participants, and by a lack of a theoretical base. Many of these characteristics may be noted, however, in much of the sport personology literature.

Some general conclusions may be presented, though. A number of studies by Morgan (Morgan & Costill, 1972; Morgan & Pollock, 1977; Morgan, Note 1) and by Kostrubala (Clitsome & Kostrubala, 1977; Gontang, Clitsome, & Kostrubala, 1977) have examined the introversion/extraversion characteristics of runners. The findings of these studies are equivocal, with some evidence indicating that runners tend to differ from other athletic subgroups in being more introverted, although not differing from the general population, and other findings suggesting that runners tend to be more introverted than the norm. Difficulty in presenting a true picture of the nature of introversion/extraversion in runners is compounded by the use of differing groups of subjects, from world class marathon runners, to runners who had completed a marathon race, to intercollegiate cross-country competitors. Differences among these samples cannot be resolved until more widespread testing is conducted.

Results from these and other studies suggest that runners are introverted, stable, low on anxiety, self-sufficient, high on self-esteem, and imaginative. Although a profile of this sort may be teased out of the data, many problems with reported research findings remain. These include the testing of many different groups of subjects, use of numerous personality instruments, univariate analyses of data, and comparison groups used. Generalizations at this point must be made with caution, and the researcher/clinician interested in the relationship of personality and running is well advised to consider the problems encountered.

One of the major questions that remains to be answered about addiction to running deals with the development of this phenomenon in the individual. One initial approach to this problem is the determination of personality characteristics associated with addiction. The association of certain traits with differing levels of addiction would suggest avenues of research to be investigated in the search for causal, in addition to correlational, factors.

The personality traits of 100 male runners from Tallahassee, Florida were assessed to examine the relationship of these factors to addiction (Sachs, Note 2). The personality traits were introversion/extraversion, neuroticism/stability, mood states, trait anxiety, and locus of control. The relationship of these constructs to running had been demonstrated in previous research. Findings, however, indicated only very modest correlations between any of the traits and level of addiction, which was measured by the score on the Carmack and Martens (1979) Commitment to Running scale. Two conclusions seemed most plausible: Either the variables selected were not good predictors of addiction, or the measures used failed to reveal the extent of the relationship of these factors to addiction. Scores of the runners were not very different from the published norms for the personality traits. Casual observation suggests that regular runners tend to be a fairly diverse group, and it is likely that general trait characterizations of the addicted runner's personality may not be meaningful. Morgan (1973) has indicated, however, the potential of consideration of state factors, such as anxiety, in research in this area.

Perhaps the most fascinating area of research in the psychology of running is the use of running, and exercise in general, as a psychotherapeutic modality. Because this topic is addressed more thoroughly by others in this volume, it will be discussed only briefly here. The use of running therapy has received increasing attention in recent years, and research and theoretical advances are being made rapidly. Its use has ranged from specific applications in successful treatment of phobias to general treatment of depression and anxiety. Hypotheses that may help explain the beneficial effects of running relate to mastery, capacity for change, distraction, symptom relief, consciousness alteration, biochemical changes, and positive habit or addiction. In addition to its application in psychotherapy, running has been used in stress management.

It is consistently reported that participants feel better after they exercise, although this is not always supported by reductions in test scores. Morgan's (Bahrke & Morgan, 1978; Morgan, 1973) findings suggest that physical activity may modify state variables such as anxiety and depression, but not trait variables as noted earlier. Depending on whom one reads, running has been categorized as a panacea for many ills and suggested as having attained the status of a religion. But beyond these overly embellished presentations, the feel-better phenomenon, the reduction in anxiety and depression, the increases in feelings of control, the physiological improvements are all positive benefits that runners consistently cite.

Given these positive benefits, it is likely that regular participation in physical activity, manifested through addiction, has important implications for the effectiveness of approaches such as that of Solomon and Bumpus (1978). Maintenance of tension reduction and management of stress through the use of exercise, for example, represent significant practical objectives.

The bottom line in the development of addiction to running is adherence. You can't develop addiction to the activity unless you participate on a regular basis. I noted earlier that a range of 4 months to 2 years has been suggested as being necessary for addiction to develop, although a time frame as short as even 1 month has been cited as sufficient for the development of running addiction. Numerous factors have been found to be related to adherence, including the role of significant others, attainment or nonattainment of exercise objectives, and injuries. Research by Dishman (Dishman, Ickes, & Morgan, 1980) suggests that prediction of exercise adherence can be enhanced by measurement of body fat and body weight, in conjunction with self-motivation scores.

This leads to a question that has not been adequately addressed: How does addiction to running develop? This addiction is generally positive, and I will operate under the assumption that negatively addicting aspects of running, which will be discussed shortly, come only after one has progressed into and through the stage of positive addiction.

One critical factor has been presented by Dishman: self-motivation. Before addiction can develop, the individual must be motivated to continue running for an extended period of time. There are many reasons for starting to run. A fair percentage of individuals soon find that running is not for them and revert to states of inactivity or try other sports. But runners who do continue are buoyed by positively and negatively reinforcing contingencies. There are the inevitable positive comments of how well one looks, how much weight has been lost, the interactions with running friends and social atmosphere at races and track club meetings, and the feeling of being in better shape. Negatively reinforcing consequences arise from fear of what might happen if one should miss a day, or if one doesn't run as much as one is supposed to on a given day.

Whatever the reasons, participation becomes a habit, a regular part of daily activity. At this stage the runner is hooked. Other aspects of life begin to be shaped around the daily run, with changes in eating and sleeping schedules, as well as in time spent with family members. These are in addition to changes in diet and leisure time activities, the latter frequently encompassing races or long runs on Saturday mornings, and voracious reading of books and magazines on running. Running has become a compulsion, a habit, an addiction. When days are missed, withdrawal symptoms become immediately apparent and generally powerful. Running has become much more than a means to the end of getting in shape; it has become the end itself. The need to run becomes omnipresent.

There is a nebulous area here, an idiosyncratic one, wherein the degree of addiction may be said to shift from positive to negative. Lest this seem an unimportant zone, we should consider that running would move from an important, but considered aspect of one's existence, to a controlling factor, eliminating other choices in life. The runner must learn where his or her fine line between positive and negative addiction exists.

But what is this negative addiction to running? We need to carefully examine the concept of running as a positive addiction. Although exercise evangelists have clearly publicized running as a positive addiction, Morgan (1979) has presented evidence concerning negative aspects of this experience. Although initially the idea of exercise evangelists may seem somewhat strong, one might cite a racing experience of former President Jimmy Carter. Carter entered a 10,000 meter race, but was forced to drop out after 3½ miles suffering from severe heat stress. Afterwards, however, he said that running was "a great thing" and urged audience members to become "evangelists" for the sport.

Morgan (1979) has noted that the development of exercise addiction does not differ from addictive processes in general. I emphasized earlier that addiction is characteristic, not of any particular substances or activities, but of the involvement that a person forms with these drugs or events. Although running may generally be classified as positive, abuse may become manifest (in other words, too much of a good thing), and negative addiction may be noted. Morgan cites a number of case studies of runners who are virtually consumed by the need to run. These runners alter their daily schedules dramatically, continue to run when seriously injured, and neglect the responsibilities of work, home, and family. Morgan indicates that the behavior of the hard-core exercise addict resembles that of other major addictions.

Those readers who are regular runners, and who may be addicted, may recognize symptoms of negative addiction in themselves or their friends. The toll of heavy training takes form in decreased ability to concentrate, listlessness, fatigue, constant thought about running, and other subtle signs. More obvious symptoms include skipping appointments because of the need to run. Because runners tend to be, on the whole, well educated, many negatively addicted participants might be able to acknowledge the existence of these symptoms and the effects of running on their lives. Accepting help is another matter, however.

I must emphasize, though, that for the vast majority of runners the development of addiction to the activity represents a positive aspect of life. For the negative addict, on the other hand, we need to give thought to programs of therapy designed to reduce the level of addiction. What form might such programs take? Initially, general information about the phenomenon of negative addiction must be provided in an effort to make negatively addicted runners aware of their dependence. Meetings should be held to discuss the concept of addiction to running in general and should focus specifically on behaviors that characterize the negatively addicted runner. Written material could be provided to highlight important points.

But the key in treating negatively addicted runners is getting them to decrease their level of involvement and to learn to cope with the initial withdrawal symptoms associated with this reduction. Eventually, one would hope that running would be incorporated as an integral part of the individual's life style, but a part that blends well with the responsibilities of work, home, family, and other aspects of human existence. Some runners, as in Morgan's studies, can accomplish this restructuring on their own. Most, though, need the help of psychologists and psychiatrists who understand this condition, are aware of the importance of running to these individuals, and are capable of helping the runners to regroup and become human again.

What happens to the addicted runner who can't run? Usually, this is the result of an injury, which virtually always must be serious for an addicted runner to take time off. I cited a number of symptoms earlier, including feelings of anxiety, restlessness, irritability, and guilt. Clearly, these runners need coping strategies for those times when exercise deprivation occurs. If the injury does not restrict participation in other sports, activities such as swimming or bicycle riding would be recommended. But even this may not satisfy the true addict; as one person indicated when a pulled Achilles tendon forced her to stop running for a period of time and bicycle for exercise: "It was like methadone maintenance for a heroin addict."

It may be important to keep in mind, however, that regular, even daily, participation does not necessarily mean that the person is addicted. Sachs and Pargman (Note 3) have proposed an hypothesized model as a clarifier of motivation for participation in running. Two axes are conceptualized, one indicating degree of psychobiologic dependence, and the other degree of cognitive-intellectual commitment. Thus it is speculated that motivation for participation in running is best examined through a two-factor, rather than a unidimensional, model.

Commitment to running may be viewed as a multifaceted phenomenon, in that numerous social, psychological, and physiological factors appear to underlie involvement in this activity. Time spent thinking and reading about running; distance involved in traveling to races and frequency of competition; money spent on books and magazines about running and on equipment and accessories; changes in eating, drinking, sleeping, and other lifestyle patterns in order to accommodate the daily run; and the duration and intensity of running itself are all variable aspects of individual participation in running.

The committed but not dependent runner is one who does not run because of opportunities for mind-bending experiences, escape from depression, or euphoria, but for other reasons. These include health and social reasons, such as running to forestall the possibility of a heart attack due to a history of heart attacks in the family or reinforcement from running with a co-worker, friend, or spouse. Additionally, factors such as money (athletes on scholarship, professionals), prestige, power, and narcissism might come into play.

The value of making this distinction lies in consideration of the use of different therapeutic approaches for addicted and committed individuals, and in the formulation of programs designed to facilitate the development of addiction. To become addicted, commitment must first develop in maintaining participation. The task, then, is to discover those factors that result in the individual moving from the state of committed but not addicted to committed *and* addicted, and facilitating this transfer as desired.

Still, underlying these thoughts lie questions about the whys of running. Graham (1979, reprinted in this volume) has suggested, for example, a grouping of participants into categories of competitors, health nuts, and quiet-time seekers. He is a quiet-time seeker, and says:

> It seems that my crowd runs partly as an escape from the pressures of life. We're the ones for whom the change into ritual clothing, the pain of running, and the shower of cleansing constitute a daily rebaptism into newness of life. For us, the time spent running is time no one else has a claim on, and the rewards are similar to those of prayer and contemplation. Indeed, such exercise may constitute a secular pietism. (p. 821)

Graham goes on to present an important concept in motivation for running. This concept is that of the anxiety of terminal helplessness. As one of the women in his study indicated: "I am going to run until I can't put one foot in front of another, and then I'll be dead. No geriatrics ward for me" (p. 821). Hope that running will save the individual from a state of helplessness, anxiety about incapacity at life's end, hope that the runner's body will not slowly decay in a modern "convalescent home" may indeed drive a considerable number of runners forward on their daily runs.

These individuals who run religiously, as it were, are among those one would categorize as addicted, perhaps even negatively so. The concept of the anxiety of terminal helplessness is another motivation factor underlying participation in running. Understanding the motivation of the runner, I would suggest, will provide further insights into the nature of addiction in the runners we see and with whom we interact.

What future directions are envisioned in research on running addiction? There are numerous questions that I would like to pose. A clearer delineation of the parameters of addiction to exercise in general, and running in particular, is needed. Of importance is an emphasis on identifying the process by which addiction develops in the runner. What are the stages through which a person passes in the development of addiction to running, and to what extent can these stages be modified?

Although a general definition of running addiction can be provided, a more comprehensive analysis must be forthcoming, particularly with reference to the stages and time frame involved in the development of addiction and the manifestation of withdrawal symptoms. Measures of addiction to running must be formulated to more clearly differentiate among levels of addiction and to identify progression through stages in the development of addiction.

The refinement of programs incorporating the development and modification of running addiction is necessary. Programs which will help runners achieve optimal levels of addiction to obtain the maximum psychological and physiological benefits from participation, yet limit the number and intensity of withdrawal symptoms are needed. As noted earlier, we must develop coping strategies for dealing with withdrawal symptoms during periods of nonparticipation. Therapeutic approaches to the treatment of negative addiction in runners is an additional important and unexplored area. Addiction to running is a very real phenomenon, and one that deserves serious and careful scrutiny in future research efforts in sport psychology.

Reference Notes

1. Morgan, W.P. *Extraversion-neuroticism and athletic performance.* Paper presented at the 15th annual meeting of the American College of Sports Medicine, University Park, Pennsylvania, 1968.
2. Sachs, M.L. *An examination of the relationship of commitment to and dependence upon running to a model for participation in running and personality typology of regular runners.* Unpublished manuscript, Florida State University, 1979.
3. Sachs, M.L., & Pargman, D. *Commitment and addiction to regular running.* Paper presented at the annual convention of the American Alliance for Health, Physical Education, Recreation, and Dance, New Orleans, Louisiana, March 19, 1979.

References

Bahrke, M.S., & Morgan, W.P. Anxiety reduction following exercise and meditation. *Cognitive Therapy and Research,* 1978, **2,** 323-333.

Carmack, M.A., & Martens, R. Measuring commitment to running: A survey of runners' attitudes and mental states. *Journal of Sport Psychology,* 1979, **1,** 25-42.

Clitsome, T., & Kostrubala, T. A psychological study of 100 marathoners using the Myers-Briggs Type Indicator and demographic data. *Annals of the New York Academy of Sciences,* 1977, **301,** 1010-1019.

Dishman, R.K., Ickes, W., & Morgan, W.P. Self-motivation and adherence to habitual physical activity. *Journal of Applied Social Psychology,* 1980, **10,** 115-132.

Glasser, W. *Positive addiction.* New York: Harper & Row, 1976.

Glasser, W. The positive addiction experiment. *Starting Line,* 1978, **2,** 2.

Glasser, W. Glasser experiment: Results. *AAC,* February 1979, Number 4, 7.

Gontang, A., Clitsome, T., & Kostrubala, T. A psychological study of 50 sub-3-hour marathoners. *Annals of the New York Academy of Sciences,* 1977, **301,** 1020-1028.

Graham, W.F. The anxiety of the runner: Terminal helplessness. *The Christian Century,* August 29-September 5, 1979, pp. 821-823.

Morgan, W.P. Influence of acute physical activity on state anxiety. *Proceedings of the National College Physical Education Association for Men,* 76th Annual Meeting, 1973.

Morgan, W.P. Negative addiction in runners. *The Physician and Sportsmedicine,* 1979, **7**(2), 56-63; 67-70.

Morgan, W.P., & Costill, D.L. Psychological characteristics of the marathon runner. *Journal of Sports Medicine and Physical Fitness,* 1972, **12,** 42-46.

Morgan, W.P., & Pollock, M.L. Psychologic characterization of the elite distance runner. *Annals of the New York Academy of Sciences,* 1977, **301,** 382-403.

Peele, S. Addiction: The analgesic experience. *Human Nature*, 1978, **1**(9), 61-67.

Sachs, M.L., & Pargman, D. Running addiction: A depth interview examination. *Journal of Sport Behavior*, 1979, **2**, 143-155.

Solomon, E.G., & Bumpus, A.K. The running meditation response: An adjunct to psychotherapy. *American Journal of Psychotherapy*, 1978, **32**, 583-592.

CHAPTER 11

Running Addiction: A Clinical Report

Michael H. Sacks

Current literature on running emphasizes its physiological and psychological benefits (Milvy, 1977), but recent reports have begun to question the validity of these claims. In particular, some individuals are showing a syndrome of addiction to running. It has been generally accepted that addiction need not only be to an intoxicating substance, but can also be to an activity such as work, eating, or in an example provided by Fenichel (1945), reading. Its application to exercise was first noted by Baekeland (1970), who was unable to recruit heavy exercisers willing to stop exercising in order to participate in a sleep study. Little (1969) described a population of outpatients heavily committed to athletics who showed a variety of neurotic symptoms following some insult to their physical well-being. He viewed these symptoms as a bereavement response and called it the athlete's neurosis. Glasser (1976) described the addictive aspects of running as a positive addiction because of the beneficial health effects, but Morgan (1979) has questioned this finding and described running in some individuals as a negative addiction. Greist et al. (1979), in a study of the antidepressant effects of running, noted that depressions reoccurred if the runner had to stop.

The running addict is characterized by a compulsive need to run at least once and sometimes twice a day. Inclement weather, illness, or physical pain due to injuries does not influence this. If prevented from running, such runners become irritable, restless, sleepless, and preoccupied with guilty thoughts that their body will decondition or deteriorate in some way. The running addict recognizes the irrationality of these feelings and thoughts, but they are inescapable and can only be relieved by running. The scheduled daily run preempts important vocational and social commitments, causing work, family, and friendships to suffer. In fact, addictive runners may totally alter their lifestyle to accommodate the priority of their running interest; this may involve changes in diet, clothing, choice of friends, and even career. During the time that these runners are not running, they often read the abundant literature now available about running despite its repetitiveness and absence of substance.

A frequent response to stress in addicted runners is to daydream about running. This often involves kinesthetic sensations of running, which may focus on pleasurable feelings of rhythmic movement, physical strength, or competitive triumphs associated with a race. Usually in the fantasy, there is a feeling of specialness, of being unique, or the memory of euphoric experiences during past runs. This euphoric feeling, the runner's high, occurs frequently. Addicted runners will continue running despite injuries and the risk of severely harming themselves in search for this high, often taking analgesics and living with pain to maintain the running. Finally, as with all addictions, runners continually increase their activity so that they run longer and more frequently, sometimes reaching mileages of 50-70 miles per week and, in some instances, 100-200 miles per week.

We have had the opportunity to examine a small number of such running addicts and have found that they began running or became addicted during a period of emotional stress. The running addiction served as an adaptive response to the stress.

Mr. X began to run during his father's prolonged illness. He soon was an addicted runner and spoke of the pleasurable feelings of strength and invincibility the running provided him. At his father's death, he experienced no grief, but felt driven to run that day for an unusually long period. Psychotherapy revealed that the running was an attempt to recapture an early relationship with the father during which they would playfully try to catch each other. Participation in the running and the weight loss which attended it was secondarily reinforced by an identification with the father's weight loss which the patient rationalized as secondary to the running. It also represented a wish to strengthen the father's failing health by making himself strong so that the father would be strong. He would breathe life into his father. Following the father's death, the patient was able to deny the loss by maintaining the unconscious fantasy that the father was running with him. This became clear when after a particularly joyous run he began to cry uncontrollably. In therapy, he was able to recall that just prior to his crying he had had a memory of his father and the eerie sensation that someone was running along side of him. When he looked and did not see anyone, he began to cry.

In this patient and in others, running provides an adaptive response to losses that affect self-esteem and produce intrapsychic pain. Given the current social and medical support for regular exercise, running readily lends itself as an acceptable symptomatic adaptation to emotional distress. What is of particular interest is the ease with which it offers itself as a possible addictive solution. With regular effort, the new runner is able to quickly achieve significant gains in endurance and strength. Following popular training programs, he or she learns a marathon can be run with only 6 months of training (Henderson, 1976). The possibility of attaining such an immense accomplishment after only a brief preparatory period may be a factor that contributes to its addictive potential. A related aspect is that running requires very little skill. Unlike participants in other sports such as golf or tennis, runners rapidly improve without spending long periods of time acquiring new motor coordination. They simply run, which involves only the process of remembering what they did as a child (Perry & Sachs, Note 1).

Perhaps the early childhood experience of mastering the upright posture and walking, the practicing period described by Mahler (1966) as accompanied by immense feelings of elation, self-efficacy, and invincibility, is recaptured by running addicts. Other runners describe more primitive experiences of ego fusion in which they feel a heightened connection with their surroundings together with a sense of timelessness and mystical awe. Seeking experiences of either fusion or a grandiose self-efficacy have been described in the dynamics of drug addiction (Milkman & Frosch, 1973). It is not clear why only certain individuals become addicted to intense compulsive physical activity as a way of managing stress. It may be that for them, physical activity or the "magic of action" has special developmental significance as a mechanism for regulating self-esteem and resolving conflict (Greenacre, 1950). This remains a hypothesis. In summary, many individuals who turn to running as a regular source of exercise during periods of stress may become "addicted" to the running as a means of resolving conflict.

Reference Note

1. Perry, S., & Sacks, M. *The psychodynamics of running.* Paper presented at the Symposium on the Psychology of Running, Cornell University Medical College, New York, October 20, 1978.

References

Baekeland, F. Exercise deprivation: Sleep and psychological reactions. *Archives of General Psychiatry*, 1970, **22**, 365-369.

Fenichel, O. *The psychoanalytic theory of the neurosis.* New York: W. W. Norton, 1945.

Glasser, W. *Positive addiction.* New York: Harper & Row, 1976.

Greenacre, P. General problems of acting out. *The Psychoanalytic Quarterly*, 1950, **19**, 455-467.

Greist, J., et al. Running as treatment for depression. *Comprehensive Psychiatry*, 1979, **20**, 41-51.

Henderson, J. *Jog, run, race.* Mountain View, CA: World Publications, 1976.

Little, J.C. The athlete's neurosis: A deprivation crisis. *Acta Psychiatrica Scandinavica*, 1969, **45**, 187-191.

Mahler, M. Notes on the development of basic moods: The depressive affect. In R. M. Lowenstein, L. M. Newman, M. Schur, & A. J. Solnit (Eds.), *Psychoanalysis—A general psychology: Essays in honor of Heinz Hartmann.* New York: International Universities Press, 1966.

Milkman, H., & Frosch, W.A. On the preferential abuse of heroin and amphetamines. *The Journal of Nervous and Mental Disorders*, 1973, **156**, 242-248.

Milvy, P. (Ed.). *The marathon: Physiological, medical, epidemiological, and psychological studies.* New York: The New York Academy of Sciences, 1977.

Morgan, W. Negative addiction in running. *The Physician and Sportsmedicine*, 1979, **7**, 56-63; 67-70.

CHAPTER 12

Worker or Runner?
The Impact of Commitment to Running and Work on Self-identification

Paul Joseph and James M. Robbins

What kinds of activities and what types of experiences do individuals find to be the most important source of self-identity? For many Americans, the answer is work. We spend the greatest part of our waking hours working. We are encouraged by our families and schools to measure our social contributions and self-esteem through our occupations, and our friends reinforce this tendency in numerous and frequently subtle ways. In our social world, we tend to locate others through their work. Success and performance are measured more through work than any other activity. When meeting strangers in social encounters, we ask "What do you do?" The answer we expect is the person's occupation.

This paper examines the issue of self-identity in the context of running boom, a particularly dramatic form of expansion of leisure which now numbers some 30 million adherents. The importance of a clear-cut sense of identity to psychological well-being is well known. Given this, our interest is focused on what kinds of individuals have shifted their self-appraisal of the relative importance of their activities from work to running, making the latter a locus for self-identity. We were primarily interested in obtaining answers to two questions. First, how does a commitment to running affect the respondent's tendency to report that running activities are a more important source of self-identity than work activities? Second, how does the work ethic and work experience, specifically job dissatisfaction, affect the tendency to rank running as more important than work?

The central concern with work evidenced in our modern Western societies is unique, at least in historical and cultural terms. Other cultures, in different historical settings and different geographical locations, have identified themselves in many other ways, including family, religion, community, kinship patterns, and a combination of different activities of which work is only one component. Indeed, social historians have collected compelling evidence that our contemporary concern with work as the activity contributing most to self-esteem and sense of accomplishment is quite unusual (Clayre, 1975; Rodgers, 1978; Yellowitz, 1976). In China, for example, people do not ask "What do you do?" but "What organization do you belong to?"

Is this concentration on work misplaced? It has been argued by some that our work-related attitudes and behavior are responsible for rapid industrial development, improved economic performance, and a comparatively open stance toward science and its practical applications (Parsons, 1960; Weber, 1930). Social change is to be expected and welcomed. Modern attitudes toward work have also been associated with cultural changes encouraging freedom of expression, willingness to participate in social experimentation, and a loosening of traditional restrictions and limitations on the individual (Hoselitz, 1957; Lipsit, 1960; Smelser, 1976).

However one assesses the impact of the Western work ethic on industrial development, it is also becoming increasingly apparent that this constellation of attitudes and norms has contributed to work-related pressures that may lead to severe personal consequences. This is true not only among occupational categories normally associated with work stress, notably blue-collar and clerical positions, but among white-collar and professional occupations as well. Studies of worker alienation no longer focus exclusively on miners, file clerks, automobile assembly line workers, and textile mill operators, but have broadened their scope to include doctors, lawyers, engineers, and teachers. Terms such as "professional burnout" and "white-collar woes" are becoming commonplace. The privilege of a career no longer guarantees protection from job dissatisfaction (Derber, 1980; Mallet, 1975).

The spread of job dissatisfaction into more prestigious occupational positions has been accompanied by changes in the work ethic itself. Some of these changes are difficult to detect, but social researchers agree the traditional value system governing the world of work is in flux (Yankelovich, 1978). Increasingly, Americans are questioning the fundamental tenets of work, such as the following:

1. Work is "instrumental," something to be tolerated as long as it provides a

decent living and some economic security.

2. Women should stay at home as long as they can afford to do so.

3. Money and status are sufficient rewards to motivate people.

4. People are tied to their jobs not only through their commitment to their families but also by loyalty to their organization.

5. People define their identity predominantly through their work while suppressing other social and personal needs.

Although each of these aspects of work have been called into question, it is the last, the relationship between work and identity, that is of particular concern in this paper.

Some questioning of the assumption that identity should be derived solely from work is perhaps inevitable. We are witnessing a quiet reaction against the current standard, and one form of that reaction is increased interest in leisure not only as activities in themselves, but as experiences that are becoming important in their own right for an individual's identity and self-location. Recent surveys indicate that family and work have grown less important and leisure more important. Renwick and Lawler (1978) report that when work and leisure are compared, only one out of five state that work means more to them than leisure. A study of Swedish men, conducted in 1955, asked "What gives your life the most meaning—your family, your work, or your leisure?" Only 13% answered "leisure." Thirty-three percent answered "work" and 45% answered "family." By 1977, there had been a dramatic shift. The percent naming work had been cut in half—from 33% to 17%. Those answering family dropped slightly to 41%. But the percent choosing leisure had more than doubled from 13% to 27%. Our purpose is to explore similar shifts from work to leisure within the running boom itself.

Method

Sampling of individuals committed to long distance running as a leisure pursuit poses particular problems for the survey analyst. Previous studies (Carmack & Martens, 1979; Glasser, 1976; Jones & Jones, Note 1; Jorgenson & Jorgenson, Note 2; Sachs & Pargman, Note 3) have relied upon some combination of race entrants, membership lists of running clubs, readers of running periodicals, friends, high school or Olympic athletes, or regular noontime runners. These samples are likely to miss the less committed and less competitive runners who comprise the majority of participants in the running boom. The American Institute of Public Opinion (Gallup, Note 4) reports that 60% of Americans jog on the average less than 2 miles a day.

To capture this group as well as the more serious runners, a scheme that combined sampling from running clubs, employees at running stores, and particular locations in the Boston area was adopted. Contacts were attempted with (a) all full-time employees in three area running stores; (b) all female members of the Greater Boston Track Club and the Cambridge Sports Union; (c) a systematic random sample of male members of those two clubs; and (d) runners at one of four regular running routes in the Boston area. At each contact, runners were given a questionnaire and asked to return it by mail. After repeated telephone follow-ups, 354 of 568 questionnaires were returned. Of those, nine were unusable, leaving 345 runners or 60.7% for whom complete information was obtained. The procedure continued the general practice of biasing in favor of more committed runners although the average number of miles run a week (median = 23 miles) is substantially less than reported in other studies. The sample thus includes a greater proportion of less committed runners (39.3% run 15 miles a week or less) and a higher proportion of female runners (40%) than is typical. The procedure thus permits systematic comparison among runners of vastly different levels of commitment.

Commitment to Running and Worker-Runner Self-identity

Our sample was asked to respond to the statement, "If I were to describe myself, you would get a better understanding of me through my running activities than through my work." Respondents were asked to rate themselves on a 7-point scale. Low scores indicated that work was more important, whereas high scores indicated that running was more important. Eight measures of commitment to running were used: number of miles run per week; how often one ran (ranging from once a week to twice daily); how often one raced (ranging from never to weekly); length of time since taking up running; whether or not one had run a marathon; how often one read books or magazines devoted to running (never to daily); how many of one's friends were runners; and how many of one's new friends, those made since taking up running, were runners. Note that these measures of commitment are not restricted to physical aspects (e.g., miles per week), but also contain indicators of the degree of involvement in the running subculture (e.g., number of friends who are runners or time spent reading running literature).

In addition, responses on these and other measures of commitment were combined to produce a typology of runners. Typing runners is not new; Pargman (Note 5) distinguishes between "addiction-dependent" and "commitment-dedication" runners. Morgan (1979) separates the "hobby jogger" from the "serious runner." Sime (Note 6) divides runners into "compliers," "adherers," and "addicts." Our classification combines both physical and subcultural items, although it is also important to note that racing performance (how fast one actually runs) does not enter the typology. A decision-tree used to classify respondents is listed in the appendix. A basic premise of our approach is that the classification has general theoretical significance regarding the relationship between leisure pursuits and other activities. Table 1 summarizes the main characteristics of each type, and a brief description of each follows.

Type I—"running as the most important commitment" ($N = 27$, 8%). For

Table 1

Modal Characteristics of Four Types of Runners

	Miles (mean)	How Often One Runs	How Often One Races	Percent New Friends Who Run (mean)	How Often Read Running Literature	Running Tapers Off in Winter	Maintain Running Log
Type I "Running as the most important commitment"	75.0	Daily	Weekly to every few weeks	75.4	Weekly	No	Yes
Type II "Running as a crucial commitment"	47.8	Virtually daily	Monthly	31.0	Monthly	No	Yes
Type III "Running as a hobby"	29.3	Four times a week to daily	Few times a year	14.9	Rarely	Somewhat	Sometimes
Type IV "The occasional runner"	12.3	Two-three times a week	Rarely to never	6.2	Never	Yes	No

this group, running may be the most important commitment of their life. They run at least 40 miles a week ($\bar{X} = 75$), race often, have runners as most of their new friends, and are immersed in the running subculture to the extent that running literature occupies their attention at least weekly.

Type II—"running as a crucial commitment" (N = 92, 27%). Mileage in this group is more variable, ranging from a low of 11 to more than 70 miles a week ($\bar{X} = 48$). These runners are also heavily involved in racing but are much less involved in the subculture. They are serious, competitive runners with perhaps enough talent to reinforce efforts at improvement.

Type III—"running as a hobby" (N = 63, 18%). Mileage in this group is also substantial, ranging from 11 to more than 40 miles a week ($\bar{X} = 29$), but improving racing performance and the running subculture are comparatively unimportant. Conceivably, this could be a pure category of commitment; a definite level of dedication is made without expecting a payback other than the joy of participation.

Type IV—"the occasional runner" (N = 163, 47%). By far the largest group, they run as much as 24 miles a week but as little as 4 or 5 ($\bar{X} = 12$). They run as infrequently as once a week but usually more. Their running tapers off or stops entirely during the winter months or bad weather. This category conforms to the popular notion of a "jogger."

The relationships between self-identification and commitment to running are presented in Table 2. As is apparent from the Pearson correlation coefficients, each of the eight individual measures of commitment is directly related to a tendency to rank running as a more important source of self-identity than work.[1] The more one is committed to running, the more one feels that he or she can be understood through running. The associations are especially strong for mileage, how often one runs, and racing frequency. Somewhat surprisingly, the associations tend to be somewhat weaker for the subcultural measures of commitment, although the number of new friends who are also runners continues to be strongly related to a tendency to understand one's self through running rather than through work.

For the four classifications of runners, the results are also predictable. The mean score on the 7-point scale (1 = worker, 7 = runner) for Type I (the most committed group) is significantly higher than the other three groups ($\bar{X} = 5.08$). For each of the successive categories of runners the mean drops, with the difference statistically significant at the 5% level between Type I and the other three groups, and between Type II and the other two groups ($\bar{X}$ for Type II = 3.94; $\bar{X}$ for Type III = 3.24; $\bar{X}$ for Type IV = 2.86.[2] These lower

---

[1]Clearly the assumptions of the Pearson correlation coefficient are violated when employed with ordinal data, although there is evidence that potential errors are not severe. Thus rank correlation coefficients were also computed where appropriate. In no instance did the nonparametric analysis fail to support the parametric.

[2]Significance tested by analysis of variance and Tukey's Honestly Significant Difference multiple comparison procedure.

Table 2

**Pearson Correlation Coefficients, Measures of Commitment to
Running and Self-identification as Runner Over Worker**

Measures of Commitment to Running	Self-identification as Runner Over Worker
Miles per week	.397*
How often one runs	.367*
How often one races	.359*
How long one has been running	.124*
Run a marathon	.323*
How often one reads running literature	.129*
Number of friends who are also runners	.176*
Number of new friends who are also runners	.298*

*$P < .01$
$265 \leq N \leq 333$

scores indicate increased self-identification with the work role as one moves toward lower levels of commitment to running.

Thus, the evidence is straightforward. As expected, the more an individual makes a commitment to running, a commitment that has been measured in several different ways, the more an individual believes that others will be able to understand his or her true self in the leisure role.

The Job Experience and Self-identity Between Work and Leisure

Attempts to analyze the relationship between work and leisure activities are often frustrated by the very terms themselves. Precisely what is meant by "work" and by "leisure"? Is the comparison based on the physical aspects of the activity (sitting at a desk, digging a hole in the ground, or running)? Or should the comparison between work and leisure be based on the meaning that each activity has for the individual (Kando & Summers, 1971). Take the issue of intensity vs. relaxation in work and in running as an example. One individual may be attracted to train for and finally experience the intensity of a marathon. Another may enjoy running for the relaxation that it presents. The individual searching for intensity in running may be merely extending a generalized need for intensity, a meaning or need that is also sought in the workplace. Or he or she may be searching for a need, such as intensity or relaxation, that has been frustrated on the job. Thus a comparison between work and leisure based exclusively on the form of physical activity is inade-

Table 3

Items and Factor Loadings for Work Needs[a]

Factor	Work Need	Loading
Self-development	Ability to have control over the outcome of my efforts	.78
	Opportunities to reach my full potential	.71
	Chance to make contribution to society	.70
	Fits in with overall values	.69
	Opportunities to see clear unambiguous results of my efforts	.56
	Helps me understand myself	.54
	Opportunities to feel good about myself	.53
	Opportunities to be intense, totally engaged	.50
	Opportunities to be creative	.48
Self-involvement	Opportunities to feel playful, to counter the seriousness of life	.78
	Chance to forget about personal problems	.68
	Opportunities for adventure and excitement	.59
	Opportunities to relax	.51
	Opportunities to be alone with my thoughts	.49
	Chance for association and friendship	.43
Material	Good working conditions	.74
	Job security	.64
	Good pay	.54
Competition	Chance to compete with others	.76
	Chance for recognition from others	.47

[a]Principle components solution with varimax rotation. Loadings greater than .40 are presented.

quate. It is important to penetrate to the level of needs or meanings that the activity holds for the participant.

To allow for a comparison between work and running based on needs, and to permit more precise discrimination among different aspects of both the work and leisure experiences, we asked our sample to rate the importance of 20 work needs and 21 reasons why people run (1 = not at all important and 7 = very important). For examining the issue of the impact of work on worker-runner self-identity, those questions asked of the workplace are especially important. Each of the 20 aspects of work or work needs was classified, following factor analysis, into one of four specific subsets. These subsets were labeled "self-development," "self-involvement," "competition," and "material." Items composing each subset are listed in Table 3.[3] This technique enables one to make statements about the impact of work on worker-runner self-identity in general and to allow for the possibility that distinct patterns may emerge when different sets of work needs are considered separately.

Respondents were asked to rate the importance of each of the 20 work needs to them in general, and the degree to which their current job provided an opportunity to experience each need. A measure of relative dissatisfaction for each need was obtained by subtracting the score on the item as answered for "current job" from the score on the item as answered for "work in general." For example, individuals ranking "ability to have control over the outcomes of my efforts" as "very important" would score a 7 on that work need in general. If they found that their current job only afforded an incomplete opportunity to experience the "ability to have control over the outcomes of my efforts" (say, a score of 4), then the level of relative dissatisfaction with that particular work need would be 3 (7 minus 4).[4] Those who value particular work needs highly will also tend to experience relative dissatisfaction. For example, two individuals who report that their particular jobs provide equal opportunities to fulfill a particular work need, say, "a chance to contribute to society," will nonetheless experience different levels of relative job dissatisfaction if one respondent rates that need highly while the other does not find it to be important. Using this procedure, a measure of relative dissatisfaction was obtained for each of the four subsets of work needs by adding the individual scores on those work needs falling within a particular subset.

Two important findings resulted from this study; the first is a modest but significant tendency for those valuing self-involvement at work in general, that is, as part of their particular work ethic, to also identify themselves through their running. These are individuals who, without experiencing job dissatisfaction, are still more likely to identify themselves through their leisure role than the rest of the sample. In this context it is also useful to point out that Type I runners, those making the highest level of commitment to running, are also significantly more likely to value self-involvement at work (Joseph & Robbins, Note 7). Those making the highest commitment to running are also more likely to value aspects of work that permit one to focus on oneself rather than on the mediation between oneself and one's work and social environ-

---

[3]Four single summated indices based on the variables loading highly on respective items were constructed.

[4]Negative scores obtained by this procedure were recoded to zero. In this manner, subjects for whom highly valued aspects of work were not present in their current job received positive scores, while subjects for whom highly valued aspects of work were present or for whom unimportant aspects of work were present received scores of zero.

ment. Self-involvement work needs are thus associated with both self-identification with the leisure role and the highest level of commitment to running. The significance of this finding will be subsequently discussed (see Table 4).

The second finding concerns relative dissatisfaction with the job. With one exception, that of material needs, dissatisfaction within each subset of needs is associated with a tendency to identify with running over work. This relationship is concentrated particularly strongly in the self-development subset. The modest correlation of .145 for dissatisfaction in self-involvement work needs and .194 for dissatisfaction in competitive work needs pale beside the .372 correlation for dissatisfaction in the self-development subset of work needs.

Table 5 examines in more detail the relationship between relative dissatisfaction in self-development work needs and identification with the runner role. Following the procedure outlined earlier, a score on an index of relative dissatisfaction was obtained for the nine needs falling within the self-development subset. Forty-four respondents (14.7%) reported no relative dissatisfaction. Ninety-six (32.0%) reported a score from 1 to 5. Sixty-six (22.0%) fell between 6 and 10. And ninety-four (31.3%) reported relatively high scores between 11 and the high of 42.

Scores on the dependent variable (self-identification on the 7-point scale between runner and worker) were classified into three groups: predominantly worker, predominantly runner, and both worker and runner. Among those reporting slight or no relative dissatisfaction, approximately 55% identified themselves as predominantly worker and approximately 10% identified themselves as predominantly runner. Among those reporting moderate levels of relative dissatisfaction, 43% identified themselves as predominantly worker and 15% identified themselves as predominantly runner. On the other hand, in the category reporting the highest level of relative dissatisfaction, almost 32% identified themselves as predominantly worker (down from 52% experiencing no dissatisfaction) and 41.5% identified themselves as predominantly runner (up from 9% experiencing no dissatisfaction). We have noted elsewhere that work dissatisfaction is *not* accompanied by a corresponding increase in mileage or in other physical or subcultural forms of commitment to running (Joseph & Robbins, Note 7). Thus, those experiencing relative dissatisfaction in the workplace, particularly in the self-development cluster, do not make a greater commitment to running but compensate with a cognitive shift in self-identity. Those who are denied the opportunity to experience individual growth through the interaction between their immediate work experience and their surrounding environment, or who are denied the opportunity to realize personal goals through external engagements, become frustrated. One method of coping with this frustration is a shift in self-identity.

Table 4

Pearson Correlation Coefficients Among Work Needs, Relative Job Dissatisfaction and Self-identification of Runner Over Worker

| | Work Needs | | | |
	Self-development	Self-involvement	Material	Competition
Self-identification as runner over worker	−.011	.138*	.064	.073

| | Relative Job Dissatisfaction | | | |
	Self-development	Self-involvement	Material	Competition
Self-identification	.372*	.145*	.020	.194*

*$P < .05$
$265 \leq N \leq 333$

Discussion

Those tending to identify themselves through their running rather than through their work role include the following: (a) those more committed to running, (b) those who value highly the self-involvement opportunities of work, and (c) those experiencing dissatisfaction in the workplace, especially in the "self-development" cluster of work needs. It may be helpful to think of the last two reasons as opposite sides of the same coin: Those associating with the leisure role are either *attracted* to a particular set of work needs, really a philosophy of work, that stress the *cultivation of the self* (a chance to relax, to be alone with one's thoughts, to counter the seriousness of life, to forget about personal problems, etc.); or they are *frustrated* by their job experience because of its failure to provide for self-development through *engagement with external referents* (control over outcomes of efforts, ability to see unambiguous results of efforts, to make a contribution to society, and to be totally engaged, etc.). Thus, those whose running identity becomes more important than their work identity tend to place higher values on aspects of their work such as opportunities to escape, for adventure and friendship (self-involvement), or they are disappointed with the opportunities for achievement and mastery (self-development) provided by their current job.

What are the deeper social factors underlying these shifts in self-identity? A precise answer is difficult to formulate, in part because the reasons for the shift do not always run in parallel. Different individuals are not motivated by the

Table 5

**Cross-tabulation of Relative Dissatisfaction with
Self-development Opportunities on the Job and Worker-Runner
Self-identification**

Worker-Runner Self-identification	Relative Dissatisfaction with Job							
	None		Slight		Moderate		High	
	%	(N)	%	(N)	%	(N)	%	(N)
Predominantly worker	52.3	(23)	58.3	(56)	43.9	(29)	31.9	(30)
Both worker and runner	38.6	(17)	31.1	(30)	40.9	(27)	26.6	(25)
Predominantly runner	9.1	(4)	10.4	(10)	15.2	(10)	41.5	(39)
TOTALS	100.0	(44)	99.8	(96)	100.0	(66)	100.0	(94)

Chi square = 38.56 with 6 degrees of freedom, $p < .01$
Cramer's V = .254
$N = 300$

same set of reasons and it is important to untangle the different aspects involved. We suggest that the social factors involved—and here we move beyond the data presented earlier—in the individual choices made above, involve four themes.

The first is the gradual rejection of the previous social norm that individuals should identify themselves exclusively through their work. We found that those more likely to reject the traditional code make a greater commitment to running and have reoriented their work philosophy by adopting a particular code of work values that stress the self. In this sense running, not just as a sport or as an activity that promotes physical fitness but as an arena of individual sustenance, can be welcomed. Running offers an alternative to work, helps to provide a balance between work and leisure, and contains meanings and significance sufficient to promote self-understanding. Here running represents a quiet but legitimate rebellion against the unwarranted hegemony of work as the primary locus of self-identity.

The second social aspect underlying the search for self-identity is the expansion of the leisure time—at least for a particular segment of the population (Kaplan, 1975). Without this historical development, the opportunity to cultivate other aspects of one's self would not have arisen. In this context, we should also note that alongside the expansion of leisure time for some social strata is another phenomenon: paradoxically that this is also a period in which more Americans are forced to take second jobs to support themselves. Those who are engaged in exploring new forms of self-identity through a sustained commitment to running are lucky.

Third, the search for alternative or supplemental arenas of self-understanding in new forms of leisure such as running is not without ambiguity, an ambiguity that is itself socially rooted. Although the norms of individualism and pragmatism have positive aspects, American culture has also been characterized by a quiet but desperate search for community and individual meaning (Derber, 1979; Lasch, 1979; Slater, 1969; Stein, 1960). If runners are searching for meaning not readily available in existing activities, a search that can take on compulsive and irresponsible features of its own, then running also contains elements of pathos, uncertainty, and insecurity. The addictive aspects of running that are clearly negative serve as only one example (Merrill, 1980; Morgan, 1979). This is not to imply that shifting one's locus of self-identity toward running is automatically evidence of individual pathology or social irresponsibility. Indeed individuals attempting to balance the arenas of their self-understanding between leisure and work may evidence higher standards of "personal health." But the greater claims that have been advanced on running's behalf have not always proved persuasive. The unsettling element to this search for self-identity in running is the implication that all is not as it should be elsewhere. By pouring ourselves into running, we unconsciously adopt a form of social amnesia toward activities that continue to be important.

The fourth social aspect concerns work dissatisfaction. The individual who substitutes a concentrated focus on leisure and running for the previous concentration on work has no doubt gained something. But at what cost? Those who have chosen to identify themselves through running because their work lives have been less than satisfactory than they wish may be engaging in a comparatively successful form of compensation. But they are also being robbed of a chance for satisfaction and fulfillment in an arena that continues to be crucial.

These findings suggest that the running boom contains layers of social and individual significance that extend deeper than health, self-improvement, personal growth, and other aspects conventionally identified with fitness and leisure. In this fashion the search for self-identity in running is merely a clue to more pervasive social themes present in our society. It is our own contention that the study of running is a useful method to focus on these developments of broader significance.

Acknowledgement

This research was supported in part by a grant from the Tufts University Faculty Research Awards Fund and NIMH Grant 5T32-MH14641-04. The assistance of Susan Goodman, Rick Lefferts, and Sara Mattes is gratefully acknowledged.

Reference Notes

1. Jones, S., & Jones, D. *Serious jogging and family life: Marathon and sub-marathon running.* Paper presented at a meeting of the American Sociological Association, Chicago, 1977.
2. Jorgenson, D., & Jorgenson, C. *Perceived changes in intrafamilial relations: A study of runners/joggers.* Unpublished manuscript, Southwest Texas State University, San Marcos, 1978.
3. Sachs, M., & Pargman, D. *Examining exercise addiction: A depth interview approach.* Paper presented at a meeting of the North American Society for the Psychology of Sport and Physical Activity, Tallahassee, Florida, 1978.
4. Gallup Organization. *Nearly half of Americans now exercising daily: 24 percent are joggers.* Gallup Opinion Index, Report 151, 1978.
5. Pargman, D. *The way of the runner: An examination of motives for running.* Unpublished manuscript, Florida State University, Tallahassee, 1978.
6. Sime, W. *Psychophysiological concomitants of running.* Paper presented at a meeting of the American Alliance for Health, Physical Education and Recreation, New Orleans, 1979.
7. Joseph, P., & Robbins, J. *Work satisfaction, political beliefs and the running boom.* Paper presented at the Symposium on Medical Aspects of Long Distance Running, American Medical Joggers Association, New York, 1979.

References

Carmack, M.A., & Martens, R. Measuring commitment to running: A survey of runners' attitudes and mental states. *Journal of Sport Psychology,* 1979, **1,** 25-42.

Clayre, A. *Work and play: Ideas and experience of work and leisure.* New York: Harper & Row, 1975.

Derber, C. *Pursuit of attention.* Boston: Schenkman, 1979.

Derber, C. *Dominated authority: Professionals at work.* Boston: G. K. Hall, 1980.

Glasser, W. *Positive addiction.* New York: Harper & Row, 1976.

Hoselitz, B. Economic growth and development: Noneconomic factors in economic development. *American Economic Review,* 1957, **47,** 28-41.

Kando, T., & Summers, W. The impact of work on leisure. *Pacific Sociological Review,* 1971, **9,** 310-327.

Kaplan, M. *Leisure: Theory and policy.* New York: John Wiley & Sons, 1975.

Lasch, C. *The culture of narcissism.* New York: W. W. Norton, 1979.

Lipsit, S. *Political man.* Garden City, NY: Doubleday, 1960.

Mallet, S. *Essays on the new working-class.* St. Louis: Telos Press, 1975.

Merrill, S. Running bums. *The Runner*, 1980, **2**(7), 68-72.

Morgan, W. Negative addiction in runners. *The Physician and Sports-medicine*, 1979, **7**, 57-70.

Parsons, T. *Structure and process in modern societies*. New York: The Free Press, 1960.

Renwick, P., & Lawler, E. What you really want from your job. *Psychology Today*, 1978, **12**, 53-65.

Rodgers, D. *The work ethic in industrial America, 1850-1920*. Chicago: University of Chicago Press, 1978.

Slater, P. *The pursuit of loneliness*. Boston: Beacon Press, 1969.

Smelser, N. *The sociology of economic life*. Englewood Cliffs, NJ: Prentice-Hall, 1976.

Stein, M. *The eclipse of community*. New York: Harper & Row, 1960.

Weber, M. *The Protestant ethic and the spirit of capitalism*. New York: Charles Scribner's Sons, 1930.

Yankelovich, D. The new psychological contracts at work. *Psychology Today*, 1978, **12**, 46-50.

Yellowitz, I. *Industrialization and the American labor movement*. Port Washington: Kennikat Press, 1976.

Appendix

Decision Rules for Runners' Typology

Type I   "Running as the most important commitment"
1. Runs 40 miles a week or more, maintains log or does interval workouts, reads running literature weekly or more, and more than 50% of friends are runners.
2. 40 miles a week or more, races at least monthly, reads weekly or more, and more than 50% of friends are runners.

Type II   "Running as a crucial commitment"
1. 11-24 miles a week, doesn't taper during winter months or bad weather, races at least monthly.
2. 11-24 miles a week, doesn't taper, races a few times a year, log or intervals.
3. 25-39 miles a week, races at least monthly.
4. 25-39 miles a week, races a few times a year, log or intervals.
5. 40 miles a week or more, races a few times a year, log or intervals, reads less than weekly.
6. 40 miles a week or more, races a few times a year, reads weekly or more, less than 50% of friends are runners.
7. 40 miles a week or more, races at least monthly, reads less than weekly.

8. 40 miles a week or more, races at least monthly, reads weekly or more, less than 50% of friends are runners.

Type III "Running as a hobby"
1. 11-24 miles a week, rarely races if at all, doesn't taper.
2. 11-24 miles a week, races a few times a year, doesn't taper, no log or intervals.
3. 25-39 miles a week, races a few times a year, no log or intervals.
4. 40 miles a week or more, races rarely if at all.
5. 40 miles a week or more, races a few times a year, no log or intervals.

Type IV "The occasional runner"
1. Runs less than twice a week.
2. Runs more than twice a week, but less than 11 miles.
3. 11-24 miles a week, but tapers.

SECTION FOUR

The Mind of the Runner

The nonrunner often finds it difficult to understand the pleasure and motivation of the distance runner. It seems to the nonrunner that the repetitive motion and regular rhythm of feet pounding the ground should result in a numbing mental anesthesia. Nothing could be further from the truth. In fact the ease of the runner's effort may permit the mind to wander freely and facilitate the attainment of pleasurable meditative-like states. In the section on psychodynamics, we focused on the intrapsychic drama enacted during the run. In this section, we focus on the special contributions to the runner's mind that arise from mortality, gender, ultramarathon distances and, finally, the historical period in which the runner lives.

In the first contribution, the runner is viewed as an individual coping with imperfection which, for theologian W. Fred Graham, derives from the existential realization of the certainty of one's ultimate mortality. In his daily run, Graham seeks a temporary relief from "terminal helplessness" or the painful awareness of his own future death. It is an adaptive effort because it enables him to return to his daily activities renewed and refreshed.

Carole Oglesby, in Chapter 14, examines the effects of gender on the woman runner. She explores the arbitrary limitations imposed on women because of their sex in sports in general and in running in particular. She argues that many of women's limitations in sport derive from traditional cultural restrictions and are not founded on any basic underlying physical deficiencies. The positive benefits of exercise, particularly running, may enable woman to successfully confront these assumptions.

In Chapter 15, Sacks and his colleagues look at the mental status and psychological coping of competitors during a 100-mile race. Although marathoners have received considerable research attention in the past 5 years, comparatively little attention has been focused on ultramarathoners. Runners were asked a series of questions during the race, and it was found, perhaps surprisingly, that thinking did not become significantly impaired, that they did not blank out or experience a high, despite what they may have reported after the race. Indeed, the runners remained remarkably sharp through the first 10 hours of the race, and only then began to exhibit some signs of mental fatigue evidenced through a slightly impaired response time. The authors examine the cognitive content of these runners as they struggle with the distance, competition, and pain.

The last article in this section is provocative, providing to some extent a counterpoint to the highly positive messages about running which appear in this volume. Joseph Epstein, a self-confessed cynic, provides historical and sociological insight into the running movement. Evangelistic proponents of the running lifestyle might be counseled to view themselves within the context suggested by the author. The potential benefits of running assume a completely different valence if one shares Epstein's conviction that they represent a desperate response to a current disillusionment with traditional values and institutions.

CHAPTER 13

The Anxiety of the Runner: Terminal Helplessness

W. Fred Graham

I have been a noontime runner for more than a dozen years. A decade ago I was a lonely figure on the campus track. But now, when the weather closes in and the geriatric jocks gather in the fieldhouse, I can count at least a hundred people at any one time between 11 o'clock and 12:30, busy with the various stages of their exercise. The once-quiet woods now gallop with activity on fine fall days; on one football-less Saturday, more than 1,200 of us put on our Frank Shorter T-shirts and ran 10 kilometers through the streets of East Lansing in times ranging from world class to plain ridiculous.

Apparently, those of us who run do not all do it for the same reasons. Some are competitors, steadily increasing time and distance, entering races where runners can really hurt themselves, and reading *Runner's World*. Others are pure health freaks who never run any farther or faster, keep to the indoor track even when the sun shines, and talk about heartbeat rates and studies of longevity among runners. It seems that my crowd runs partly as an escape from the pressures of life. We're the ones for whom the change into ritual clothing, the pain of running, and the shower of cleansing constitute a daily rebaptism into newness of life. For us, the time spent running is time no one else has a claim on, and the rewards are similar to those of prayer and contemplation. Indeed, such exercise may constitute a secular pietism.

I

At one time the division of runners into competitors, health nuts, and quiet-time seekers satisfied my need to analyze the motivation for an activity that I engage in almost every working day. Recently, however, two tasks have opened up to me a deeper level of motivation. One project was to read and classify the responses of women runners to a questionnaire. The second was an analysis of my own daydreams, especially those that cluster about the act of running. I discovered through these efforts a more profound explanation for the phenomenon of the jogger in modern society, one that discloses another angst to place alongside Paul Tillich's listing of the anxieties of death, guilt, and meaninglessness, and psychologist J.F.T. Bugental's addition of the anxiety of loneliness.

It was the questionnaire that first set me thinking. A woman runner and I, planning an article for a university publication about the growing number of women runners, devised a set of questions that probed for motivation. Some of the answers were ones we expected—they testified to the sense of well-being that comes from a regular running program:

> I like it when people make over me a lot because I run two miles a day.
> Things never go right the rest of the day if I don't run.
> I know that if I can run a mile a day I can also . . . [fill in the blank with everything from "lose 50 pounds" to "live without my husband"].
> It's the only thing I do that's all mine.
> I was so fat and out of shape.

The other motivation—the one that set me thinking afresh—was one expressed in one way or another by 19 of the 20 women who responded to the survey: "I am going to run until I can't put one foot in front of another, and then I'll be dead. No geriatrics ward for me."

What these women were articulating was the hope that running will save them from a state of helplessness. Incapacity at life's end is the new anxiety that modern medical technology has given Western society, and I am convinced that running has gained so many converts in recent years because people hope to guarantee that their bodies will not slowly decay in a modern "convalescent home." Runners want to remain active and independent until they die. Hidden somewhere in the pursuit of regular exercise is the notion that if one keeps moving, one will never be caught in the wires and tubes and sterile unprivacy that the aged suffer today.

II

Let me describe the running phenomenon itself by borrowing Suzanne Langer's "tension-act-release" curve.

Many noontime runners begin their working day by planning their daily run. If it appears that the way is clear, that no luncheon appointments or meetings will interfere, then all is well. Runners forget the advent hour of pleasure-pain and do the work set before them. But let a conflict appear, and a cloud obscures the sun. Sometimes one can work around it by rearranging the hour of exercise. But when necessity simply allows no free time, the runner works less enthusiastically, participates in luncheons and meetings grudgingly, and gains a reputation for obduracy. A colleague once snapped at a friend of mine: "You'd be department chairman if you'd quit running!"

The "trigger" that signals the reappearance of tension will vary. For the secretary it may be the approach of noon; for the faculty member, the end of a class or advising time. Something signals, and the attention turns to the track even if other activities intervene. I have no idea how morning runners can arise from slumber and immediately begin to run, though Annalies Knoppers, Michigan State University's volleyball coach and a daily 13-miler, argues that the need to run is tension enough. If morning joggers miss their miles, she says, tension is the result. For the new runner, a fresh decision often requires recollection of the original motivation—perhaps the remark of a friend or spouse about the need to lose weight. I used to recall the pain and humiliation of hitting a home run in a softball game, only to be so crippled by the dash around the bases that I couldn't return to center field next inning. I quit softball and started to run.

The motions that follow may differ, but each person goes through a pattern during which tension grows. A typical agenda would require traveling to the site of action, changing into ritual clothing, entering the place of exercise, doing calisthenics, and talking with others about the projected run.

My daydreams during this stage are of two kinds that have in common only that they are self-regarding or self-praising. The first usually centers on several unpublished books I have written (theological mystery thrillers!), and the scenarios always include publication, instant adulation, and generous remuneration. The second fantasy is more significant: I have retired from university teaching (but still write best sellers, of course), and have become pastor of a rural church. Sometimes the setting is Scotland. There, because of my engaging personality, mature wisdom, and natural genius (with God's grace as an afterthought), the church flourishes mightily. The whole community finds a home there. As my due reward, I am asked to give lectures at seminaries—lectures in which I tell the professors what's wrong with theological education today.

These two fantasies I entertain while walking or biking to the fieldhouse. The first is mere wishful thinking, though it surely responds to the anxiety of death and the desire to create something to outlive me. But the second reveals my hope of remaining vital and active even in advanced age. In that daydream, I write, preach, learn to play the piano, give tennis lessons, and much else—and always I continue to run. Rarely, death-thoughts arise: death always comes with an auto sending this aged but still jogging carcass hurtling to its end.

iii

The act of running itself is the simplest of the three stages. To the aging competitor, time and distance are important; to the health-centered and quiet-time runner, they mean less. But for any runner, a forced lay-off from running is agony; the anxiety of helplessness insistently whispers its message of "time-is-passing" and "the-body-is-aging."

Why one person is satisfied to run a mile in 10 minutes and another must run 13 miles at an 8-minute pace—such mysteries are lost in the unconscious. But that labyrinth is also where the sibilant voice of anxiety insinuates. And it must be quieted before the course can be finished, even at some risk or at great inconvenience. Runners often prolong simple respiratory infections because they refuse to take a week off. Minor foot and muscle injuries cripple runners whose determination not to quit overstrains their ligaments. It is this anxious voice grown demonic in intensity that transforms casual joggers into fanatics who can't stop until they have run 10 miles a day. Tillich was right: the demons take our anxieties and magnify them into raging psychic needs whose feeding threatens our sanity.

My fantasy during the act of running is always the same. In real life I have four daughters. But in the midrun fantasy I have an adopted son. He is a fantastic athlete—unbeatable at any sport—and he always wins an Olympic gold medal in the 1,500 meter run. Now, of course, a son means a kind of immortality. But this son has a living father, who, though old in years, is young in heart, in stride, and in accomplishment. If the daydream of the son quiets the anxiety of death, the presence of the father who shares in his victory quiets the modern anxiety of terminal helplessness.

The third stage in the act of running, that of satiety, needs little comment. Seldom are there daydreams. Instead, there is the rebaptism of the shower—a reward well deserved and gladly received, except by the puritan few who take it icy cold. Secular clothes are donned, and I find myself no longer fantasizing. My mind is free to plan. I plot lecture outlines, study committee responsibilities—in short, I am free of anxiety and able to enter refreshed into real life. My imagination, now free of self-aggrandizing and self-preserving daydreams, is released to cope with the rest of my life.

One runner I know has said: "I'm going to run till I'm 90. If the weather is bad on my last day, I'll collapse and die on the indoor track. Don't let anyone try to keep me alive, Fred. Just take a pushbroom and shove me off the running surface. Then, when you've finished your run, call the coroner."

A second runner related to me a dream in which he has reached advanced years and is killed in an accident. A surgeon is handed his heart on a tray so it can replace the diseased heart of a younger person. As the cardiac specialist picks up my friend's heart, he looks at it, whistles admiringly, and says, "What a beauty. Too bad the youngster who had this is dead."

From my own study of the Tillichian anxieties of death, guilt, and meaninglessness, I am convinced that death is the deepest-rooted, the basic anxiety. But, as Tillich saw, cultural presumptions and pressures heighten other anxieties and give them warped significance. He showed why the guilt anxiety prevailed at the time of the Reformation, and he confronted brilliantly the anxiety of meaninglessness in post-World War culture. Our ancestors scarcely knew the anxiety of terminal helplessness, at least in its present form. When illness laid them low in their advanced years, pneumonia quickly finished them off. But we today know that we could live for years lying in a hospital bed. Thanks to penicillin and the turning of comatose patients in their beds, people may sleep a score of years and never know their surroundings. Millions languish in homes for the aged, their minds and spirits exhausted but their bodies helpless to die.

I do not believe that the tap-root anxiety, the anxiety of death, is dealt with by running. The geriatric jogger is not engaged in what Ernest Becker called "an immortality project," because that anxiety surfaces early in life and is handled more or less adequately in other ways. (One of those "projects," by the way, is the publication of books and articles that will outlive the author.)

But the anxiety of living death, of helplessness, pervades civilized societies today. Running is a scientifically approved way of extending life; runners, however, do not so much want to gain an extension as they want to ensure mobility until death comes. "I'll run until I drop," one woman wrote in her questionnaire. Running, as a secular salvation that works no better than other secular saviors, poses questions for the ethicist, the theologian, and the student of religion and modern culture, but especially for the pastor and church member. The church as a community of believers bears a special responsibility in addressing the anxiety of terminal helplessness.

IV

The individual who lives outside of a caring community is powerless to face the reality of terminal helplessness in any way other than suicide. My own 2-or 3-mile run along the banks of the Red Cedar River will someday become a 10-foot shuffle from bed to bathroom with an attendant's hand supporting me, unless I determine to stumble into the river some day and drown.

Only community responds adequately to terminal helplessness. The Armenian and Chaldean ethnic communities in Detroit are known never to allow their aged to be taken into institutional care. Death for them is an "at home" event whenever possible. The concept of a hospice for the dying—especially those dying of cancer— is also essentially a community idea. The hospice staff members give patients medication to ward off pain, give

people some choices in their struggle to live through their death, and surround them with the persons and accouterments of home.

My father died summer before last. An apparently healthy man in his late
70s who had taken care of my bedfast mother through the half-decade of her
decline and death, he had spent a busy day with me and my family. We had
taken him on a short trip to renew our acquaintance with the hamlet where
my mother grew up. Then we had shared dinner with my sister's family and
turned on the television to watch the Cincinnati Reds get trampled. My father
never cared who won baseball games, but he cheered mightily when Pete
Rose and company lost. So we all went to bed happy. The next morning
when I went to awaken him, I found—to borrow my mother's language—that
"the Lord had called him during the night." It was a happy death, for he
never experienced what millions of the elderly go through, that living death of
helpless inactivity as medical miracles and institutional care prolong their existence. That night as I tried to sleep, I thought of my running and of my need
to keep moving. I knew at once that the effort was hopeless. I can only pray
for a death like my father's; I cannot guarantee it. I can only watch myself
carefully until I see the signs and then put an end to my life. Or I can find a
community that will allow me to die and help me as I prepare to be with the
Lord.

V

Paul Tillich, in his classic study of existential anxiety, does not seem to
realize the paralysis of this kind of helplessness. He subsumes the "anxiety of
powerlessness" under its more powerful companion, the "anxiety of death."
But by lumping powerlessness with death, Tillich fails to treat it with the care
he gives the anxieties of guilt and meaninglessness. I believe that death
should be singled out as the generic root of all our disease. Following that,
helplessness as a general anxiety, and terminal helplessness as a peculiarly
modern case in point, need special focus.

But more important, Tillich does not treat any anxiety as if its primary an-
tidote were to be found in community. Instead, corporate responses to anxiety are labeled as "courage to be as a part," and one is warned against
succumbing to "heteronomy" as an escape from anxiety. Certainly it is true
that people have sought to avoid the persistent agonies of the human condition by losing themselves in some group or nation-state or ideology that promises health and meaning, while it destroys freedom. All this Tillich meant by
heteronomy. Perhaps Tillich's secular existentialist heroes who exhibit the
"courage to be as oneself," do stand taller than any crowd, even a caring, life-
enhancing one as the church can be. Whether such heroes help us much is a
different thing. I think Tillich had no experience of real community. He lived
through the collapse of German society after World War I, and taught as an
exile in America most of his life. There is little evidence to be found in the section on the church in Tillich's *Systematic Theology*, Volume III, that church-

as-community (or Body of Christ) was real to him. My wife, Jean, who has read the spate of Tillich biographies, tells me that, except for his being rebuked for not attending chapel at Union Seminary, a worshiping community does not enter his life in America. In this, he is definitely a modern man. He is also of no help with the anxiety of terminal helplessness.

Certainly, the anxiety of death has been overcome for many by the church's proclamation of the resurrection of Jesus Christ. For many, the anxiety of guilt and condemnation has been overcome by the gospel declaration of pardon, usually made within the Body of Christ. The anxiety of meaninglessness, writes Tillich, can be overcome only by "the courage to accept acceptance." Yet for most of us that acceptance is found first in human community, not in metaphysical pursuit of the "God beyond the God of Theism." One can, of course, substitute other communities for the church, if within them human anxieties are accepted and confronted, and opportunity for meaningful sharing and response is afforded.

Of all human anxieties, the response to the anxiety of terminal helplessness is peculiarly community-bound. Yet ours is a time when community consciousness about the plight of the terminally helpless is uncertain, and ways of handling it are confused. Our age exalts youth and shunts the aged aside. I confess with shame that the sight of the very old or terminally ill fills me with dread. I dodge, sidestep—do anything but confront those who bear in their fragile bodies my helpless future. I run! So our society with great relief allows the professionals to take dying out of our hands.

Until the time comes when church and synagogue can reaffirm a place in community for the aged and dying, suicide and suicide pacts have a "good sense" ring to them, even if they affront Christian theology. There are, to be sure, numerous church-sponsored homes for the aged that really *are* homes, not merely institutions for terminal care. Perhaps church-hospice arrangements can also humanize the last weeks of life that could otherwise be devoid of choices in convalescent homes for the aged and busy hospitals.

VI

I began with jogging and the daydreams that surround it; I end with a plea for community. The church must try to deal specifically with the environments of the terminally ill and the terminally aged. As hospices make their way into abandoned maternity and pediatrics wings of local hospitals, churches can push for their acceptance and church people can serve on boards of directors and aid in ministering to dying patients and their families.

Second, the whole problem of aging has to be rethought by churches that are determined to be the Body of Christ. It is a restatement of the obvious, but it is a fact that mainline churches cannot really "discern the Body" (I Corinthians) in our "speaker-audience" style of worship; nor can we take seriously our aged as part of the Body until they are as much a part of our church communities as puzzled parents, youthful rebels, and businessmen. And that reality must be expressed and experienced first in public worship.

I suspect that these suggestions should be reversed. First, the pastor's mentality and the service of public worship must be restructured so that all can discern that they are part of the body of Christ regardless of age or health. Then extending the church's ministry to all will be as natural as breathing—or helping.

CHAPTER 14

The Women Who Run: Arbitrary Limitation or Freedom

Carole Oglesby

A whole new poetry beginning here.

Adrienne Rich

The above quotation, from one of a collection of poems by Adrienne Rich, captures some of my feelings about being a sportswoman living in the United States today. There is a sense of beginning and potentiality. Newspapers and magazines tick off some of the important events of the recent past (Varro, 1978):

1. Diana Nyad attempted a Cuba-Key West swim and wept when she was forced to abandon the effort after 40 hours;

2. Stella Taylor, 48, swam 140 miles from Bimini to Florida, trailed by a shark which had to be killed;

3. Robyn Davidson, dubbed the camel-lady, trekked alone across 1,200 miles of sand dunes in Australia;

4. In September 1978, 10 women attempted and 2 were the first Americans to succeed in scaling the 26,545 foot peak Annapurna. This was the first American Women's Himalayan Expedition.

These are amazing occurrences and certainly only the tip of the iceberg with regard to women's

increasing involvement in sport and challenging physical activities of which
running is an important example. But an uneasiness assails me: Why did this
take so long to happen? Why are there so many women still untouched, unin-
volved, and unknowing about their own bodies? In this paper, with the
foregoing considerations in mind, I shall explore three themes: That women
who run (a) have overcome elemental social-psychological obstacles in order
to incorporate this activity into their lives; (b) derive great benefit from running
as a flow/synthesis experience which provides opportunity for defining and
extending personal limits; and (c) could be multiplied and the quality of their
experience enhanced by specific assistance from the medical profession and
other health-related professions and agencies.

The Myth of Female Limitation for Sport

A fundamental obstacle to the realization of potential by a woman who runs
(or who may contemplate taking up running) is the sense of arbitrary limitation which is both self- and other imposed. To incorporate running (or any
activity with deep involvement) into the self-concept often requires a "conversion," she must be "born again," for the activity initially feels outside the
boundaries of her sex role and perceived femininity. As the sociology of
knowledge has shown, our perception of reality is socially constructed (Loy,
1978). In *The Crack in the Cosmic Egg,* Pearce (1971) details the social formation of an individual's world view. He agrees that reality, truth, and logic
are variables formed and discarded by cultural agreement.

For most women, the social reality surrounding sporting contexts has been
that they are out-of-bounds: masculine, part of male, not female, sex-
appropriate behavior. Felshin (1975) states that "the dramatic equation of
sport has yielded a stylistic and social formula for manhood . . . the athletic
and masculine models (of competition, power, and dominance) are inter-
changeable" (p. 31).

This social reality has been informed and legitimated by virtually all professions and disciplines. I will utilize samples from psychology, sociology,
history, and exercise physiology to illustrate my point. First, psychologist
Carolyn Sherif (Note 1) notes the following:

Until a few years ago, U.S. textbooks on adolescence contained research data
that the physical skills and capacities of young males increased during the period
while those of adolescent females declined as though from premature senility.
The differences were considered 'natural' sex differences. They *were* differences
reflecting the near opposite demands placed upon adolescent males and
females at the time the data were collected; they were not 'natural'.

From a sociological viewpoint, Birrell (Note 2) states that the sport role has
not been considered a salient one for women, young or old. She points out
that Coleman's classic work on the adolescent society did not consider at all

the social consequences of female involvement in sport. The silence on the matter of two replicative studies published in 1972 and 1973 indicates that the lack of salience remained at that time.

The perusal of historical accounts of significant events and significant persons in sport does little to transform a woman's perception that she has no place in sport. For example, it is said of Baron Pierre de Coubertin, founder of the modern Olympic Games, that:

> Although Coubertin had no particular objection to the sports of swimming and tennis for women, he drew attention to the fact that fencers, horsewomen, and rowers also existed and that soon, perhaps, there would be women soccer players and runners who would also wish to be included in the Olympic program. Such sports, practiced by women, he felt, would not constitute an edifying sight before assembled crowds for Olympic contests. (Leigh, 1974, pp. 21-22)

Now, we could respond to this with sophisticated amusement: What a quaint story! Unfortunately, the Baron had quite a bit of power and women had to work from 1900 to 1922 to finally obtain a regularized, albeit limited, role in the Olympic Games. Unfortunately also, the heirs of the Baron have, as yet, not allowed any women's running events beyond 1500 meters in the Games, although the track and field program has 21 events for men and 13 for women.

These are the elemental obstacles females face as they contemplate becoming a "woman who runs." Not only is there obvious secondary status in the world around them but most debilitating of all, their own encompassing world view is structured with concepts of limitation.

The published data on sex differences in physiological characteristics of sportsmen and women *can* seem but a litany of the inferiorities of the female system. Dr. Waneen Spirduso, exercise physiologist, introduces the following cautionary notes into our interpretations:

> 1. Results about sportswomen from exercise physiologists using valid experimental designs and reliable sophisticated equipment are few and have been accumulated only over the past 10 years;
> 2. Age ranges of sportswomen studied have been quite varied, which limits the generalizability of the whole information pool;
> 3. The cultural climate for development of female athletes in this country . . . has not been highly favorable. Women are probably *far from their athletic and physiological potential* and current understandings of them are only descriptions of the emerging female athlete. (cited in Gerber, 1974, p. 457)

Exemplifications of Spirduso's viewpoint are presented by Hudson (1978) in a recent publication in which she reviewed the literature on lean body fat ratios of female college "athletes" from 1967-73. One study showed gymnasts at 15.5% but five other studies reported average values from 20.8% to 26.9%. Hudson proposes that the female college athletes of this time period were not significantly different from "normal" college women and that present increases in intensity of training will be followed by different profiles on measures such as lean body fat. Hudson suggests further that East German female swimmers seem to exist in an environment which is both top class and equitable with their male counterparts. Table 1 illustrates that these female swimmers are performing at 91 to 97% performance levels of their male counterparts under these conditions.

Stefani, an expert in computer simulation, has gone another step in developing performance projections for the 1980 Games as well as for those of the year 2000. Stefani (1977) calculated a male/female percent of improvement between 1952 and 1976 and projected it through a least squares procedure. He shows that women are improving their performances more quickly than men and that this improvement will be increasingly true in the future. Table 2 illustrates the decreasing percent of difference in performance in selected events for women and men.

The Myth of female limitation *for* sport is exactly that: a myth. The legitimation of the myth can be discounted if people with access to information choose to do so.

Female Limitation in Sport

The arbitrary limitation of women in sport is no myth. It is an ever-present reality. The aspect of arbitrary limitation I wish to highlight is exclusion. In the past, much of boys/men-only sport has been legitimized by notions of dramatic biogenetic-based psychological differences in the two sexes. Maccobey and Jacklin (1974), after a massive review of the literature, reflect on the tentativeness of present understandings of this biogenetic base. One might think that, in the face of tentative data, administrative and bureaucratic regulation would be flexible, but this has not been the case in many sport in-

Table 1

Comparisons of Best Times by Country in the Montreal Olympics (1976)

Event		USA Female	USA Male	USA(%) Female/Male	GDR Female	GDR Male	GDR(%) Female/Male
Freestyle	100	56.81*	49.99[b]	88.0	55.65[b]	53.93	96.9
	400	4:10.46*	3:51.93[b]	92.6	4:09.89[b]	4:02.20	96.9
Backstroke	100	1:06.01	55.49[b]	84.1	1:01.83[a]	57.22	92.6
	200	2:17.27*	1:59.19[b]	86.8	2:13.43[a]	2:08.02	96.0
Butterfly	100	1:01.17*	54.35	88.9	1:00.13[bc]	55.09	91.6
	200	2:12.90	1:59.23[b]	89.7	2:11.41[b]	2:00.02	91.3

*American record
[a]Olympic record
[b]World record
[c]Tie

Table 2

Average Percent Difference Between Men and Women for 100 M Freestyle, 400 M Freestyle, 100 M Backstroke, 200 M Breaststroke

Olympiad	Average % Difference
1952	12.2
1956	11.3
1960	9.7
1964	10.9
1972	11.6
1976	9.9
1980	9.5
2000	7.4

stances. In the main, the consequences of arbitrary limitation are that boys/men are allowed and encouraged to test themselves to the outer limits of their abilities, whereas girls and women are encouraged and required to remain well inside their limits.

The exclusion of women from any running event beyond 1500 meters in the Olympic Games is a perfect case in point. The women's long distance running committee of the Amateur Athletic Union (AAU), the National Association for Girl's and Women's Sport, and the Avon International Running Circuit are among groups pressing the AAU and the International Amateur Athletic Federation (IAAF) (the governing federation) for the inclusion of a marathon for women.* One can hope that someday the politics will be right and women will be included. But in how many years? How many marathoners will be passed by in the interim? Where are the medical data to support the obvious reality of women by the hundreds running marathons all over the US and the world (Switzer, Note 3). Again, self-limitation is just as debilitating to females if not more so. Far too many women accept and even affirm these exclusions and myths of unsuitability. We, who know better, must do all we can to "convert" women to new beliefs about their physical potentialities. As Oliver (1978) has stated, "we are entitled to all our potentialities, *including those of which we cannot yet conceive*" (p. 3).

Running as a Flow/Synthesis Experience

The thrust of my own "lifework" is to enable women and men to open themselves to the psychological development which can occur through

---

*Editor's note: In 1981 a marathon for women was approved for the Olympic Games, beginning in Los Angeles in 1984.

movement participation. In this section I will briefly indicate how running and other sport-as-flow experiences benefit the women and men who run.

John Loy provides us with one framework by which to understand the meaningfulness that running may engender. Loy teases out from sport forms (like running) various expressive and instrumental functions which participation may fulfill. For example, running may fill expressive needs for play, release, sociability, or may even serve as a condition for the occasional experience of ecstasy. Similarly, when participated in as an institutionalized activity (i.e., consistent training, entering races, working towards progressive performance goals), these instrumental values may function for the individual as a socialization into dominant values of American society.

Loy (1978) sees the history of sport as a paradoxical tension between its expressive and instrumental aspects. He proposes a future synthesis in sport wherein expressive/instrumental, intrinsic/extrinsic, means/ends dichotomies will be transcended. This kind of transcending capability has been described, in human personality, as androgyny (Duquin, 1978). Duquin has demonstrated that at present, for a variety of reasons, sportswomen are more likely than sportsmen to reflect the desirable qualities of androgyny.

Another way to view running as a synthesis activity is to see it and other movement activity as potential healers of the deep mind/body dichotomy so prevalent in our thinking processes. Research seems to support the notion that activity and physical competence enhancement is accompanied by positive psychological development. Of the two categories of research on this relationship, one uses psychiatric patients as subjects and activity (often jogging) as an adjunct to psychotherapy, and the second has "normals" as subjects with activity as a treatment group.

In a recent review of this literature, Griffin (Note 4) found positive results reported in the programs of both categories utilizing jogging, although only three were found which included female subjects. Griffin concluded that "the consistency of results and existential reports of increased feelings of psychological well-being attributed to the level of participation in activity is difficult to ignore." Sachs (Note 5) has identified a body of literature which also supports the notion that psychological benefits are derivable from running.

Several psychotherapy models postulate running as a crucial aspect. Among these are the following:

1. Running therapy, originated by Kostrubala;

2. The meditation model, wherein the repetitive and rhythmical aspects of running function in the same manner as the mantra;

3. The brain function model which focuses on increased blood flow to the brain, flushing in a psychopharmacological sense and exhaustion of the left cerebral cortex yielding a beneficial time of right cortex dominance; and

4. Zen sport, described by Gallwey and Kriegel. (Griffin, Note 4)

Griffin states that although clear statistical evidence supporting these formulations does not exist, research has begun.

A third and related way of seeing the potential benefit of running is to view it as a flow experience. Csikzentmihalyi (1975), in attempting to discover what makes any activity enjoyable, developed a theoretical model which identifies the criteria for a flow experience and the contexts in which it is most likely to occur. Games and play, including running, were identified as potentially excellent for flow experience. In flow there is (a) merging of action and awareness; (b) self-forgetting or the loss of self-consciousness; (c) centering of the attention on the activity; (d) effortless control over self and environment; (e) coherent, noncontradictory demands for action and clear, unambiguous feedback to action; and (f) no need for extrinsic goals or rewards. Flow occurs only when the challenges of the activity are evenly matched with participants' skills.

One of the most important concomitants of "running free" as a flow/synthesis experience is the opportunity it provides for authenticity; in this case the finding of one's own present limits of distance, speed, strength, endurance. In keeping with Heidegger's concept of MAN, sic WO(MAN) (Berger, 1963), when a woman says to herself, "I could never run 26 miles. 'Women' are not built for that kind of stress," she lives inauthentically. When the IOC states, as it implicitly does, that "Women" cannot run a marathon safely, an opportunity for full authenticity is denied the many women who have conclusively demonstrated they can (Switzer, Note 3). Certainly only a few women will be Olympic performers, or life-riskers like those who climb mountains, or spacecraft pilots, and so forth. But we, each of us, must find these things for ourselves or we have not lived fully. Certainly many men have stirred us with their lives, strengths, bravery, compassion. Wives, daughters, sisters; we need such role models—of our own kind—to better form our visions and entitlement.

Conclusion

The medical and health-related professions can help women gain the freedom to find their own limits, by taking the five steps that follow:

1. Research institutions and laboratories should review and evaluate their on-going projects in regard to the following kinds of concerns: Is there a balance of work on female and male subjects? Are projects which have significance for women's potential being addressed? Are efforts being made to recruit women to the staff and to medical research in general? Spirduso has stated, "The basic questions, some of them asked as long as 60 years ago, still remain (as regards female performance) . . . . Little systematic attention has been given these questions by American doctors or physiologists" (cited Gerber, 1974, p. 486).

2. Unrecognized sexist biases must be considered as potential contaminants in research projects. The institutional review processes, which protect the rights of human subjects (Lally, 1978), should be designed to be sensitive to pervasive sexism as well.

3. For those in clinical work, it is proposed that well-planned exercise programs be recommended whole-heartedly for women, unless specific prohibiting complications exist. Although this may sound simplistic, the physician needs to be attentive to strong linkages in female patients between perceptions of femininity and qualities such as passiveness, dependency, and subordination of self-concerns. The adoption of a systematic training regimen is particularly difficult when these linkages exist; secondary support from physician, family, and friends may need to be marshalled.

4. The presentation of fitness standards for males and females must be considered. Sherif (Note 1) has stated that "the level at which one's own standards of performance are set are governed by standards prevailing in one's reference group and relative to other groups with whom the reference group compares itself." In light of the history of obstacles to women developing their potential in physical performance, so-called "norms" of performance for girls and women must be regarded as self-fulfilling prophesies, artifacts, and relics. Through medical advisory roles to groups like the President's Council on Physical Fitness and Sport, local school districts and the like, policy recommendations must be forthcoming which call for publication of norms for females of all ages based on data provided by females who have been active and trained for good performance.

5. As implied in point 4, the medical community could be an ally to the women's sport community in the politics which surround sport. For example, if for bureaucratic reasons the sport governing agencies choose not to expand the program of the Olympic Games to add a women's 5000 meter run, a 10,000 meter run, and a marathon, let them be faced with the truth of that. Let them not propose that their hesitancy arises from concerns for females' tenuous health and welfare. Public positions by medical groups must clarify these issues and frame them as political and not as scientific or medical issues.

Reference Notes

1. Sherif, C. *Women's emancipation, femininity, and sport: A psychologist's view.* Unpublished manuscript, International Congress of Physical Activity Sciences, Quebec, 1976.
2. Birrell, S. *The neglected half of the adolescent society: Status and consequences of high school athletic participation for girls.* Unpublished manuscript, University of Massachusetts, 1976.
3. Switzer, K. *A report on women's long distance running.* New York: Avon International Women's Running Circuit, 1980.
4. Griffin, P. *Play and sport experiences: The flow experience and self-knowledge education.* Unpublished manuscript, University of Massachusetts, 1978.
5. Sachs, M. *Exercise addiction.* Paper presented at NASPE Sport Psychology Academy Pre-convention Symposium, Detroit, Michigan, 1980.

References

Berger, P. *Invitation to sociology: A humanistic perspective*. Garden City: Doubleday, 1963.

Csikzentmihalyi, M. *Beyond boredem and anxiety: The experience of play in work and games*. San Francisco: Jossey-Bass, 1975.

Duquin, M. The androgynous advantage. In C. A. Oglesby (Ed.), *Women and sport: From myth to reality. Philadelphia, PA: Lea & Febiger, 1978.*

Felshin, J. Sport, style and social mode. *Journal of Physical Education and Recreation, 1975, **46,** 31.*

Gerber, E. *The American woman in sport*. Reading, MA: Addison-Wesley, 1974.

Hudson, J. Physical parameters used for female exclusion from law enforcement and athletics. In C. A. Oglesby (Ed.), *Women and sport: From myth to reality*. Philadelphia, PA: Lea & Febiger, 1978.

Lally, J.J. The making of the compassionate physician-investigator. *Annals of the American Association of Political and Social Scientists*, May 1978, p. 437.

Leigh, M. Pierre de Coubertin: A man of his time. *Quest*, 1974, **22,** 19-24.

Loy, J.W. The cultural system of sport. *Quest*, 1978, **29,** 73-102.

Maccobey, E., & Jacklin, C. *Psychology of sex differences*. Stanford, CA: Stanford University Press, 1974.

Oglesby, C.A. (Ed.) *Women and sport: From myth to reality*. Philadelphia, PA: Lea & Febiger, 1978.

Oliver, S. Defining our territories. *Quest: A feminist quarterly*, 1978, **4,** 3.

Pearce, J.C. *The crack in the cosmic egg*. New York: Pocket Books, 1971.

Rich, A. *The dream of a common language*. New York: W. W. Norton, 1978.

Stefani, R.T. Trends in Olympic winning performance. *The Athletic Journal*, December 1977.

Varro, B. Because it's there: Women invade male area of competition. *Chicago Sun Times*, August 21, 1978, p. 41.

CHAPTER 15

Mental Status and Psychological Coping During a 100-Mile Race

Michael H. Sacks, Paul Milvy,
Samuel W. Perry, and Lloyd R. Sherman

What happens in the minds of runners attempting distances greater than the marathon? What are they thinking about? How well do they think at all? These are the questions which we were interested in answering.

Anecdotal reports suggest that during long-distance runs thinking becomes impaired—that runners are unable to calculate their pace or think clearly, and at times they may even blank out (Chodes, 1978; Sheehan, 1978). For example, one runner described a 50 miler: "The last twenty miles were sort of a blur of pain and fatigue" (Fixx, 1979, p. 23). We could find no study in the literature which documented this impairment in thinking during an actual distance race (Maron & Horvath, 1978), and studies of psychological coping in marathon runners have yielded mixed findings. Morgan distinguished two groups of marathoners: the "associaters" who focus predominantly on the race and on their bodies, and the "dissociaters" who use various mental devices to take their minds off the race and off of their pains (Morgan & Pollock, 1977). Sime (Note 1) found that some runners employ both strategies. Sachs (Note 2) confirmed this, but could find no simple characterization of cognitive coping strategies in the runners he studied.

A possible source of error in these investigations and in the numerous published anecdotal accounts is that the data were collected after the race was over. The runners may not have remembered accurately what was going on in their heads *during* the race or, for whatever reasons, may have provided a distorted representation. In an attempt to diminish this retrospective distortion, we tested the mental states of runners during the process of a 100-mile run. We wanted to see if the clarity of thinking declined over time, if performance was in any way related to mood (highs or lows), and if ultramarathoners used any particular kind of psychological coping mechanism while they ran.

Method

Two hours before the start of a 100-mile road race, we obtained permission from 10 male runners who agreed to participate in the study. Approximately every 3 hours one of the investigators bicycled alongside of a runner as he was starting another 2½-mile lap. The investigator handed the runner a lightweight portable tape recorder about the size of a cigarette pack. Without changing pace or breathing, the runner then answered a series of questions, which took about 9 minutes. The questions were as follows:

1. How are you feeling? Physically? Emotionally?
2. What has been on your mind the last lap?
3. Have you noticed any times that your mind sort of went blank?
4. Remember the following three items—I will ask you to repeat them in a few minutes. (The runner was then asked a set of three nouns, such as pen, pie and, spoon. A different set was asked during each questioning period.)
5. Repeat the following numbers. (A 4-digit number was then stated—such as 6,894—and the runner was asked to repeat it. The same process was then followed for a 5-digit and a 6-digit number.) Repeat the following number backwards. (The runner was then given a 4-digit number to repeat backwards, then a 5- and a 6-digit number. The set of numbers was changed for each questioning period.)
6. Spell this word backwards. (A set of 3-, 4-, and 5-letter words were then given separately, such as tack, house, and number. A different set was given during each question period.)
7. Add these numbers. (A 2-digit number was then followed by another 2-digit number, such as 48 and 63. A different set of three such additions was given during each questioning period.)
8. Recall the three items I asked you to remember.
9. If 100 is the best you could ever feel and 0 is the worst you could possibly feel and 50 is normal, with what number would you rate yourself now?

The investigators had on their bicycles a clipboard with the prearranged series of questions and the specific recall items. The advantages of using a small tape machine were that the answers did not have to be recorded immediately and that the time required to answer the questions could be measured. This method provided measures of accuracy and response time. We expected both would be influenced by the elapsed running time.

Results

The results are recorded in Tables 1 and 2. In Table 1 are the errors, response times, and mood evaluations for the runners. Because there were so few errors, we averaged all the runners to provide errors per runner. The response times were derived by averaging the findings of two independent listeners to the replaying of the tapes.

A nonstatistically significant decline in the number of errors per runner occurred over the 13 hours of the race. In any event, this finding could undoubtedly reflect a practice effect caused by increasing familiarity with the procedure. The response time decreased similarly over the first three periods but then increased, except when runners were spelling backward in the 11-13 hour range. Although this finding is not statistically significant, there appeared to be a trend in the latter part of the race for the runner to slow down mentally but not, however, to make more errors.

The mood ratings show a progressive decline during the race. Only one runner said he felt a "100" in the first 2 hours; no one else rated his mood as better than his normal 50 during the race. At 11-13 hours, the runners as a group reached their lowest point. The individual mood ratings listed in Table 2 showed a progressive decline in all runners except for Runner 2, who finished higher than he began. His "55" was obtained just after the race and after he had been told that he had established an excellent time. We will discuss this table in more detail later in the paper.

Discussion

The data support the general impression obtained during the interviews themselves that the thinking of these runners during the race remained sharp and clear for the first 8-10 hours. The recall of three items was excellent, indicating no impairment in short-term memory. Attention span, concentration, and immediate memory were also efficient, as indicated by the digit recall, the digit reversals, and the spelling reversals. The mental arithmetic revealed no deterioration in the ability to calculate. We also found no deterioration in the time between the finish of a question and the response by the runner.

After 10 hours, there was no increase in the number of errors, although there was an increase in the average response time. Even though this increase was not statistically significant, it does indicate a trend. Because response time

Table 1

Average Response Time, Number of Errors, and Mood Evaluation

	2-4 hrs (sec)	5-7 hrs (sec)	8-10 hrs (sec)	11-13 hrs (sec)
Numbers, Fwd.	2.57	2.35	2.17	2.18
Numbers, Bkwd.	3.09	2.02	2.03	2.22
Spelling, Bkwd.	4.75	4.40	3.41	4.39
Addition	4.21	3.89	2.01	3.48
Memory	6.53	5.59	6.07	8.05
Average Time/Rsp.	4.23	3.65	3.14	4.06

	2-4 hrs	5-7 hrs	8-10 hrs	11-13 hrs
Errors/Runner[a]	1.5	1.4	1.6	1.0
0-100 Mood Eval.	53	47	36	30
No. Participants	10	8	5	4

[a]There were 15 questions asked of each runner during each test period: 3 recall, 3 numbers forward, 3 numbers backward, 3 spellings backward, and 3 addition. The differences found were not significant.

Table 2

Mood Ratings For Each Runner

Runner	2-4 hrs	5-7 hrs	8-10 hrs	11-13 hrs
1	60	65	40/35	10 (finished)
2	45	40 (withdrew from protocol)	—	55 (finished)
3	44 (stopped)	—	—	—
4	50	45	40	40 (stopped)
5	45	40/70 (stopped)	—	—
6	45	35 (stopped)	—	—
7	40	35	20	10 (finished) in 18 hrs)
8	75	50	35	35 (stopped)
9	100	45	40	30 (stopped)
10	25	(stopped)	—	—

is a more subtle indication of mental fatigue, a cautious conclusion is that the four remaining runners were beginning to show some deterioration. Remarkably, however, this deterioration was quite mild.

We, of course, were interested in a correlation between mental acuity and physical performance. We could find no such correlation. Even in runners who dropped out because of "exhaustion," "pain," or "feeling too shitty," no evidence of impaired thinking by our measurements was present. We also found no correlation between performance and temperament. Although irritability often accompanies physical tiredness, only one runner out of 10 was slightly irritable and asked us to leave him alone because he didn't want to be bothered. In this study, however, he was unique. The other runners were remarkably cooperative and polite. For example, after one of the investigators nearly ran over a runner with his bike in an earlier interview, in the last lap this runner cordially asked if he could skip this series of questions because he wanted to be alone.

No correlation was found between how a runner rated his mood and whether he continued or dropped out. The median at the start was 40. The runner who rated his mood at "100" said he felt fantastic and seemed to be caught up with an initial intense excitement that separated him from the rest of the runners. In fact, the investigator was not even sure that this runner understood the mood question. In contrast, however, at the beginning of the race most of the runners felt a little worse than usual. The scores continued to drop during the next 4-6 hours, but a decline in mood did not necessarily herald that the runner was about to drop out. For example, one runner reported a 40 at 5-7 hours and a 55 just before he finished. A front runner rated his mood as 10—but then finished, whereas another runner rated his mood as 40 but dropped out because he "no longer saw any point in it." A runner who started with a mood rating of 45 dropped out after only 2 hours, feeling a 70 psychologically and a 40 physically. Most strikingly, one runner rated his mood as 10 for the last 4 hours of the race, but nevertheless continued and finished. Nothing in our data supported the belief that these runners experience a high during a race.

In response to the less structured questions about thoughts and feelings, the ultramarathoners turned out to be a terse bunch of individuals. Their answers were laconic and, for the most part, psychologically sparse. At this point, we must admit to a certain bias. All of the investigators are marathoners, yet the notion of running four times that distance inspired in us a certain awe. Appreciating what was required to run 26.2 miles, we were unable to grasp how one could run much further. We viewed the ultramarathoners as somehow attaining an excellence of endurance that was beyond us. If we struggled to run "only" a marathon, what might we find out about these special, inspiring, giant marathoners? The research was therefore partly motivated by a barely concealed envy.

This bias produced what we realized in retrospect was a serious shortcoming in our methodology. Although the runners were generally willing to talk while they ran and several even welcomed the opportunity, we were hesitant about asking the runners to elaborate their answers or in any other way challenge them. We expected these "supermen" to be greater than life and did not want to reduce them to mere mortals by asking probing questions about their very human concerns. At the time, we rationalized our hesitancy by saying that we did not want to disturb the runners, but we suspect now that they would have been more cooperative had we not been so uneasy ourselves.

So, we remain uncertain whether it was our reluctance to probe or the runners' terse style that produced such sparse psychological material. We are certain that instead of extraordinary insight into questions of endurance and motivation, we obtained very ordinary answers. For example, the question "What have you been thinking about during the last lap?" produced the following answers from one world class runner:

At 5 hours, 13 minutes: "Well, not really anything."

At 8 hours, 7 minutes: "Mostly that muscle [in his knees], I guess."

At 10 hours: "Same thing as usual. Forty miles to go. That little muscle in my left leg around the knee hurts."

At 14 hours: "Just keep going. That's about it."

On the surface, these comments appear to illustrate "associative thinking." Morgan defines associative thinking as occurring when runners focus primarily on what is necessary to accomplish the race—on their body, on the terrain, and on the competition. During dissociative thinking, runners focus on things to distract them from the race—on grade school teachers, on Beethoven's symphonies, and on complex mathematical formulas. Applying these criteria, the ultramarathoners were clearly not dissociative thinkers. They monitored the race and themselves closely. For instance, after 2 hours one runner said he was worried about a very slight blister which might give him trouble in 5 or 6 hours, then added, "I know how far I have gone, how far to go, and roughly what my pace is." Other runners showed this same meticulous attention to detail and did not permit themselves to be distracted because the race required careful pacing. As one runner put it, "One hundred miles is more of a mental challenge than the marathon because you have 10 more hours to think about it while doing it." Another runner said, "The last 4 miles of the marathon are mental; in a hundred-mile race it is the last 40."

But before simply concluding that ultramarathoners primarily use associative thinking, let us look at the data more closely. Although the runners only *volunteered* thoughts that were focused on the run, by collecting data during the process of the race we were able to infer that other thoughts were occurring as well. For example, at 2 hours 27 minutes the investigator asked a runner if his mind went blank at any time. One can "read between the lines" of the following responses.

Runner: "Well, I daydream, if that's what you mean."

Investigator: "What do you daydream about?"

Runner: "Anything. Nothing in particular."

And at 5 hours 13 minutes, the investigator asked what was on the runner's mind during the previous lap.

Runner: "Well, not really anything."

Investigator: "You don't recall what you were thinking?"

Runner: "I don't remember."

During both questioning periods, the runner indicated that he was occupied with other thoughts but did not reveal them. This runner was more than willing to elaborate his associative thoughts about the race, yet gave little attention or "could not remember" his other thoughts, his daydreams. We hypothesize that the runners were willing to emphasize their associative thinking even though much of the time their thoughts were elsewhere. This implies that the "other thoughts" had no emotional investment and simply passed through their minds: "I'm not thinking about much"; "nothing of much magnitude"; "I'm thinking lap by lap—in other words I have to think of it in laps so I can finish another one, and most of my thoughts are good"; "thinking mostly about that muscle, I guess"; "just keep going, that's about it," and so on.

In addition, we were interested not only in what the runners reported but also in what the runners did *not* report. The data clearly suggest that the runners were not always monitoring the race and their bodies even though these associative thoughts were the ones they volunteered. Some of the time during the 4-8 hours their thoughts were elsewhere. Where were they? In trying to answer that question, we have concluded that those "other thoughts" are irretrievable. They simply "passed through" without holding any emotional investment or meaning.

We are not suggesting that the ultramarathoners use dissociative thinking, because as Morgan defines it, dissociative thinkers are focused on something other than the race. These runners were spending hours focused on nothing, simulating a meditative process in which any ideas, feelings, or images simply run through the mind and fade from view. We are *not* saying the runners were "free associating." In the analytic situation, "free thoughts" are believed to be laden with significance and are therefore closely observed by both the analyst and the analysand. The runners' free thoughts were not imbued with this importance.

As more runners are interviewed during the process of races, we suspect Morgan's original thoughts about associative and dissociative thinking will be modified. A third kind of thinking—meditative thinking—may prove to occupy most of the time during the race. During this kind of thinking, runners are focusing neither on themselves nor on some distracting thought, but rather they are not particularly focusing at all. As one runner summed it up: "The more the race is on, the more you try to concentrate on the race. The mind goes in circles. First on one thing, then the pace, then something else, and then the pace." The "something else," however, may have nothing at all to do with the race or the runner's body.

In fairness to Morgan's distinction, one must note that the ultramarathoner is running a slower race than the marathoner. Although it is longer, the slower pace in the ultramarathoners might permit the runner to play what one author has called "mind games" (Zinman, 1979). He quotes Park Barner, a world class ultramarathoner, describing how he lets his thoughts wander and daydream: "It's the same thing as when you're driving a car hour after hour on a turnpike." This is very similar to the quotation above regarding the "mind going in circles" if we assume that Park Barner means that while driving a car his thoughts come and go but do return to the car itself—its speed, the amount of gasoline in the tank, the traffic conditions, and so on. Having made these judgments, he then returns to meditative thinking.

We were, of course, also interested in how these runners coped with the problem of pain. Interestingly, all the runners talked about pain, but never as something that would make them consider stopping. When pain occurred, they responded to it by noting its presence, altering their stride, taking aspirin, or wondering what the pain might mean or forecast—but pain was considered more of a signal, a sign, than something distressing in itself. By some mental trick or conditioning, pain for these ultramarathoners was seen as a sensation rather than an unpleasant experience in itself. Only one of the eight runners who stopped mentioned pain as the reason, but even this explanation was ambiguous. At 80 miles, he said, "I am sick to my stomach and I have become less tolerant to the pain in my legs." His statement implies that the pain had been around for some time, and only his tolerance for it had changed.

Finally, we attempted to discern why the other runners stopped, but no clear pattern emerged. One runner who stopped after 10 hours explained that he was depressed and disappointed that he didn't feel like he ordinarily felt in a 100-mile race. Another said that he stopped because he was worried about a race he had entered 3 weeks hence. Of note, only one runner openly acknowledged that he dropped out at 77 miles because of feeling defeated by the other runners: "Guys were walking by me, not quite, what's the point of it? I felt I had lost my pace psychologically." To the investigator, he seemed defeated and lost. He did not at this point mention anything about the pain.

Interestingly, however, 3 weeks later he returned a questionnaire we had sent him, stating that he had dropped out because of the pain and had been troubled by this: "I felt depressed with my inability to overcome physical problems. I was later plagued with doubt that my dropping out was not justified by the extent of the injuries I had incurred." This statement is noteworthy because it demonstrates how this runner may have used pain retrospectively to explain his dropping out of the race even though *at the time* he emphasized the psychological and competitive aspects. The significance of the pain to this runner appears to have changed as the race became more a thing of the past. While running, he responded to the pain not as something that hurt, but as a signal informing him about his stride and capacity to continue. Days later, the pain assumed a different significance. If this finding is replicated by others, it would cast the entire lore of the runner's pain and masochism into a different perspective. Pain may become a more precise way of describing after the race what was difficult to define during the race, such as what one is thinking about and why one drops out.

Perhaps the most interesting question was not asked and was therefore not answered: Why did any of these runners want to run 100 miles? In general, runners showed a remarkable absence of competitive feelings with the other runners and a far greater preoccupation with their own personal best performance. Only one runner mentioned that he wished to finish near the top; all the others set as their goals their own particular times and then raced to achieve that. Even if we asked the runners why they ran, we doubt we would have received a satisfactory answer because these runners appeared to be motivated by forces outside of their own awareness. For example, one runner volunteered the following reason for attempting the feat: "I want to get one of those tee shirts that say 'I Ran 100 Miles.' It's a way of being different. Not many people could do that. If I don't finish, I'll cop one of them." He may have been running to be different. We doubt that he was running for a tee shirt.

Conclusion

By asking questions during the process of an ultramarathon, we did not find that thinking became significantly impaired, that runners blanked out, or that runners experienced a high. They remained remarkably sharp up to 10 hours and only then began to show a slightly impaired response time that might indicate some mental fatigue. Although we found that runners' mood fell over time, there was no correlation between a low mood and stopping the race. The runners volunteered "associative thoughts" about the race and about their bodies but implied that daydreaming was occurring during large portions of the race. These daydreams simply "passed through" their minds in a meditative manner without becoming invested with meaning or feeling. Pain was viewed as a signal of what was going on in their bodies, but was not experienced as an overwhelming, unpleasant sensation or as a reason in itself for stopping. One runner's questionnaire, however, completed weeks later, suggested that the pain may be viewed quite differently in retrospect. In general, competitive feelings were neither the reason for running the race nor the reason for stopping. Why the runners ran and why they stopped were questions we did not satisfactorily answer. The main advantage of our method was that we avoided retrospective falsification and were therefore able to demythologize previous anecdotal reports.

Reference Notes

1. Sime, W. *Association/dissociation and motivation in marathon runners.* Unpublished manuscript.
2. Sachs, M.L. *On the trail of the runner's high — A descriptive and experimental investigation of characteristics of an elusive phenomenon.* Unpublished doctoral dissertation, Florida State University, 1980.

References

Chodes, J. *Corbitt.* Los Altos, CA: Tafnews Press, 1978.

Fixx, J. Frontiers. *Running,* 1979, **4,** 23.

Maron, M.B., & Horvath, S.M. The marathon: A history and review of the literature. *Medicine and Science in Sports,* 1978, **10**(2), 137-150.

Morgan, W.P., & Pollock, M.L. Psychologic characterization of the elite distance runner. In P. Milvy (Ed.), *Annals of the New York Academy of Sciences,* 1977, **301,** 382-403.

Sheehan, G. *Running and being.* New York: Simon & Schuster, 1978.

Zinman, D. A matter of perspective. *Running,* 1979, **4**(4), 49-51.

CHAPTER 16

Running and Other Vices

Joseph Epstein

Whenever I see someone jogging by, body glistening with sweat, face contorted with pain, I think of a fellow with whom I went to high school, one Taxicab Rabinowitz by name. Rabinowitz earned his vehicular sobriquet, as W. C. Fields might have put it, from traveling almost exclusively by cab. I did not know him well, but on those occasions when I did see the Cab, as intimates called him, he inevitably appeared to be either emerging from or entering into yet another taxicab. Taxicab Rabinowitz was one of those boys who go directly from early childhood to middle age without ever stopping at youth. I imagine he began shaving around the age of nine. He wore pointed-toed shoes with alligator trim. He was wide in the flanks, soft in the middle; the omnipresent cigarette on his lip—a Pall Mall, unfiltered, if memory serves—was as much a part of his physiognomy as his well-pomaded hair. Taxicab Rabinowitz was of course unthinkable in a gym suit or athletic togs of any kind, with the exception of a checkered suit to be worn at the track. He was, with his cabs and cigarettes and puffy body, the very antithesis of all that is implied by the phrase "in shape."

"In shape?" I can easily hear Rabinowitz asking. "In shape for what?" That is not a bad question, to which I shall return presently, but first I want to say that the reason I think of Taxicab Rabinowitz whenever I see a jogger is that he, the Cab, is the last man in the world I can imagine jogging. Miami Beach, Las Vegas, Palm Springs, whichever pleasure spa Taxicab Rabinowitz now inhabits, he is surely not running around it but is much more likely to be seated—most probably in the back of a cab, from where he must long ago have concluded that cab meters, not human beings, are for running.

If Taxicab Rabinowitz is the last man in the world I can imagine taking up a regular regimen of running, then I am the next-to-the last man. I am, if only in the physical realm, too virtuous as it is. Here is my dismal record: I drink, but scarcely ever to excess. I weigh exactly what the weight charts inform me I ought to weigh (the result of avoiding too frequent indulgence in fattening foods, every one of which I love). I play racquetball, usually twice a week. My cholesterol count is where it ought to be; my blood pressure is normal. I have recently quit smoking cigarettes, a habit of more than 20 years' standing. I both retire and rise early. Quite sickening, is it not? Also a bit worrisome. Enjoying such good health has of late caused me to think myself a perfect potential victim for being run over by a school bus. ("He was in his prime, Emily, never sick a day in his life.") But to enter upon a running regimen is more virtuous than even I care to be.

No mistake, it is the virtuousness of runners that appalls—the notion that their running makes them a select breed, an elite of sorts, whose elitism, though anchored in physical activity, goes well beyond the physical. Early last year the *Wall Street Journal* ran an article about people in cars harassing joggers and runners along roadsides: honking at them, spitting at them, nudging them with front bumpers, in some instances running them off the road. The motive, the joggers and runners assumed, was envy of their superior health. Ah, how readily the scene sets itself in the mind! A jogging couple, resplendent in polyester warm-up suits, blond brows aglow with a fine coat of perspiration; then up drives a long Lincoln, one of those gas guzzlers that got us into the energy crisis to begin with; the fat, beetle-browed driver behind the wheel shifts a cigar stub in his jaw, slips the Lincoln out of Cruisomatic, and, muttering obscenities, aims his car toward the jogging couple—who embody good health, sensible economy, and (let's face it) everything America could, and indeed ought to, be.

Implicit in this scene, too, is the notion that joggers and runners are an endangered species of sorts, though few things could be further from the truth. For 26-mile marathon races in Boston, New York, and Chicago, runners turn out by the thousands; soon the mark of a bush-league town will be that it does not have a marathon. Yet marathon runners are but a minuscule portion of people who run noncompetitively: those who run before work in the early morning or after work in the early evening, the weekend runners, and those who run whenever they can. They have become part of the landscape, these joggers and runners, sometimes the first thing one sees out the window in the morning. One sees them chugging alongside the Potomac in Washington, up and down every street and footpath in Eugene, Oregon, at sunup in Manhattan, in middle western parks. Chicago has already had a jogging rapist whose victims have been women jogging in forest preserves. A commonly cited figure for the American running population is 25 million.

This surging pedestrianism seems to disregard strict social confines. Running/jogging is not something done chiefly by the upper middle class, nor is it preponderantly suburban. The young go in for it in great numbers, of course, but the middle-aged are padding along with them, and even the quite old are huffing not far behind. Running is unisex at all but the competitive levels, and as many (perhaps more) women as men seem to be swept up by it. Motives for running seem as varied as the backgrounds of runners; among them are wanting to lose weight, gain muscle tone, take fresh air and exercise, feel achievement, extend and test physical capacity. More arcane motives for running, if they were not present to begin with, have since been supplied. Running "highs" are now spoken of. In some of the books about running, not simply exercise but "ecstasy" is held to lie just down the path. In short, the oily fingers of the consciousness movement have taken hold. "Sweat reaches places nothing else reaches," says Dr. George Sheehan, one of the gurus of running. "Sweat cleanses you."

And the purveyors of running gear, one ought quickly to add, pick you even cleaner. Among the advantages of running, one might suppose, is that it would seem to require so little in the way of equipment; shoes, shorts, a road—doesn't that about cover it? Not quite. No sooner had the fad of running begun in earnest than abreast of it trotted up the publishers, manufacturers, merchandisers. These running dogs of capitalism are even now running all the way to the bank. They founded magazines, such as *Runner's World* and *The Runner*, that seek to proselytize even as they preach to the converted. Books in plenty continue to appear: practical manuals like *Guidelines to Successful Jogging, Aerobics for Women, Computerized Running Training Programs;* books holding out hope and promise such as *The Joy of Running* and *Run for Your Life;* biographies of long-distance runners; and books of philosophic purport such as *Running and Being: The Total Experience* (this last by Dr. Sheehan, who has become something of a J. P. Sartre in an athletic supporter).

Riffling through the pages of the new magazines devoted to running, one could conclude from the advertisements that there are more kinds of running shoes now on the market in America than there are feet. But this is not to speak of such auxiliary items as special arch supports, heel protectors, insoles; nor of fog-repellents for glasses, or skin lube to prevent chafing under the arms, or runner's mittens; nor of warm-up suits, singlets, socks, and shorts (one manufacturer sells shorts that he advertises as "almost like running nude"). Then there are metric conversion scales, chronographs and stop-watches, wallets that attach to running shoes, pouches to fit on the back of shorts. One of my favorite items is a "jogging stick," comparable to a military swagger stick, to be carried along while running and to be used, apparently, for beating off dogs, muggers, perhaps smokers.

Ours is an age of health, and the runner is surely our most fanatical seeker after health, a Hassid at the altar of Hygeia. Various explanations have been adduced for the excessive concern with health in our day. The novelist Mary Gordon, for example, feels that it has to do with politics taking a turn inward. Unable to control the external world of events, she explains, we seek to control the internal world of our bodies. "If we can't stop Seabrook," writes Miss Gordon, "maybe we can lengthen our Achilles tendons." There may well be something to this. Others seem to feel that a political profile can be discerned among running folk; as I write, a comedy revue in the Middle West carries the title *Great Jogging Liberals*. But I think something rather more fundamental is entailed. I think it is, at bottom, the fear of death that keeps joggers and runners jogging and running. This seems to me a reasonable enough fear, and one we all share. The only difference between joggers and runners and the rest of us, when it comes to the fear of death, is that they are doing something about it: they are running from it.

Our own age of health has a historical precedent in the early and middle Victorian age in England. The setting for the 19th century concern with health seems to have been rampant sickness and arbitrary death. In a recent book, *The Healthy Body and Victorian Culture* (Harvard University Press), Bruce Haley notes: "Nothing occupies a nation's mind with the subject of health like a general contagion." England in the 1830s and 1840s according to Professor Haley, was lashed by three tidal waves of contagious diseases: "the first, from 1831 to 1833, included two influenza epidemics and the initial appearance of cholera; the second, from 1836 to 1842, encompassed major epidemics of influenza, typhus, smallpox, and scarlet fever; in the third, from 1846 to 1849, there were occurrences of typhus, typhoid, and cholera." As a result of such devastations, the English became health-minded, and the body became a thing to be cultivated as sedulously as the mind—perhaps even more so. In England this was the time of the rise of many sports, among them mountaineering, cycling, lawn tennis, rugby, rowing, badminton, and roller skating. This was the time of the installation of games into the regular life of public schools. (The Battle of Waterloo won on the playing fields of Eton and all that—which, according to Professor Haley's researches, the Duke of Wellington never in fact said.) This was, finally, the time of the rise of what was known as muscular Christianity.

The analogy between the Victorian setting and our own is not altogether tidy, but it does have some things to recommend it. We currently live under no fear of contagion, but every one of us has had to shiver at the black prospects of cancer or heart disease. Much of our concern with diet in recent years is about these grim prospects. We must not choke up the arteries with fat, or send the blood pressure rocketing, or breathe the bad air, or swallow anything on Dr. Nader's Index of Prohibited Foods. ("Whoso speaks on Health," wrote the Victorian G. H. Lewes, "is sure of a large audience"—which might serve as a gloss on Ralph Nader's career.) Like the Victorian age, too, our own has seen an efflorescence of sport, and not alone spectator sport. Over the past decade alone, participants in tennis, skiing, backpacking, racquetball, and jogging and running have all grown hugely in number. In part this growth has had to do with an increase in leisure and a fairly steady level of affluence—what is nowadays considered an acceptable pair of ski boots runs to around $250—but in even greater part it has had to do with our slightly terrified concern about not getting proper exercise, being healthy, staying in shape. If the Victorians went in for muscular Christianity, we, in our more secular age, appear ready to settle for simple muscularity.

The late Robert Hutchins, when chancellor of the University of Chicago, used to say that whenever he felt like exercising he would lie down till the feeling passed, which inevitably it did quite soon. Hutchins also said that if you have to watch the meter, don't take a cab. (These two apothegms ought to qualify him as Taxicab Rabinowitz's man for all seasons.) But Hutchins's advice had certain limitations. Tall and slender, absolutely princely in carriage, Robert Hutchins was one of those fortunate creatures who came by his physical elegance naturally. (He probably also had most of his cab fares paid by other people or by expense account.) Hutchins was, it will be remembered, the man who dropped football from the University of Chicago; implicit in his decision was the idea that the life of the mind need have no further traffic with the life of the body—once the majoritarian view among intellectuals and academics. Hutchins believed and they believed, along with Montaigne, that it was sufficient to maintain "the soul and reason in good trim."

In an extraordinary reversal, it now often appears that the best way to maintain the soul and reason in trim is first to have the heart and legs and lungs in trim. This, too, is not altogether new. Professor Haley quotes a character in a Charles Kingsley novel of 1871: "Believe me, it may be a very materialist view of things: but fact is fact—the *corpus sanum* is father to the *mens sana*." Most regular runners would seem to hold to this notion. Attend, for example, to James F. Fixx, author of *The Complete Book of Running*, arguing *against* the idea of running as a religion:

> It's easy enough to see how running got confused with religion. Running can, it's true, make you imagine yourself a better person than you are. Yesterday, I ran for an hour through a seaside park near my home in Connecticut. The last of the leaves were tumbling in the wind. I ran past three imperturbable skunks, a raccoon, a family of squirrels busily laying in a winter's supplies. A pheasant noisily took to the air at the sound of running shoes on gravel. By the time I got home, I felt refreshed and beautified. I know of no human activity, except perhaps sex, that can do so much in so brief a time, and do it so wonderfully.

Mr. Fixx is a temperate, no doubt altogether reasonable man. He does not talk about being in touch with the spirit while running; he does not confuse sweat with salvation. Neither does he equate modern-day runners with a persecuted religious sect, as I have heard another running maven, a man named Joel Henning, do. Yet when I read a passage like Mr. Fixx's above, why do I wish its author, not exactly ill, but a plague of life's little inconveniences? As he runs through his seaside park, I hope that he will one day perturb those three skunks sufficiently for them to loose their most noxious perfume upon him; that the raccoon will take a small bite out of his, Mr. Fixx's, running shoe; that the pheasant who now noisily takes to the air at the sound of Mr. Fixx's foot on gravel will instead smile at the sound of the same foot squishing in pheasant droppings.

Quite a little animus I seem to have built up here. Whence does this animus derive? From, I suspect, Mr. Fixx's and other runners' avowed self-satisfaction, from their not altogether suppressed smugness. Note, for example, the nudging reference to sexual activity in Mr. Fixx's last sentence. He is saying that his running is splendid, no question about it, but that his sex is even better. This leads one to think that a jackpot awaits the author of a guidebook to be entitled *Sex While Running*.

If my animus is strong, it is not solitary. More than one person has remarked upon the great boringness of running as a conversational subject. The vanity of the long-distance runner has become notorious. Tom Wolfe, among his series of monthly drawings in *Harper's*, has a particularly devastating drawing of a grotesquely misshapen middle-aged couple running through a Marin-County-like suburb. The drawing is entitled "The Joggers' Prayer," and the prayer reads:

> Almighty God, as we sail with pure aerobic grace and striped orthotic feet past the blind portals of our fellow citizens, past their chuckroast lives and their necrotic cardiovascular systems and rusting hips and slipped discs and desiccated lungs, past their implacable inertia and inability to persevere and rise above the fully pensioned world they live in and to push themselves to the limits of their capacity and achieve the White Moment of slipping through The Wall, borne aloft on one's Third Wind, past their Cruisomatic cars and upholstered lawn mowers and their gummy-sweet children already at work like little fat factories producing arterial plaque, the more quickly to join their parents in their joyless bucket-seat landau ride toward the grave—help us, dear Lord, we beseech Thee, as we sail past their cold-lard desolation, to be big about it.

The smugness of runners, their vanity, may be inherent in the very activity of running itself. Runners chalk up achievement daily, or at least on each day that they run. They have had the body out for a tune-up, a cleaning, an overhaul, whereas the rest of us haven't. Their situation is akin to that of the woman whose car is just out of the car wash or the man who has just had a shoeshine. How grubby, at such moments, everyone else's cars and shoes look! A pity, really. One would think people would have enough self-respect not to let their personal possessions get so run down. A man named Joe Henderson, a consulting editor to *Runner's World*, remarks in that magazine about not missing his daily run in nearly 4 years: "That's what I'm proudest of: There's something in the way I run that keeps me eager and healthy." Implicit in that sentence is the thought, "And you, Pudge, your *not* running is doubtless what keeps you logy and sickly." Reading the writings of runners, listening to them talk, one is reminded of Proust describing Albertine on her first appearance at the beach at Balbec, leading her little band of friends who all had "that mastery over their limbs which comes from perfect bodily condition and a sincere contempt for the rest of humanity."

The contempt of joggers and runners for the rest of humanity is often quite sincere, but I am not sure that it is deserved. Apart from competitive long-distance runners, who tend to be a self-enclosed and solitary lot in a lonely and grueling sport, most joggers and runners are not, at least in my experience and observation, among the best athletes. This may have to do with the fact that running has never been rated very high by serious athletes, other than as a means to an end. Often it has been used by coaches and trainers as a salubrious punishment for such misdeeds as reporting in overweight at the beginning of a season, missing a practice, fouling up in one way or another. Few athletes who have known the pleasure of sport at a fairly high level can content themselves with running as a source of satisfaction in and of itself. Serious athletes understand the need to be in shape, but in shape for something quite palpable: the game that they play. Joggers and runners are people who are content merely to be in shape for its own sake.

The pleasure of jogging and running is rather like that of wearing a fur coat in Texas in August: the true joy comes in being able to take the damn thing off. And because the runner or jogger regards running and jogging as its own end, an element of puritanical fanaticism easily insinuates itself. Thus a writer on the subject named Tom Osler, who does "not wish to be numbered with those who make claims of special life-extending benefits from it [running]," turns out to have run once for 24 hours straight, covering a distance of 114 miles (not, surely, everybody's idea of a day well spent). Thus *Runner's World* informs female readers that it is quite all right to run pregnant, right up to the day of delivery. There are people who are now beginning to run up mountains. Soon, doubtless, races will be held in which the contestants will wear lead in their shoes, or carry snow tires in their arms, or strap their accountants on their backs. If it feels good to remove a fur coat in Texas in August, how much better it will feel to remove a fur coat, leather leggings, and a tank helmet in Yucatan.

Committed joggers and runners would dispute all this. As for the argument that others use running as a means to an end while for them it is an end in itself, this they wouldn't concede at all. Running is not merely getting in shape per se; it is, many runners would reply, getting in shape for life. "Since I started running regularly, my outlook is better, my confidence greater, my self-regard higher"—such is the kind of testimonial one finds in the letters columns of the running magazines. Besides, what is the matter with getting in shape per se? Is not good health one of those things worth pursuing as an end in itself?

It is, up to a point. The point is when the concern with good health becomes unseemly—almost, one is tempted to say, unhealthy. The most cheering thing about good health is that it allows one not to think about one's health. Think too closely about it, dwell on it too long, and, lo, it will depart. Has there ever been a less robust crowd than the customers (and usually the clerks) in health food stores—with their sallow skins, dull eyes, bony carcasses, the human equivalent of horses ready to be shipped off to the glue factory? Joggers and runners, though they look rather better, are similarly preoccupied, even obsessed, with their bodies. "I eat bread sparingly," writes Tom Osler. "In the summer, I consume large quantities of fruit juices . . . . I do not use salt at the table or at the stove. I do not use sugar, because it seems to make my skin break out in acne." In an article titled "Running Through Pregnancy" in *Runner's World,* we learn that runners "have little trouble with irregularity. Some even experience a frequency increase in bowel movements." In the pages of the same magazine Joe Henderson reports that he thinks of a running high "as the way we're supposed to feel when not constipated." If one did not know what was being talked about—running—one might feel like an eavesdropper listening in on conversations in a nursing home for the elderly.

As it turns out, many joggers and runners do seem to require a certain amount of nursing, and the precise benefits of jogging and running are very much in the flux of controversy. As nearly as I can make out, internists appear to think jogging/running quite a good thing for circulation, respiration, general metabolism. Orthopedists, bone and joint men, appear to deplore it, citing its potential for injury: shin splints, stone bruises, tendonitis of the knee or ankle, spinal troubles. All physicians agree that great care must be taken, especially if one is past 40 years old, when too strenuous a running program can be dangerous. To die from a heart attack while jogging seems neither a glorious nor a philosophical death. The French used to speak of dying as "stumbling into eternity," which seems to me far preferable to running toward the same destination.

While runners come from a diversity of backgrounds, there is much to unite them. An article in *The Runner* puts it thus: "The enemy lines are drawn. Divergent lifestyles foster a see-saw phenomenon. One side must be put down for the other to go up: smoker versus non-smoker, vegetarian versus meat-eater, runner versus non-runner." If ever two groups were opposed, surely these two groups are runners and smokers. Running is one of the few things that cannot be done while smoking, and smoking is one of the chief things runners despise. The same article in *The Runner* notes that "a lot of runners are extremely obnoxious about that [smoking]. They're pompous. They're rude. They go and take a cigarette out of someone's hand."

Yet why, pressed to a hasty generalization, do I tend to prefer the company of smokers over that of runners? The most obvious reason is that smokers are not always talking about their smoking and their bad health in the way runners, when not on crutches, tend to talk about their running and good health. Smokers as a group tend therefore to be rather less boring than runners. But the reasons, I think, go deeper.

Although Robert Coles has not yet written a book about them, smokers are today something of a persecuted minority in the United States. A friend who works in a large corporation reports to me that at least one department head there refuses to hire smokers because other people in the department stridently complain about the smoke. States and municipalities have of late held referendums—and some have put laws upon the books—outlawing smoking in public places. We may one day be headed for a new Volstead Act prohibiting smoking. Smokers meanwhile have come to take on the hesitant manner of the persecuted. "Do you mind if I smoke?" once the most perfunctory of questions, is perfunctory no longer. "Damn right I mind, buddy!" can come shooting back in response.

"The exquisite vice," as Oscar Wilde called smoking cigarettes, has become the nasty habit. Where once the cigarette was an accoutrement of elegance—think of Andre Malraux, Humphrey Bogart, Franklin Delano Roosevelt, all of whom could almost be said to have worn cigarettes, and worn them very well—the cigarette has now become a mark of enslavement to a shameful habit. "God gave us tobacco to quiet our passions and soothe our grief," says a character in Balzac. But no longer. Nowadays it is said that around 80% of all smokers would like to be able to quit.

That roughly 100,000 of the 390,000 annual deaths owed to cancer can be linked to smoking, that smoking is a great stimulus to heart attack, that it reduces sexual appetite in men, that some 37,000,000 people will shorten their lives because of smoking—none of this would most smokers dispute. As I believed it as a smoker, so do they believe it. The fact is that smoking has nothing to do with belief, or with rationality. But quitting smoking is one of the world's great small nuisances—"Quitting smoking is easy," said Mark Twain, a cigar smoker, "I have done it a thousand times"—so difficult in its way that comparing nicotine addiction with that of alcohol and heroin, while far-fetched, is not altogether crazy. Having finally succeeded in stopping smoking after many abortive attempts, I now find that I have exchanged one habit for another, and today spend half my waking hours with a hard candy or lozenge in my mouth. I may be one of the first men in history to die of tooth decay.

Yet smoking, and struggling to quit smoking, does give one a keen sense of human imperfectibility. My attempts to quit smoking—so small and mean a thing, as I keep telling myself, to ask of so large and generous an intelligence—long ago killed off the last remaining vestiges of utopianism in me. I do not mean to imply that smoking makes anyone more intelligent. Given all that is known about smoking, it is a supremely unintelligent thing to do. Toward the end of my struggle I found myself smoking less and despising myself more. But this most pertinacious and exasperating habit teaches a healthy regard for human limitation.

Runners, on the other hand, are full of thoughts of human possibility. If one runs 7 miles in the spring, perhaps by autumn one can do 10 miles. The pages of the running magazines revel in the mention of runners in their seventies and eighties. I have read about a new magazine calling itself *Nutrition Health Review*, which (according to an ad in the magazine *Mother Jones*) asks, "Can You Live to Be 100?" The question is rhetorical, and the answer is that, watching what you eat and imbibe, you can indeed. But why stop at 100? Why not 120, or 150, or 200?

"What!" Frederick the Great is supposed to have said to a general who informed him of his troops' refusal to go into battle. "Do they expect to live forever?" Runners, like all truly self-absorbed perfectibilitarians, do seem to expect to live forever. Perhaps they do not expect to run forever—only up to the age of (say) ninety, at which point many could be got to agree to taper off. "I grow old . . . I grow old . . . ? I shall wear the bottoms of my trousers rolled," says J. Alfred Prufrock. But were he a runner, he would doubtless add: "But, look, above my rolled-up trousers I wear the two-toned singlet of tricot from Sport International, which prevents chafing and whose mesh bottom prevents it from clinging, thus helping me keep dry. While below I wear the Wildcat running shoe, from Autry Industries, Inc., whose thick heel and ankle padding helps protect my Achilles tendons." Our new Prufrock shall no longer walk but now run upon the beach/no longer hear the mermaids singing, each to each/but only the pounding of blood in his ears/drowning out thoughts of death and other legitimate fears.

SECTION FIVE

Psychobiology of Running

Running is not just another psychotropic agent. Running is not merely another method of self-hypnosis. Running affects more than just the psyche . . . . There is no place . . . for a bodiless psychiatry or psychology . . . . there is no way of helping a person's psyche without first attending to his body. (Sheehan, Chapter 17 in this volume, pp. 189-191)

Although some may take issue with Dr. Sheehan's analysis of the relative importance of the body discussed by the speakers at the Psychology of Running Seminar in October 1979, few would dispute the importance of his statement. Sheehan's message sets the tone for this section on the psychobiology of running.

Alexander and Selesnick (1966) have noted the complexity of human beings both as physiological organisms and as cognitively, verbally oriented beings, and have suggested that people should be studied psychologically and physiologically at the same time. Sheehan, in Chapter 17, reinforces the significance for the researcher/clinician in incorporating an understanding and study of the body *as well as* the mind in order to thoroughly investigate the nature of behavior. Studying the mind without the body or the body without the mind does indeed present an incomplete picture of a complex interaction.

In Chapter 18, Dienstbier and his colleagues present an excellent and complex study integrating the mind and body in an examination of changes in stress tolerance, mood, and temperament as a result of running. Across both psychological and physiological dimensions, moderate running was found to positively influence the individual's tolerance for subsequently induced stress. Highly committed runners expected and achieved more positive benefits from their running than expected and achieved by runners lower in "running self-concept," a measure of the individual's commitment to participation.

Both Dienstbier and Sheehan suggest that character, as well as the body, is affected by maintenance of a running program. Dienstbier, in particular, offers evidence that perhaps running (and other activities as well, if one generalizes the findings) can result in an increased capacity to tolerate stress and some degree of character change over the long term.

Mandell, in Chapter 19, and Riggs, in Chapter 20, examine the intricate relationship of brain chemistry to psychological and physiological effects of the running experience. Opiate-like peptides known as the endorphins have recently begun to receive considerable attention for their potential effects on the quality of the run, particularly in the experience of the phenomenon known as the "runner's high," and on addiction to running (see Section 3).

Mandell examines the "second second wind," which can incorporate at times mystical experiences more appropriately categorized as altered states of consciousness and peak experiences. He relates the psychophysiological aspects of this second wind to a possible kindling effect in a primitive part of the brain that is associated with processing pleasurable sensations. The distance runner is able, over time, to lower the threshold at which electrical discharge in that part of the brain occurs, producing an increased capacity and capability for experiencing pleasurable states of altered consciousness. To provide a further explanation of these aspects, Charles Riggs has examined the literature on neurotransmitters. Of special interest is the work on the endorphins, and how these newly discovered opiate-like peptides may relate to pain tolerance and the high which most distance runners claim they experience.

Although many questions remain to be resolved, such as the differential effects of these biological changes across individuals, these articles highlight the beginning of an exciting area of research in the psychophysiology of running. They are important beginnings which, if successful, will not only provide us with an insight into how running produces a state of well being, but will also contribute to our understanding of the psychophysiology of abnormal mental states.

Reference

Alexander, F.G., & Selesnick, S.T. *The history of psychiatry*. New York: Harper & Row, 1966.

CHAPTER 17

Body and Soul

George Sheehan

I sat in the last row of the amphitheatre listening to the speakers who preceded me. They were psychiatrists presenting papers in a seminar on "The Psychology of the Runner." For most of the morning they had been dissecting the runner's psyche. Using slides and graphs to establish changes in mood and feelings and temperament, they presented a case for running as a form of psychotherapy.

As the morning progressed I became more and more restless. I am no psychiatrist, but I know the effects of running are much more complicated than those experts were saying. Running is not just another psychotropic agent. Running is not merely another method of self-hypnosis. Running affects more than just the psyche.

I realized then what I would tell them. Minutes before I was to speak I went to the men's room and put on running clothes. When I was introduced I descended the stairs and took the floor in full racing gear—shirt, shorts, and shoes. Then, shivering a little, I turned and faced the audience. "Ladies and gentlemen," I said, "I have brought an exhibit with me: the human body."

That was what the other speakers had left out. The body and its effect on the psyche. In a way this was odd. The unique contribution of psychiatry to medicine has been its emphasis on the whole person. Because of psychiatrists, psychosomatic disease is now understood, diagnosed, and treated.

I have come to suspect, however, that the reverse is not true. The psychiatrists, unfortunately, have not come to understand the effect of the soma on the psyche. In this seminar they viewed runners as psyches and very little else. Running to them was not a physical, but a psychological act. It was time to hear it for the body.

I told them about a runner I met at a race in upstate New York this past summer. He was in his late 50s and in superb shape. He was 175 lb. of bone and muscle and very little else. "When I began running," he told me, "I weighed 230 lb., smoked three packs of cigarettes a day, and drank five quarts of booze a week."

Running had transformed him. He stopped smoking and limited his drinking to an occasional beer. He had become an athlete—the person William James called "a secular saint."

If he had seen a psychiatrist 2 years ago, what would have happened? I looked up at my colleagues in medicine and suggested a scenario. The psychodynamics of his two addictions would have been explored, then appropriate therapy prescribed. Eventually, his smoking might have stopped, his drinking might have curtailed.

Suppose they had been able to accomplish this, what would they have seen in front of them? A 230 lb. wreck. A man who had given up things he still needed and had made no progress toward becoming the person he was meant to be.

If, on the other, he were to come into the office today, they would have to say, "Oh! That's who you are." Because there finally would be the man seen incognito 2 years ago.

Do psychiatrists recognize this problem? Do they realize that the fully functioning person must have a fully functioning body? That the self-actualized individual must reside in a self-actualized body? That you cannot reach excellence or integrity or personal perfection without the body?

This man had found his own cure. He had healed himself. He had taken health and growth and happiness into his own hands. He had become his body. Through his own efforts he had become the person he was meant to be.

There is no place, therefore, for a bodiless psychiatry or psychology. I concede that there are patients who have such damaged psyches that no amount of drugs can help their hearts. George Burch, the great cardiologist, once said that the expressions he saw on peoples' faces when he walked the streets—the depression and discontent, the hostility and fear—made him despair of helping them. Psychiatrists should have similar feelings when they look at their patients' bodies. They should know that there is no way of helping a person's psyche without first attending to his body.

Wittgenstein once said that the body was the best picture of the soul. In denying this truth about the body, those who practice psychiatry and psychology deprive themselves of the one clear vision of the soul: the soul-sick, and the soul-healthy.

CHAPTER 18

Exercise and Stress Tolerance

Richard A. Dienstbier, James Crabbe, Glen O. Johnson, William Thorland, Julie A. Jorgensen, Mitchel M. Sadar, and Dennis C. LaVelle

Presented in this paper is research designed in part to show that although moderate running by well-trained runners plays a significant role in *reducing* stress response to subsequently introduced stressors, running at the level of marathon competition alters psychological and physiological dispositions in a manner not conducive to reduced stress responses. In these demonstrations, the choice of our psychological and physiological dependent measures was guided by a larger theoretical framework concerning the relationship of exercise to temperament. We will discuss this larger view first because it provides a theoretical perspective that is useful in considering our specific hypotheses.

We believe that regular aerobic exercise, with its requirements for sympathetic nervous system (SNS) activation and associated endocrine activity, leads to chronic reduction in the individual's experienced stress responses to psychological stressors. As long as two decades ago, Michael (1957) suggested that regular exercise would allow greater steroid reserves—reserves available to counter stress. Other similar views include that advanced by Edington and Edgerton (1976), who posit that extending the capacity of the adrenal medulla to generate the catecholamines through exercise may help to reduce the experience of stress. Moorehouse and Miller (1971) have suggested that exercise may "increase the size and lower the threshold of stimulation of the adrenal glands," resulting in greater reserves of antistress steroids and shorter response times to stressors.

For reasons related to the limits of permissible research with human subjects, those ideas concerning the possible relationship of exercise to stress tolerance remain speculative. We do, however, have access to other empirically based knowledge which will allow reasonable inferences about this relationship. We know that physiological responses to exercise and to physiological or psychological stressors are very much alike in broad outline, with both exercise and stress responses calling for activation of the SNS and the generation of steroids and catecholamines. Adaptation to cold requires a similar physiological response pattern. Logically, then, if we can establish a reasonable case that regular exposure to (manageable) psychological or physiological stressors or to cold leads to increased stress tolerance, we could infer a similar result for regular exercise.

The most convincing evidence that regular activation of the stress response leads to chronic changes in temperament is found in animal research, where it has been demonstrated that the gentle stress of daily handling or even the daily shocking of young rodents leads to an enlarged adrenal capacity *and* a calmer or less emotional temperament in adulthood (e.g., Denenberg, 1967). With humans, several lines of modern evidence suggest a relationship between increased hormonal and/or SNS response capacity and a more calm and stress-tolerant human temperament. Several years ago, Dienstbier investigated the relationship of cold tolerance to temperament. Students who indicated that they could tolerate cold temperatures with minimal discomfort (indicating a high ability to generate and sustain SNS arousal) indicated less fearfulness, more emotional control, and a greater preference for emotional and suspenseful forms of entertainment. Recently, Frankenhaeuser (1979) has demonstrated that school children rated as more emotionally stable and competent than their classmates indicate *greater* catecholamine responses to classroom challenges than do their less emotionally stable classmates.

In summary, several lines of evidence suggest that greater SNS and hormonal capacities are associated with more positive responses to stressful situations, and with temperaments generally characterized by less anxiety and emotional upheaval. Considering that most researchers concerned with stress responses in the psychological and medical areas organize much of their thinking on the principles of the General Adaptation Syndrome developed by Selye (1976), these findings should constitute no surprise. That is, it follows from Selye's approach that if an individual is able to develop a more intensive physiological reaction during the stage of alarm or a more prolonged response during the stage of resistance, then the stage of exhaustion is postponed or even avoided (if the stressor is eliminated during those early stages of the stress response sequence). A major block in our recognizing the positive features of an ability to develop and sustain larger SNS and hormonal stress responses was probably the recognition of those responses as a sign of stress, and hence, as a sign that "something is going wrong." That previous conclusion may be most applicable in situations in which the stressor is largely psychological *and* where activity to combat the stressor is not available or not undertaken. In support of this idea, Gal and Lazarus (1975) have recently suggested that stress reactions as indicated by hormonal indices are experienced as more uncomfortable and are associated with more somatic symptoms only when activity is not undertaken; they suggest that the positive benefits of activity may exist even when the activity is not directly related to the stressor.

To return to our major point, if running changes the capacity of our hormonal system and our SNS response through the regular use or "exercise" of those systems, then one should anticipate long-term positive changes in temperament from running. Although we would like to be able to state that our research has demonstrated that such long-term personality benefits do follow from regular running, the best we are able to do is to demonstrate the interrelationship of exercise to short-term stress tolerance *and* to changes on psychological dimensions relevant to personality or temperament. Then we may infer the relationship of exercise to personality, but our inferential leap will be substantial.

We did not look for long-term personality changes mainly because we did not have the resources to overcome the very difficult control group problems which must be addressed to adequately confront this issue. Others, such as Ismail (Young & Ismail, 1976), who has shown an exercise program to influence personality or temperament, have not used control groups with expectancies for change which would be similar to those held by their exercising subjects. It is therefore difficult to know if the personality shift indicated over time is due to the exercise per se or to changes in expectation. As Morgan recently suggested (Morgan & Pollock, Note 1), another major difficulty with such studies is that subjects involved in exercise programs often "get religion," changing their intake of drugs and stimulants, and modifying eating, sleeping, and other living habits. In addition, it is extremely difficult to abstract those personality changes which might be due to our physiological response to a rigorous exercise program from those personality changes related to the sense of accomplishment, improved body image, and other psychological factors. Indeed, the difficulties of such an analysis are such that I know of no serious attempts to control such factors. These criticisms are not meant to denigrate previous research attempts but to suggest that doing conclusive research in this area is a most complex and difficult undertaking; as will be shown, our own research does not overcome all possible interpretive difficulties. Although we have avoided the pitfalls of the before-after research designs detailed earlier, we have not avoided the need for significant inferential leaps from our data to our theoretical perspectives.

To make our inferential leap, we will attempt to develop two types of empirical evidence. First, we will demonstrate that in the short term, running has a complex influence on our tolerance for psychological (loud noises) and physiological (cold) stressors introduced after the exercise; our measures of stress tolerance will also be both psychological and physiological. Success in such a short-term demonstration will lend weight to our overriding theory that long-term exercise may have comparable long-term effects by demonstrating in a convincing fashion that exercise does have an impact on the relevant variables. Secondly, when we refer to long-term differences in stress tolerance and other chronic dimensions of emotional functioning, the term temperament is relevant and appropriate. Using a standard psychometric instrument for measuring temperament, we will attempt to demonstrate that short-term differences in subjects' responses to that instrument follow from different prior exercise levels. This demonstration, too, will add weight to our inferences about chronic personality changes from a long-term exercise program by showing that in the short run the relevant exercise variables do have impact on the relevant temperament dimensions. Finally, using the same temperament inventory, we will attempt to demonstrate that our running subjects' expectations about the impact of short-term exercise do *not* match perfectly the real changes in temperament. This will allow us to conclude that the changes we do observe are probably due to more than the operation of mere subject expectancies.

The basis for our short-term hypotheses concerning the positive impact of moderate exercise on stress tolerance is that running provides an activity outlet for possible physiological imbalances caused by past stress, preventing a large cumulative stress response to a subsequent moderate stressor. In addition, it is possible that a "priming" function is realized by the prior exercise in the form of prestimulation of hormones and steroids and other energy-mobilization factors necessary to combat stress. In this latter regard, Edington and Edgerton (1976) have suggested that "pretreatment with mild stressing agents protects and aids the body in responding to the second independent stress." Past research addressing this issue using psychological measures has usually assessed anxiety on a standardized inventory or checklist following a prior short-term exercise session of usually up to ½ hour of treadmill walking or bicycle ergometer work. (For a recent review of exercise and anxiety studies, see Morgan, 1976). Other research on this hypothesis has employed physiological measures. For example, using the anticipation of a test as a stressor, Sime (Note 2) has demonstrated that 12 minutes of treadmill exercise leads to reduced muscle tension and blood pressure during the later stress. Our research attempted to go beyond those previous approaches by looking at changes on a wider variety of physiological and psychological dimensions following three different exercise conditions which range from no exercise to marathon competition. As suggested earlier, psychological dimensions were chosen to allow us a conceptual bridge back from our findings of acute differences to inferences about chronic or personality changes following a sustained exercise program.

We hypothesized that following marathon competition the exhaustion of the SNS and of hormonal capacity would lead to reduced capacity to tolerate subsequent stressors, exaggerating psychological and physiological stress responses. In formulating this hypothesis we were aware of "contradictory" data such as those developed by Morgan (1976) suggesting that even exercise "to exhaustion" is followed by anxiety reduction as indicated by performance on anxiety questionnaires. Our assumption that our runners would not perform similarly was based upon the belief that no laboratory exercise could ethically impose effort or exhaustion which would be comparable to that which our runners would drive themselves to in the course of marathon competition.

Mood and Temperament Hypotheses

Our hypotheses about mood were that although those moods relevant to anxiety would be exaggerated by not running (NoR) and by marathon (MarR) competition relative to a short run (ShR), those moods related to vigor would be reduced by NoR and MarR conditions, relative to ShR. Unlike the more global activation concept which has dominated psychological thinking until recently, our theory therefore implies a multifactor concept of activation. The mood measure used was the Mood Adjective Check List (MACL) (Nowlis & Green, Note 3).

To measure temperament, we employed a psychological measure devised by Buss and Plomin (1975) which contains items designed to assess the temperament factors of Emotionality, Activity, Sociability, and Impulsivity (EASI). In his work with this instrument, Buss concluded that all four of those dimensions were highly influenced by hereditary factors. It was our assumption that the high heritability of temperament dimensions such as Emotionality and Activity existed because those psychological dimensions depend, in part, upon physiological predispositions such as those associated with the SNS and related hormonal capacities. We noted earlier that both the work of Frankenhaeuser (1979) with children and that of Denenberg (1967) with rodents supported this link between physiological characteristics and the temperament dimension of emotionality. Relevant to our change-through-exercise hypothesis is that Denenberg's work also suggested some plasticity or "training effect" of the emotionality dimension following systematic subjection of animals to regular doses of tolerable stress. We therefore hypothesized that temperament factors might be influenced by the temporary physiological states induced by running. Of the temperament dimensions of the Buss inventory, we predicted that ShR would decrease Emotionality and increase Activity relative to NoR and MarR. Although many of the Buss items are worded in "chronic" terms, subjects were asked to interpret each item as if it were asking about how they felt "right now."

Subjects and Procedure

Our research was conducted in spring 1978 with a class of students who were training, under our direction, to run a marathon. Members of the class were recruited via various informal communications networks of students and runners.

Although the majority of our participants were students from the University of Nebraska, several nonuniversity members of the Lincoln running community enrolled for the course. Of the 30 runners who participated in the course, 23 completed their training and five were women.

Research Scheduling

At the beginning of the semester, all participants filled out a series of questionnaires including one concerning the centrality of running to their self-concept. Near the semester's end, all subjects were to participate either in a marathon or in a criterion run of over 20 miles (hereafter referred to as the marathon). Most of the data reported in this paper were gathered from three sessions scheduled for each subject. The sessions were separated by approximately 2 weeks, with each subject reporting at the same time in the afternoon (or within ½ hour) as his/her other sessions. One of the sessions followed the marathon run (MarR), one followed a day in which the subject did not run prior to the research (NoR), and one followed a "short" run (ShR). On ShR days, subjects ran approximately 6 miles at an easy pace. The order of MarR, NoR, and ShR conditions was determined randomly for subjects, with the restriction that condition and order were counterbalanced across subjects.

Research Tasks and Physiological Measures

Upon arrival at the laboratory, subjects were seated in an overstuffed chair which was isolated by a curtain from the physiograph used to monitor their physiological responses to a "stress" tape. The tape presented various loud (92db) sounds separated by approximately 30 seconds. The sounds included glass crashing, automobile crashes, a loud electric drill, and a circular saw cutting wood; the tape ended with a balloon being blown up until it burst.

Capillary constriction in the finger in response to the sounds on the tape (indicating SNS activity) was measured by a pulse transducer attached to the middle finger of the left hand. Galvanic skin response (GSR) was measured with electrodes attached to the wrist of the left hand as a further check of SNS activity.

After the sound-tape session ended, each subject went to another room where he/she rated the subjective stressfulness of the sound tape, filled out a Mood Adjective Check List (MACL) (Nowlis & Green, 1957), filled out the Buss and Plomin (1975) temperament inventory, and sat for 5 minutes in a 60 degree (F) room prior to rating the subjective discomfort of that cool temperature. Because acute cold adaptation is accomplished through SNS activation with the accompanying catecholamines of noradrenalin and adrenalin, it was anticipated that subjective comfort in the cold would be greatest following ShR, with NoR and MarR being characterized by relative discomfort.

The procedure of physiological monitoring and psychological testing described above was repeated on each of the three sessions for each subject. At the end of the third session, subjects were asked to fill out the Buss temperament inventory three additional times reflecting the way they *typically* feel after conditions of NoR, ShR, or MarR. This procedure was undertaken to study the degree to which actual differences between feelings on those days corresponded with the subject's expectations of differences following different running conditions. It was predicted that, in general, subjects' expectations would reflect an exaggeration of those between-condition differences found on the three experimental days. Scores from GSR and capillary constriction monitoring in response to each of the 17 discrete sound events on the sound tape were derived from the print-out of the continuously recording physiograph as discussed above. Single GSR scores and capillary constriction scores were created for each subject by combining the scores obtained in response to all the taped sounds. In order to statistically control for possible adaptation effects between sessions, physiological scores were standardized between the three sessions.[1]

Results

After a preliminary examination of the data, it became apparent that the subjects' degree of commitment to running was an important moderator variable influencing how they responded to our dependent measures. Therefore, for the analyses subsequently presented, subjects were divided into approximately equal halves, based upon how central running was to each person's self-concept. Those individuals in the high running self-concept (Hi RSC) group had indicated that running was "very central to my self-concept

---

[1]Scores were standardized around a mean of zero and a standard deviation of 100. For example, the GSR measures for all subjects reporting for their first physiological monitoring session (approximately ⅓ of those in each of the three running conditions) were equated with the mean and standard deviation for the data from the remaining two sessions. This standardization was permitted by the almost perfect counterbalancing of running conditions within order. Effects due to the factor of running condition could therefore by analyzed as a main effect in analyses of variance without the intrusion of the theoretically meaningless dimension of adaptation to the sound tape across the three sessions. More importantly, with the introduction of the running self-concept dimensions as a moderator variable, this normalization of physiological scores allowed the selection of two subgroups for which perfect counterbalancing of running condition within session did not exist. Because session effects had been previously removed statistically, they could not confound comparisons between such imperfectly matched groups. (Actually, the counterbalancing within the two running self-concept subgroups was reasonably similar between the groups.)

. . . one of the first things I think of when I think about defining who I am"; or that running was "moderately central . . . important, but not one of the two or three most important aspects of self-definition." Those indicating that running was "important but not central . . . not one of the dimensions I usually think of in defining myself"; and those indicating running was "not very important . . . while I take some pride in running, it's no big thing," were classified as low in running self-concept (LoRSC). (Other options indicating even less commitment were available, but none of our subjects chose those less-involved-with-running self-definitions). The data were mainly examined through two by three factorial analyses of variance with two levels of running self-concept as a between-subjects variable and the three running conditions of NoR, ShR, and MarR as a within-subjects variable.

Overview of Negative Mood Factors

We predicted that the mood and temperament factors usually characterized as negative would be reduced (or improved) in the ShR condition as compared with NoR; additionally, it was predicted that indicators of stress reactions such as GSR and capillary constriction would also change in a positive direction, indicating reduced stress in the ShR condition as contrasted with NoR. We predicted that many of those negative mood and stress indicators would be higher following MarR than following the ShR condition. Negative mood factors were Anxiety, Skepticism, Aggression, Fatigue, and Sadness; in addition to those multiple-item factors, we included the single-item mood terms of Disgust, Guilt, and Sick. Negative EASI temperament factors were Impulsivity and Emotionality; we were, however, particularly interested in the part of the Emotionality score consisting of fear-related items, (contrasted with the anger items). (Although each of the four temperament factors except Sociability were composed of several subfactors, only emotionality was examined at the subfactor level.) Negative scaled items consisted of the rating of the discomfort experienced from the 5-minute stay in the 60 degree room, and ratings of the stressfulness of the sound tape played during the physiological monitoring. Those negative dimensions of major theoretical interest and/or indicating large between-condition differences are presented in Table 1, along with statistical analyses. Those dimensions are also illustrated in Figures 1 and 2, along with these positive dimensions indicating large between-condition changes.

Every negative dimension of mood, temperament, physiological change, or scaled item, except the rating of cold discomfort, changed in the predicted direction of reduction from NoR to ShR conditions. Although the degrees of change for the measures not reported in Table 1 were often not statistically significant or substantial, this almost perfect directional support across a variety of different types of measures suggests a remarkable improvement in well being for our running subjects after a moderate run.

The pattern of results following MarR is somewhat less clear, for some of the negative dimensions of interest did not differ between ShR and MarR con-

Table 1

Means[a] and F-Ratios for Dependent Measures by Running Condition (with Running Self-concept for Some Measures)

Measure	Run Self-concept	N	Means by Running Condition			ANOVA F-Ratios		
			NoR	ShR	MarR	Running Condition	Running Self-concept	Interaction (RC × RSC)
Anxiety	All	21	11.75	9.39	9.42	3.28*	<1	<1
	Low	11	11.91	10.18	9.64			
	High	10	11.60	8.60	9.20			
Fatigue	All	21	7.76	6.69	9.36	5.04*	1.77	<1
Vigor	All	21	6.07	7.41	4.70	9.50**	<1	1.09
Elation	All	21	8.04	9.17	11.10	8.41**	<1	<1
Social affection	All	21	6.85	7.51	7.65	1.23	<1	<1
Temperament Factors								
Emotionality	All	23	17.16	16.70	15.69	<1	<1	1.17
	Low	12	16.82	19.00	17.18			
	High	11	17.50	14.40	14.20			
Emotion-Fear	All	23	5.68	5.30	4.47	<1	4.49*	4.61*
	Low	12	5.37	7.00	6.09			
	High	11	6.00	3.60	3.40			
Activity	All	23	17.66	18.03	13.65	5.20*	<1	<1
Sociability	All	23	3.80	4.77	4.06	1.40	2.47	<1
Physiological Measures								
GSR	All	20	72	-277	115	2.15	<1	<1
	Low	11	-130	-270	29			
	High	9	274	-285	201			
Capillary constriction	All	19	332	-104	-67	2.81	<1	6.75**
	Low	11	-43	-65	306			
	High	8	708	-143	-440			
Scaled Items								
Temperature discomfort	All	20	2.40	2.40	2.45	<1	<1	2.56
	Low	10	2.10	2.20	2.80			
	High	10	2.70	2.60	2.10			
Sound tape rating	All	18	3.89	3.28	3.50	1.60	2.26	<1
	Low	9	3.67	3.00	3.22			
	High	9	4.11	3.56	3.78			

*Significant at $p < .05$
**Significant at $p < .01$
[a]All negative dimensions (e.g., anxiety, emotionality, sound tape rating of stress, and the physiological indicators) are scored so that a larger mean indicates more negative or greater indicators of stress; with positive factors, a higher score indicates more of that positive dimension or less stress.

ditions (i.e., moods of Anxiety, Skepticism, Aggression, and Disgust; Capillary Constriction, and temperature discomfort), whereas others indicated less negative feeling or stress following MarR compared with ShR (i.e., temperament factors of Impulsivity and Emotionality and its component, Fear). Most dimensions, however, did indicate more negativity follow-

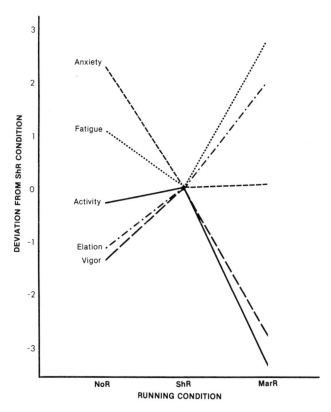

Figure 1. Mood and temperament scores by running condition. To clearly illustrate differences of NoR and MarR from ShR conditions, the dependent measure scales are arranged so that they overlap at ShR.

ing MarR contrasted with ShR (i.e., moods of Fatigue, Sadness, Guilt and Sick—the latter at a statistically significant level, the physiological measure of GSR, and the stressfulness of the sound tape). As discussed below, this somewhat unclear picture is improved with the division of subjects into those high and those low in RSC.

Overview of Positive Factors

The prediction that positive dimensions would be found to be higher following ShR compared with NoR was upheld with every dimension studied (i.e., mood factors of Social Affection, Elation, Vigor, Surgency, and Elation; temperament factors of Sociability and Activity).

Differences between ShR and MarR for the positive dimensions were less definitive, as was the case with the negative dimensions. Although the mood of Elation went up dramatically following MarR, the mood of Vigor declined, as did the temperament scores on Sociability and Activity. Moods of Surgen-

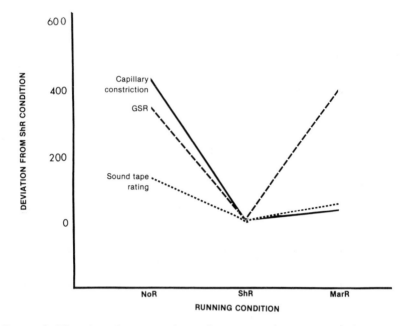

Figure 2. Physiological scores and sound tape rating by running condition. As in Figure 1, the dependent measures are arranged so that they overlap at ShR.

cy and Social Affection indicated no change. Because the reasons for these changes are, in most cases, quite apparent, and because RSC did not appear to be a major moderator variable for these dimensions, the remainder of this paper will be devoted largely to the negative dimensions. Those positive dimensions of relatively major interest and/or those indicating the greatest change are included in Table 1 and shown in Figures 1 and 2.

Specific Issues and Consistencies

Attention to the temperament factor of Emotionality was given because it is a central concept in our approach to the impact of exercise on personality. Two important subfactors in Emotionality are Fear and Anger. Although Anger did not vary between conditions for all subjects or when subjects were divided by RSC, the subfactor of Fear yielded a statistically significant interaction on the running condition and RSC dimensions with LoRSC runners, indicating a slight increase in fear in ShR and MarR conditions (over NoR), but with HiRSC runners indicating a fear reduction with ShR or MarR (see Table 1). Because it is to be expected that the mood factor of Anxiety should resemble the Fear factor, even without the justification of a comparable statistically significant interaction for Anxiety, both factors are shown in Figure 3 for comparison. As illustrated in the figure, HiRSC subjects indicated a large drop in anxiety and fear from NoR to ShR, with no further changes of any magnitude

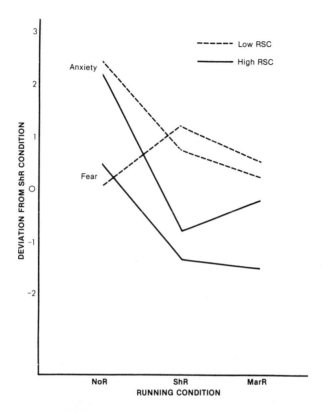

Figure 3. Anxiety (MACL) and Fear (EASI) scores by running condition and by running self-concept.

from ShR to MarR. With a far less consistent pattern, LoRSC individuals, who indicate similar NoR baserates of anxiety and fear to HiRSC individuals, evidence far less positive change following either ShR or MarR. In general, where interactions of the RSC and Running Condition factors exist on the various dependent measure dimensions, this pattern of greater change from NoR to ShR or MarR with HiRSC subjects is repeated.

The two physiological measures yield a somewhat similar picture to that formed by the dimensions of Anxiety and Fear. That is, as demonstrated in Figure 4, while the HiRSC subjects evidence a dramatic decline in physiological responses to the stressful sound tape between NoR and ShR conditions, comparable differences for the LoRSC group do not exist, with practically no NoR to ShR physiological differences. (Although the differences between RSC groups across running conditions are reflected in a statistically significant interaction for capillary constriction, as indicated in Table 1, comparable differences for GSR are far from statistically significant;

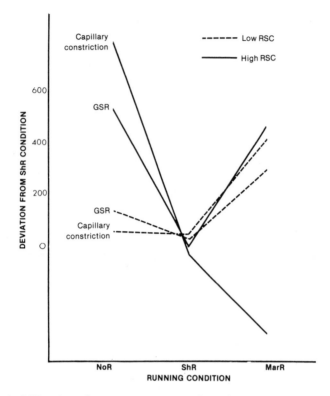

Figure 4. GSR and capillary constriction scores by running condition and by running self-concept.

these discussed similarities between the two measures are therefore only moderately supported by statistical analyses.)

Differences in the physiological measures from ShR to MarR between RSC conditions also exist, with GSR and capillary constriction both indicating increased stress responses for the LoRSC group following the marathon, whereas only GSR indicates such increased stress responses following MarR for the HiRSC group. No significant assistance is given to the interpretive problem suggested by these data from the sound tape rating or temperature discomfort as indicated in Figure 5. On the one hand, the temperature discomfort scale suggests that the HiRSC subjects are more stress-tolerant following the marathon than at any other time (contrasted with the opposite pattern for LoRSC subjects, as indicated by an interaction approaching statistical significance). Yet ratings of stressfulness of the sound tape are almost identical for the two RSC groups, giving no illumination to the problem of blood flow differences between the two RSC groups (but giving weak support to the hypothesis of lowest stress response following ShR).

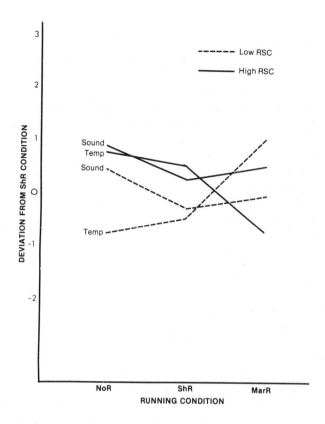

Figure 5. Sound tape rating and temperature discomfort scores by running condition and by running self-concept.

The array of data illustrated in Figures 3, 4, and 5 leads to the conclusion that although runners in both RSC groups experienced reductions in psychological and physiological indicators of stress from NoR to ShR, HiRSC runners indicate a stronger and more consistent improvement following moderate running. Less certainly, it appears that for the HiRSC runners running in a competitive marathon does not entirely eliminate the psychological and physiological benefits accrued after a moderate run, possibly even reducing stress responses to some stimuli on some measurement dimensions. For the LoRSC runners, not only are their benefits from ShR less certain, but there is no strong evidence that they retained any significant psychological or physiological stress response benefits at all when they extend their running to a competitive marathon level.

Runners' Expectations

Keeping in mind the pattern of results described previously about the real

psychological and physiological benefits derived from running, the temperament data gathered in each runner's last experimental session allows some
comparison with the benefits runners believed they achieve from their running. As indicated above, on that final day runners were asked to fill out the
EASI temperament inventory three additional times, *as if* they had just completed NoR, ShR, or MarR. Table 2 indicates results from the four EASI factors plus the subfactors of Anger and Fear comprising the Emotionality factor.

The Imaginary means of Table 2 reveal that the HiRSC participants expected their Emotionality to decrease dramatically when they ran longer
distances, whereas LoRSC subjects anticipated only a slight drop (with the
differences between the groups across conditions statistically significant, as indicated by the interaction F-ratio). Comparably large expectations for Fear
and Anger reductions by the HiRSC subjects also exceeded expectations for
Fear and Anger reductions by the LoRSC subjects. The low expectations for
change by the LoRSC subjects were reasonably accurate, for their feelings on
Anger and Fear did not change appreciably across running conditions.
However, although the positive expectation of change by HiRSC subjects
was reasonably accurate for Fear, their considerable expectations for Anger
reduction reflected no similar trend in the real between-running condition
mean changes. The relative accuracy of both RSC groups with prediction and
realization of greater changes across running conditions is also reflected on
the Activity and Impulsivity dimensions.

The relatively small predicted change on the Sociability dimensions is
reflected in the real scores on that dimension. In conclusion, it appears that
highly committed runners expect and achieve more positive benefits from
their running than expected and achieved by LoRSC runners. Furthermore,
with the possible exception of the unfulfilled anticipation of anger reduction
following running, runners' expectations of the benefits they achieve from
their running generally reflect reality.

Of course, it could be objected that the responses given on NoR, ShR, and
MarR days reflect nothing more than the expectations which, in more salient
form, account for the between-running condition scores obtained under imaginary conditions. First, however, the very real physiological differences
noted between running conditions in response to the sound tape suggest basic
stress-tolerance differences resulting from running. It seems quite likely that
those differences would have an impact upon both mood and temperament
scale responses (when the latter are framed in terms of immediate rather than
chronic feelings). Secondly, the directional similarity between imagined and
real scores is not perfect. If real between-running condition differences
reflected only expectations of change, we should not expect any situations
such as demonstrated by the HiRSC subjects anticipating dramatic drops in
Anger with running, while indicating no comparable trend in data gathered
after real NoR, ShR, and MarR condition. Similarly, the dramatic drop expected by LoRSC subjects in Impulsivity across running conditions is not
reflected in the real data generated by those subjects.

Table 2

Means and F-Ratios for Real and Projected Temperament Scores Following Real and Imagined NoR, ShR, and MarR

| | | Imaginary | | | | | | Real | | | | | | Imag. vs. Real F-Ratio |
| | | Means by Running Condition | | | F-Ratios | | | Means by Running Condition | | | F-Ratios | | | |
Measure	Run Self-concept	NoR	ShR	MarR	Run Cond	Run Self-conc	RC × RSC	NoR	ShR	MarR	Run Cond	Run Self-conc	RC × RSC	Interaction Real vs. Imag. by RC
Emotionality	All	20.08	15.96	13.61	9.98**	<1	3.92*	17.16	16.70	15.69	<1	<1	1.17	2.27
	Low	17.17	15.92	14.67				16.82	19.00	17.18				
	High	23.00	16.00	12.54				17.50	14.40	14.20				
E-Fear	All	5.81	4.60	4.12	8.34**	<1	3.32*	5.68	5.30	4.74	<1	4.49*	4.61*	<1
	Low	5.08	4.83	4.33				5.36	7.00	6.09				
	High	6.54	4.36	3.91				6.00	3.60	3.60				
E-Anger	All	6.47	5.07	4.36	5.62**	<1	3.46*	4.66	4.76	4.85	<1	<1	<1	2.63
	Low	5.58	5.42	5.08				4.82	5.00	4.91				
	High	7.36	4.73	3.64				4.50	4.50	4.80				
Activity	All	19.42	19.24	14.08	7.76**	<1	<1	17.66	18.03	13.65	5.20*	<1	<1	<1
	Low	19.67	19.75	15.33				16.73	17.36	14.00				
	High	19.18	18.28	12.82				18.60	18.70	13.30				
Sociability	All	4.96	5.24	5.04	<1	<1	1.26	3.80	4.77	4.06	1.40	2.47	<1	<1
Impulsivity	All	7.11	3.95	1.47	17.60**	<1	<1	4.88	4.22	3.70	<1	<1	<1	3.45*
	Low	5.50	3.17	0.75				5.36	5.64	4.91				
	High	8.73	4.73	2.18				4.40	2.80	2.50				

*Significant at $p < .05$
**Significant at $p < .01$

Conclusions

Our major hypothesis, that moderate running would positively influence tolerance for subsequently introduced stress, was confirmed by these data in a consistent manner across physiological and psychological dependent measure dimensions. Although it has been suggested by Morgan (Bahrke & Morgan, 1978) that the positive impact of running on feelings of well being and improved stress tolerance may result from nothing more than the run being a "time-out" period from the stresses of daily living, several aspects of our data do not support that explanation. First, although most laboratory studies using controlled exercise periods test subjects within a brief period following that exercise, we usually tested our subjects several hours following their ShR and an average of 5 hours following MarR. Intuitively, it does not seem that the impact of a brief time away from the usual activities of life would retain its impact so well after several hours of return to usual activities. Secondly, the differences between our running self-concept groups, with greater impact for the HiRSC subjects (from ShR relative to NoR), would not seem to support a time-out hypothesis, for there is no logical reason why "time out" should have a more significant impact on individuals for whom running is an important part of self-concept than for less committed runners. Finally, we might argue that the "time out" encountered on a marathon day is the ultimate "time out," for irrespective of the stressfulness of the marathon itself, runners are unlikely to engage in stress-producing activities following that long Sunday run. Yet marathon running did not seem as effective as more moderate running in consistently indicating positive changes on our dependent measure dimensions.

The second part of our major hypothesis, that MarR conditions would lead to increased indications of stress and an elimination of positive benefits predicted and found for ShR, was not consistently confirmed. That hypothesis had been based upon the assumption that the SNS and associated catecholamines, steroids, and other body chemicals which are activated by moderate exercise would be depleted by MarR, so that they would not be available for later stress resistance. Prior to our research, however, we were not aware of Appenzeller's remarkable data suggesting that well-trained marathoners sustain no apparent exhaustion of the SNS and related hormones during or following such competition. Appenzeller (Note 4) has demonstrated that total catecholamines increase by a factor of three (over baseline) during the early miles of a marathon, and increase after 20 miles to a level of six-fold over baseline. Had we been aware of those data, our initial hypothesis would have been presented in a more articulated manner, with distinctions made concerning the predicted impact of MarR on stress tolerance for different levels of runners. In fact, the data from this study do support such an articulated hypothesis, especially the capillary constriction differences on MarR between the LoRSC and HiRSC groups, indicating better physiological stress tolerance for the HiRSC subjects following MarR.

Our theoretical interest concerning the potential impact of running on long-term personality dispositions of stress tolerance and temperament was supported as well as possible, given the large inferential leap we had to make from our data to that conclusion. The relevant data show a remarkably consistent impact on psychological and physiological indicators of stress tolerance following moderate running, suggesting that those physiological dispositions underlying stress tolerance are indeed influenced by exercise. The data following MarR (and the data from other work such as that of Appenzeller) suggest that extensive endurance exercise may sufficiently tax SNS and hormonal systems that some adaptation or "training" responses in the form of gradually increasing capacity and/or efficiency may result. Given the documented role such physiological systems play in temperament (particularly the dimension of Emotionality) the inference of long-term personality changes following long-term endurance training seems warranted.

It may well be, however, that significant individual differences exist between individuals in the ability of their SNS and related hormonal systems to adapt and adjust to such an endurance program. Indeed, the early identification of potential world-class athletes in East Germany is accomplished in part by monitoring and correctly predicting individual differences in the ability of physiological systems to adapt and respond to training. The psychological and physiological benefits from our running program were obviously not realized equally by all of our runners. It seems likely that the truly committed or addicted runners (see Sachs & Pargman, Note 5) become so committed because they are more able to derive benefits, such as those studied in our research, from their running.

Acknowledgement

Our thanks to Dwight Heil and Brian Plank for their assistance with the data gathering.

Reference Notes

1. Morgan, W.P., & Pollock, M.L. *Physical activity and cardiovascular health: Psychological aspects.* Paper presented at the International Congress of Physical Activity Sciences, Quebec, July 12, 1976.
2. Sime, W.E. *A comparison of exercise and meditation in reducing physiological response to stress.* Paper presented at the annual meeting of the American College of Sports Medicine, Chicago, May 1977.
3. Nowlis, V., & Green, R.F. The experimental analysis of mood. *Technical Report, Office of Naval Research.* Contract No. Nonr-668, 1957.
4. Appenzeller, O. Personal communication. June 8, 1979.
5. Sachs, M.L., & Pargman, D. *Addiction to running: Phenomenon or pseudo-phenomenon?* Paper presented at the North American Society

for the Psychology of Sport and Physical Activity. International Congress
in Physical Education, Trois-Rivieres, Quebec, Canada, June 28, 1979.

References

Bahrke, M.S., & Morgan, W.P. Anxiety reduction following exercise and
    meditation. *Cognitive Therapy and Research,* 1978, **2,** 323-333.

Buss, A.H., & Plomin, R. *A temperament theory of personality development.*
    New York: Wiley, 1975.

Denenberg, V.H. Stimulation in infancy, emotionality reactivity, and ex-
    ploratory behavior. In D. C. Glass (Ed.), *Neurophysiology and emotion.*
    New York: Rockefeller University Press, 1967.

Edington, D.W., & Edgerton, V.R. *The biology of physical activity.* Boston:
    Houghton Mifflin, 1976.

Frankenhaeuser, M. Psychoneuroendocrine approaches to the study of emo-
    tion as related to stress and coping. In H. E. Howe, Jr., & R. A. Dienstbier
    (Eds.), *Nebraska symposium on motivation, 1978* (Vol. 27). Lincoln:
    University of Nebraska Press, 1979.

Gal, R., & Lazarus, R.S. The role of activity in anticipating and confronting
    stressful situations. *Journal of Human Stress,* 1975, pp. 4-20.

Michael, E.D. Stress adaptation through exercise. *Research Quarterly,* 1957,
    28, 50-54.

Moorehouse, L., & Miller, A.T., Jr. *Physiology of exercise.* St. Louis: C.V.
    Mosby, 1971.

Morgan, W.P. Psychological consequences of vigorous physical activity and
    sport. *Proceedings of the New York Academy of Science,* 1976, 15-30.

Selye, H. *The stress of life.* New York: McGraw Hill, 1976.

Young, R.J., & Ismail, A.H. Personality differences of adult men before and
    after a physical fitness program. *Research Quarterly,* 1976, **47,** 513-519.

CHAPTER 19

The Second Second Wind

Arnold J. Mandell

The first thirty minutes are tough, old man. Creaks, twinges, pain, and stiffness. A counterpoint of breathless, painful self-depreciation. Like driving a mule. You brain-heavy jerk. Keep going! Challenged, I smile with pride and follow my orders. That's what professional football players call playing hurt. Maybe if I were bigger I could have done that, that macho thing in shoulder pads. The first thirty minutes hurt until the body gets the message that you're serious.

Thirty minutes out, and something lifts. Legs and arms become light and rhythmic. My snake brain is making the best of it. The fatigue goes away and feelings of power begin. I think I'll run twenty-five miles today. I'll double the size of the research grant request. I'll have that talk with the dean . . .

Then, sometime into the second hour comes the spooky time. Colors are bright and beautiful, water sparkles, clouds breathe, and my body, swimming, detaches from the earth. A loving contentment invades the basement of my mind, and thoughts bubble up without trails. I find the place I *need to live if I'm going to live. The running literature says that if you run six miles a day for two months, you are addicted forever. I understand. A cosmic view and peace are located between six and ten miles of running. I've found it so everywhere. In Munich, running in the rain at five in the morning so I could lecture sanely at eight, I was stopped by a confused German policeman. It was in Oklahoma City at 104 degrees when I was bitten by a frightened dog. It was in Ann Arbor, buried in two feet of snow; outside coal-foggy London; on the Hebrew University track, a block away from the Arab killings of Jews that morning; along the Seine in a Paris winter of 4 degrees, chased by barge watchdogs; in Central Park past torn women's garments scattered on the bridle path; at eight thousand feet in Aspen on a high-school track; embellished by manure smell along the farms of the Sacramento Valley; in the hot dryness of Palm Springs; in the hot wetness of Houston.*

After the run I can't use my mind. It's empty. Then a filling begins. By afternoon I'm back into life with long and smooth energy, a quiet feeling of strength, the kind wisdom afforded those without fear, those detached yet full. The most delicious part is the night's sleep. Long an illusive, fickle dealer with me Father Sandman now stands ready whenever I want. Maybe the greatest power of the second cycle is the capacity to decide when to fall asleep. (Mandell, 1977, pp. 50-57)

Sudden shifts in states of behavioral activation, arousal, felt energy, or mood—sometimes the same thing and sometimes not—are well documented in clinical psychiatry. The above example of my two gear shifts during a daily 13-mile run have also been described by others (Leonard, 1975; Sheehan, 1978). The first "energy" appears suddenly in the middle of painful fatigue and feels like assertive power; the second, arriving at the time of the second fatigue, now closer to despair, feels mystical.

In the psychopathologic realm, sudden changes in psychic energy are exemplified by the day of the "switch" in the course of manic-depressive disease—a patient changing from bedridden lethargy to uncontrollable mania within a period of minutes or hours (Bunney, Murphy, Goodwin, & Borge, 1970), attacks of catatonic excitement (Gjessing & Gjessing, 1961), and the release of a sequence of driven and automatic behavior within a psychomotor seizure (Gibbs, Gibbs, & Fuster, 1948).

Within the realm of "normal" psychology we have the accounts of the sudden emergence into a long lasting state of high energy and loving empathy following a period of dysphoria in religious conversion by James and Underwood (James, 1929; Underwood, 1925) and episodes of "rising *Kundalini*" in the literature of meditation (Benson, Beary, & Carol, 1975; Krishna, 1975). The sudden arrival of new energy feels spontaneous—i.e., not decided or willed, although the brain might increase its probability of occurrence by particular activities. This energy is not locked into a specific instinctual psychobiologic scenario like a temper tantrum, an episode of out-of-control night eating, or the invasion by sexual obsession driving a conflicted homosexual into a well-policed men's room.

The *first* second wind we would analogize to the effect of cocaine, bringing new energy with which to practice old behaviors, the instinctually driven stereotype of obsession and compulsion, thoughts driven by a newly energized dualistic view, the conflictual but optimistic energy of Freud's (1954) and MacLean's (1958) *individual survival* limbic system. The *second* second wind is the energy of transcendence, the correlate of MacLean's (1958) pleasure-driven *species survival* circuit, no longer subject to instinctual pressure (Freud's "genital overflow"), beyond fear, a state of bliss, dualism gone in a feeling of unity, making old conflicts seem irrelevant (Mandell, 1978c). It is mimicked pharmacologically (given an appropriate brain, set, and setting) by the actions of small doses of hallucinogens (Huxley, 1977).

In the literature, "kindling"—the induction of lower thresholds for the elicitation of limbic slow waves, hypersynchrony, and seizures by either electric stimulation (Andy & Akert, 1955) or such drugs as cocaine, amphetamine, or LSD (Adey, Bell, & Dennis, 1962; Post, 1977), when studied in animals, has two phases. The first is associated with high-voltage waves in the hippocampal-septal circuit without spread to the amygdala, during which the animal stares and manifests autonomic changes and episodes of treading (the movements, usually before sleep, with which a small kitten expresses milk from its mother's breast), purring, or sexual lordosis. These behaviors can be interpreted as reflecting pleasure (Delgado & Selvillano, 1961; Parmeggiani, 1962). In man, as revealed by depth electrodes, sexual thoughts, marijuana smoking, and hallucinogenic drugs invoke similar hippocampal-septal activity (Heath, 1972; Heath & Mickle, 1960).

The second phase of kindling, as seen in cats, invading the amygdala (Delgado & Selvillano, 1961), is behaviorally characterizable by face movements, forced general motor movement, rage attacks, defensive postures, and, finally, seizures (Delgado & Selvillano, 1961; Hunsperger & Bucher, 1967; Post, 1977). In man, amygdala hypersynchronous activity is more associated with negative affectivity, such as unpleasant thoughts (Lesse, Heath, Mickle, Monroe, & Miller, 1955) and anger (Sherwood, 1960). In the case of the temporal-lobe epileptic, the paroxysmal activity of his seizure is very likely to involve the entire limbic system, including amygdala hypersynchrony (Brazier, 1968), but his other typical paroxysmal disturbance, *interictal ecstasies*, often interpreted as visitations from God, can be speculated to induce hypersynchrony in the limbic pleasure system, the hippocampal-septal circuit, and has been shown to be associated with long-lasting, good-natured disposition and metaphysical preoccupations (Dewhurst & Beard, 1970; Waxman & Geschwind, 1975).

Thus, there appear to be two kinds of limbic energy, one of pleasure and ecstasy, the other of fearful defense and rage. Amphetamine and cocaine elicit both, the hallucinogens only the former (Adey, Bell, & Dennis, 1962; Mandell, 1978c; Post, 1977). We will see how changes in biogenic amine-inhibitory regulation by drugs and such exercises as long-distance running

and meditation can modulate these two forms of temporal-lobe limbic activity. MacLean (1959) concluded that the pleasure and the fear-rage limbic
systems were reciprocally innervated, like the extensor and flexor systems in
the spinal cord, so that one in action inhibited the other. Whereas the
amygdala hypersynchrony is short-lasting (Cherlow, Dymond, Crandall,
Walter, & Serafetinides, 1977), the hippocampal discharge, with its unusual
feed-forward facilitation (Spencer & Kandel, 1961), has long-lasting after-
discharges that go on for hours, days, or weeks (Adey, Bell, & Dennis, 1962;
Spencer & Kandel, 1961); perhaps they are permanent.

Recent work portraying the asymmetric anatomy, physiology, and
behavioral aspects of the brain (Harnad, Doty, Goldstein, Jaynes, &
Krauthamer, 1977) has suggested that in addition to cognitive style and
language, there is affectual specialization. The left-sided stroke victim exag-
gerates his difficulties (the "catastrophic" reaction); the right-sided one bland-
ly and happily denies illness (Weinstein & Kahn, 1955); intracarotid amytal
releases fear and depression on the left and joy on the right (Rossi &
Rosadini, 1967; Terzian, 1964), and temporal-lobe epileptic interictal spikers
are more obsessional, paranoid, and depressed with left-side lesions and
more hypomaniac, hysterical, and impulsive with disinhibited right lobes
(Bear, 1977; Bear & Fedio, 1977; Flor-Henry, 1976). In a recently reported
split-brain case manifesting linguistic abilities on *both* left and right sides, affectual specialization was nonetheless present. The right side was consistently
more negative in rating behavior than the left side (LeDoux, Wilson, & Gazzaniga, 1977).

It is likely that each temporal lobe represents a different world view, intrinsic
to its cognitive style: the pain of verbal analytic thinking on the left, obses-
sionally working at potential dangers; a visually intuitive, hysteric, op-
timistically impulsive mode on the right. Both are active in the ambivalent and
continuing internal dialogue of living, either being preponderant at different
times of the day, the month, even the year. We have recently described what
appears to be a lateral shuttling inhibitory mechanism involving serotonin
transmission to each temporal-lobe limbic system that might be responsible for
the changing relative degree of expression of consciousness of each side
(Mandell, 1978c; Mandell & Knapp, in press; Mandell, Knapp, & Geyer,
Note 1).

It was Glick and his co-workers (Glick, Jerussi, Waters, & Green, 1974)
who first reported a bilateral asymmetry in brain dopamine concentration in
rats that was exaggerated by amphetamine. There is a clinical case report of a
rapidly cycling manic-depressive with marked asymmetry in EEG alpha per
cent in both the manic and depressed state that was made more symmetric in
association with clinical normalization following lithium (Harding, Lolas-
Stepke, & Jenner, 1976). We have shown that lithium increases serotonin
synthesis by stimulating tryptophan uptake into serotonergic neurons
(Mandell & Knapp, 1977), and when studied in rats lithium makes limbic
serotonin concentrations, originally asymmetric, more symmetric (Mandell &

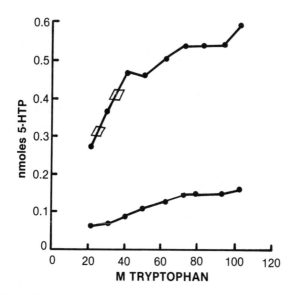

Figure 1. Tryptophan hydroxylase from rat midbrain was dialyzed for 16 hours and assayed with and without calcium. The more hyperbolic upper curve represents the calcium activation effect, seen also following cocaine administration which (a) increases the affinity of the enzyme for substrate, (b) makes substrate inhibition occur at lower tryptophan concentrations, reducing brain serotonin levels, and (c) leads to greater bilateral asymmetry of serotonin synthesis (represented by the two stippled parallelograms) because of the steeper slope of the kinetic function. Lithium, perhaps by blocking the calcium site, produces the more sigmoidal conformation, which has decreased affinity for substrate, inhibits substrate at relatively high tryptophan levels—increasing brain serotonin—and leads to decreased bilateral asymmetry in serotonin concentrations (Glowinski et al., 1973; Mandell & Knapp, in press).

Knapp, in press; Mandell, Knapp, & Geyer, Note 1). Cocaine, blocking tryptophan uptake into serotonin neurons and reducing serotonin synthesis (Knapp & Mandell, 1976), makes limbic hippocampal serotonin concentrations more asymmetric between the hemispheres (Mandell & Knapp, in press). It appears that such behaviorally activating influences as stimulants or starvation increase the asymmetry, whereas tryptophan loads, lithium, and behaviorally suppressant drugs make serotonin distribution more symmetric (Knapp & Mandell, Note 2).

The mechanism appears to involve the substrate dynamics and the conformational properties of tryptophan hydroxylase, the rate-limiting enzyme in serotonin biosynthesis. As shown in Figure 1, increasing tryptophan tends to move enzyme activity such that the levels of serotonin produced (represented by the stippled parallelograms) are closer to each other along the asymptotic portion of the velocity dimension (less asymmetry); in addition, one can see that there is more than one kinetic form of the enzyme, the upper curve tending to suggest a hyperbolic function with a high probability of asymmetry, the lower curve becoming more sigmoidal, promoting less asymmetry. Such changes in enzyme shape affecting activity properties are called conformational alterations (Monod, Changeux, & Jacob, 1963). They are often responses to chemical messages requiring metabolic adaptation and have been shown to be a property of biogenic amine biosynthetic enzymes (Mandell, 1978b) and to have the capacity to occur suddenly through a phase transition. In biosynthetic systems in bacteria or in such mammalian organs as the liver, a metabolic product serves as the feedback allosteric regulator (Hammes & Wu, 1971; Koshland, 1963); in the brain it may be a reflection of neural function—e.g., depolarization, with the influx of calcium serving as the feedback message.

With the above setting as an all-too-brief description of the machinery and the prematurity of this sort of speculation acknowledged, it is nonetheless instructive to see where using these mechanisms will take us in a psychobiologic analysis of two forms of psychic energy, each emerging "spontaneously" against the background of another feeling.

The serotonin cells of the brain are driven by sensory input and a wide variety of neurovegetative stresses (Aghajanian & Wang, 1978), and the uptake of tryptophan into these neurons has been shown to be coupled with raphe serotonin cell discharge (Glowinski, Hamon, & Hery, 1973). Thus, driving the system functions like moving the tryptophan substrate curve to the right in Figure 1, which can gradually change the relative degree of serotonin inhibition to each limbic and striatal system (Mandell, Knapp, & Geyer, Note 1) by moving the place on the substrate curve. However, increasing substrate (or increasing intracellular calcium, which occurs as a function of discharge rate) (Blaustein, Ratzlaff, & Kendrick, 1978), also has the capacity to change the shape of tryptophan hydroxylase in an allosteric transition—the enzyme maintaining its old shape until some threshold is reached, at which time it changes—so there would be a sudden shift in the differential inhibition of the hemispheres, perhaps reflected in the first second wind in the form of the abrupt release of right-lobe optimism.

These effects are mimicked by cocaine, which induces a more active, hyperbolic enzyme form, with more asymmetry in serotonin distribution (Knapp & Mandell, 1976; Mandell & Knapp, in press). Impulse gets more energy at the expense of rumination, like a burst of assertive resolve. The restricted stereotypy of amphetamine or cocaine (Post, 1977) is like instinctual compulsion—the energy of Darwin, Marx, and Freud.

In my daily run's first second wind I shift from near surrender to the ruminations about muscle and joint pain to a suddenly strong internal monologue of angry talk at the dean for his last slight, a once-and-for-all announcement of limits to my (only slightly) rebellious son, a diatribe at the car mechanic. Under the rhythmic driving or running, the serotonin cells pick up sufficient tryptophan or calcium to reach a threshold at which enzyme conformation is suddenly changed, along with the degree of symmetry of my limbic system's inhibition. I suddenly see things another way.

The *second* second wind is different. Our speculation is that it results from driving the serotonergic (or other amine) system so far that, given an exquisite sensitivity to its own transmitter (serotonin turns off serotonin cells—Aghaja-nian & Wang, 1978), it is arrested, releasing both hemispheric temporal-lobe limbic structures completely rather than changing their bilateral distribution or inhibition. This effect is imitated by LSD, an autoreceptor inhibitory agonist that has a higher affinity than serotonin (Aghajanian & Wang, 1978; de Mon-tigny & Aghajanian, 1978). Another way to reduce this inhibition is by quieting the brain and its sensory driving of the raphe system (Jacobs, 1978) by meditation (Benson, 1975). In the long-distance runner the second se-cond wind is beyond pain, hunger, thirst, anger, or depression: transcendent.

After years of training, the prolonged hippocampal-septal afterdischarge in-vades the life with a transcendent high, the same continuing high energy following the rising *Kundalini* of the meditators (Underwood, 1925). This ac-tivity, beyond the regulatory dualism in the asymmetry of two temporal-lobe world views, provides a high-energy bliss, an awareness of both sides at once, William James's "unity" (James, 1929) inhibiting rage (MacLean, 1959) and, as an accompanying event, the depression of rage (Freud, 1925) as well.

These two energies can be conceptualized as sequentially evoked defenses against despair. Imagine a tribe of prehistoric men walking in the hot desert without water to escape from enemies. Their first second wind spent, they lie down to die. Suddenly in the brain of one (and perhaps then infectiously in many) there is an attack of ecstasy and "luminescence" (James, 1929), serotonergic cell arrest, a new and transcendent energy emerges (unlike true mania, this state is empathic, loving, tolerant of differences), allowing the group to rise again and go several more miles to find water. A recent MMPI study of well-conditioned athletes shows that though their mania scales were elevated, it was not true mania in that there was a *reduction* in irritability and an increase in imperturbality (B. Smolev, Note 3). Over a million years such second second wind might be selected as a group-survival mechanism.

The dying patient, perhaps by the same sudden arrest on the oxygen-sensitive serotonergic system (Brown, Snider, & Carlsson, 1974), may also get a transcendent rush and hippocampal-septal slow-wave afterdischarge. *The Tibetan Book of the Dead* is a textbook used for thousands of years to prepare the dying to accept the ecstasy of that moment without panic (Evans-Wentz, 1960). Almost all of the features of the phenomenology of dying (Moody, 1976) have been reported by Penfield as occurring during temporal-lobe stimulation (Penfield, 1955).

These concepts have implications for psychiatric treatment: the possibility that treatment can be designed to normalize brain function by "transcendence training." The Russians think that hippocampal-septal slow waves, seen on the cortex of man as theta waves, represent the best state for learning and memory (Vinogradova, 1975). Benson (1975) reports marked improvement in cardiovascular measures following its induction. It may be the optimum state of the brain for living.

The story told to patients by psychiatrists would not be: let's straighten out your problems and you'll feel better; rather, it would be: let's feel better and then your new healthy brain will take care of its own problems. This may be the major difference in treatment strategies between the psychologies of East and West. Techniques for the induction of transcendent consciousness (loving hypomania) range from asceticism to long-distance running, from religious activity to mountain climbing, from sexual frustration to pleasant thoughts, from alpha conditioning to small doses of hallucinogens (MacLean, 1958). Perhaps the positive transference as frustrative nonreward—shown to induce this brain activity in animals—has been the power of psychotherapy.

A cautionary note. It has been shown recently that disinhibition of hippocampal CA_3 cells—gates to the hippocampal-septal hypersynchronous activity—leads to their excitation and, because of their unique feed-forward properties (Spencer & Kandel, 1961), more excitation, and then cell death (Nadler, Perry, & Cotman, 1978). These are the cells that are missing in the "pure" temporal-lobe epileptic manifesting interictal ecstasies and personality changes (Dewhurst & Beard, 1970; Malamud, 1966; Waxman & Geschwind, 1975). There is the possibility that "transcendence training," already shown to get more facile with practice, might disinhibit and kill these cells, releasing this system (Winson & Abzug, 1977) and producing transcendent consciousness permanently. When this is done in monkeys by amygdalectomy, they wander off from their tribe (Dicks, Myers, & Kling, 1969). The disarticulation of families and changing interpersonal relations in the life of the hallucinogen and pot user in our culture are known (Kolansky & Moore, 1972). In addition to the induction of changes in the quality of object relationships, the progressive disinhibition of the temporal-lobe limbic system leads to "intensification" of personality traits (Geschwind, 1965; Mandell, 1978a). I have seen some ardent meditators become more obsessional and some become more hysteric, perhaps as a function of which disinhibited temporal lobe is dominant. I've seen runners change in both directions as well. Sometimes it's more of both.

Long-term follow-up of daily runners and meditators using personality and psychosocial indicators would be instructive. In my clinical experience, these changes in long-distance runners require years to become fully expressed. The time required for the interictal personality changes to evolve fully in the temporal-lobe epileptic has been estimated to be about 14 years (Bear, 1977). One could argue that the popularity of meditation and running and the increasing acceptance of a weak hallucinogen as a common recreational drug (marijuana) both reflect and are causing a changing national consciousness, through neurochemical disinhibition, kindling, of the temporal-lobe limbic system. It's been called by some "the new narcissism," and indeed the new state does have implications for the quality of object relationships (Mandell, 1978a). No longer driven by socioeconomic necessities of the sort that pervaded the neighborhood when Darwin, Marx, and Freud took a walk near their homes (the energy of the first second wind), we seek another source—from the energy of the first to that of the second second wind.

Acknowledgement

The neurochemical research reflected herein was supported by USPHS grant DA-00265-07.

Reference Notes

1. Mandell, A.J., Knapp, S., & Geyer, M. Lithium reduces bilateral asymmetry in mesolimbic and mesostriatal serotonin concentrations. Submitted to *Science*, August 18, 1978.
2. Knapp, S., & Mandell, A.J. Article in preparation.
3. Smolev, B. Unpublished observations.

References

Adey, W.R., Bell, F.R., & Dennis, B.J. Effects of LSD, psilocybin and psilocin on temporal lobe EEG patterns and learned behavior in the cat. *Neurology*, 1962, **22**, 591-602.

Aghajanian, G.K., & Wang, R.Y. Physiology and pharmacology of central serotonergic neurons. In M. A. Lipton, A. DiMascio, & K. F. Killam (Eds.), *Psychopharmacology: A generation of progress*. New York: Raven Press Publishers, 1978.

Andy, O.J., & Akert, K. Seizure patterns induced by electrical stimulation of hippocampal formation in the cat. *Journal of Neuropathology and Experimental Neurology*, 1955, **14**, 198-213.

Bear, D. The significance of behavioral change in temporal lobe epilepsy. *McLean Hospital Journal*, June 1977.

Bear, D.M., & Fedio, P. Quantitative analysis of interictal behavior in temporal lobe epileptics. *Archives of Neurology*, 1977, **34**, 454-467.

Benson, H. *The relaxation response*. New York: William Morrow, 1975.

Benson, H., Beary, J.F., & Carol, M.P. Meditation and the relaxation response. In S. R. Dean (Ed.), *Psychiatry and mysticism*. New York: Nelson-Hall, 1975.

Blaustein, M.P., Ratzlaff, R.W., & Kendrick, N.K. The regulation of intracellular calcium in presynaptic nerve terminals. *Annals of the New York Academy of Sciences*, 1978, **307**, 195-212.

Brazier, M.A.B. Studies of the EEG activity of limbic structures in man. *Electroencephalography and Clinical Neurophysiology*, 1968, **25**, 309-318.

Brown, R.M., Snider, S.T., & Carlsson, A. Changes in biogenic amine synthesis and turnover induced by hypoxia and/or footshock stress. II. The central nervous system. *Journal of Neural Transmission*, 1974, **35**, 293-304.

Bunney, W.E., Murphy, D.L., Goodwin, F.K., & Borge, G.F. The switch process from depression to mania: Relationship to drugs which alter brain amines. *Lancet*, 1970, **1**, 1022-1027.

Cherlow, D.B., Dymond, A.M., Crandall, P.H., Walter, R.D., & Serafetinides, E.A. Evoked response and after-discharge thresholds to electrical stimulation in temporal lobe epileptics. *Archives of Neurology*, 1977, **34**, 427-531.

Delgado, J.M.R., & Selvillano, M. Evolution of repeated hippocampal seizures in the cat. *Electroencephalography and Clinical Neurophysiology*, 1961, **13**, 722-733.

de Montigny, C., & Aghajanian, G.K. Tricyclic antidepressants: Chronic treatment increases responsivity to rat forebrain neurons to serotonin. *Science*, 1978, **202**, 1303-1306.

Dewhurst, K., & Beard, A.W. Sudden religious conversion in temporal lobe epilepsy. *British Journal of Psychiatry*, 1970, **117**, 497-507.

Dicks, D., Myers, R.E., & Kling, A. Uncus and amygdala lesions: Effects on social behaviors in the free-ranging monkey. *Science*, 1969, **165**, 69-71.

Evans-Wentz, W.Y. *The Tibetan book of the dead*. New York: Oxford University Press, 1960.

Flor-Henry, P. Lateralized temporal-limbic dysfunction and psychopathology. *Annals of the New York Academy of Sciences*, 1976, **280**, 777-795.

Freud, S. Mourning and melancholia. In *Collected Papers 4*, (1925). London: Hogarth, 1925.

Freud, S. The origins of psycho-analysis. In *Letters to Wilhelm Fliess, drafts and notes, 1887-1902*. New York: Basic Books, 1954.

Geschwind, N. Disconnexion syndromes in animals and man. Part I. *Brain*, 1965, **88**, 237-294.

Gibbs, E.L., Gibbs, F.A., & Fuster, B. Psychomotor epilepsy. *Archives of Neurology and Psychiatry*, 1948, **50**, 331-339.

Gjessing, R., & Gjessing, L. Some main trends in the clinical aspects of periodic catatonia. *Acta Psychiatrica Scandinavica*, 1961, **37**, 1-13.

Glick, S.D., Jerussi, T.P., Waters, D.H., & Green, J.P. Amphetamine-induced changes in striatal dopamine and acetylcholine levels and relationship to rotation (circling behavior) in rats. *Biochemical Pharmacology*, 1974, **23**, 3223-3225.

Glowinski, J., Hamon, M., & Hery, F. Regulation of 5-HT synthesis in central serotonergic neurons. In A. J. Mandell (Ed.), *New concepts in neurotransmitter regulation*. New York: Plenum, 1973.

Hammes, G.G., & Wu, C. Regulation of enzyme activity. *Science*, 1971, **172**, 1205-1211.

Harding, G.F.A., Lolas-Stepke, F., & Jenner, F.A. Alpha rhythm laterality, lithium and mood. *Lancet*, 1976, **2**, 237.

Harnad, S., Doty, R.W., Goldstein, L., Jaynes, J., & Krauthamer, G. (Eds.). *Lateralization in the nervous system*. New York: Academic Press,

1977.

Heath, R.G. Marihuana. Effects on deep and surface electroencephalograms of man. *Archives of General Psychiatry*, 1972, **26**, 577-584.

Heath, R.G., & Mickle, W.A. Evaluation of seven years experience with depth electrodes in human patients. In E.R. Ramey & D.S. O'Doherty (Eds.), *Electrical studies on the unanesthetized brain*. New York: Hoeber, 1960.

Hunsperger, R.W., & Bucher, V.M. Affective behavior produced by electrical stimulation in the forebrain and brain stem of the cat. In W. R. Adey & T. Tokizane (Eds.), *Structure and function of the limbic system*. New York: American Elsevier, 1967.

Huxley, A. *Moksha*. New York: Stonehill, 1977.

Jacobs, B. Dreams and hallucinations: A common neurochemical mechanism mediating their phenomenological similarities. *Neuroscience and Biobehavioral Reviews*, 1978, **2**, 59-69.

James, W. *The varieties of religious experience*. New York: Modern Library, 1929.

Knapp, S., & Mandell, A.J. Cocaine and lithium: Neurobiological antagonism in the serotonin biosynthetic systems in rat brain. *Life Sciences*, 1976, **18**, 679-684.

Kolansky, H., & Moore, W.T. Toxic effects of chronic marijuana use. *Journal of the American Medical Association*, 1972, **222**, 35-41.

Koshland, D.E. The role of flexibility in enzyme action. *Cold Spring Harbor Symposia on Quantitative Biology*, 1963, **28**, 473-482.

Krishna, G. *The awakening of Kundalini*. New York: E. P. Dutton, 1975.

LeDoux, J.E., Wilson, D.H., & Gazzaniga, M.S. A divided mind: Observations on the conscious properties of the separated hemispheres. *Annals of Neurology*, 1977, **2**, 417-421.

Leonard, G. *The ultimate athlete*. New York: Viking, 1975.

Lesse, H., Heath, R.G., Mickle, W.A., Monroe, R.R., & Miller, W.H. Rhinencephalic activity during thought. *Journal of Nervous and Mental Disease*, 1955, **122**, 433-446.

MacLean, P.D. The limbic system with respect to self preservation and the preservation of the species. *Journal of Nervous and Mental Disease*, 1958, **127**, 1-11.

MacLean, P.D. The limbic system with respect to two basic life principles. In *Second conference on the central nervous system and behavior*. New York: Josiah Macy Foundation, 1959.

Malamud, N. The epileptogenic focus in temporal lobe epilepsy from a pathological standpoint. *Archives of Neurology*, 1966, **14**, 190-195.

Mandell, A.J. *Coming of middle age: A journey*. New York: Summit, 1977.

Mandell, A.J. Psychoanalytic narcissism projected. *Journal of Nervous and Mental Disease*, 1978, **166**, 369-373. (a)

Mandell, A.J. Redundant mechanisms regulating brain tyrosine and tryptophan hydroxylases. *Annual Review of Pharmacology and Toxicology*,

1978, **18,** 461-493. (b)

Mandell, A.J. Toward a psychobiology of transcendence, God in the brain. In J. M. Davidson & R. J. Davidson (Eds.), *The psychobiology of consciousness.* New York: Plenum, 1978. (c)

Mandell, A.J., & Knapp, S. Regulation of serotonin biosynthesis in brain: Role of the high affinity uptake of tryptophan into serotonergic neurons. *Federation Proceedings,* 1977, **36,** 2142-2148.

Mandell, A.J., & Knapp, S. Regulatory properties of tryptophan hydroxylase determine the degree of bilateral asymmetry in mesolimbic serotonin synthesis: A model for mood control. *Federation Proceedings,* in press.

Monod, J., Changeux, J-P., & Jacob, F. Allosteric proteins and cellular control systems. *Journal of Molecular Biology,* 1963, **6,** 306-329.

Moody, R.A. *Life after life.* New York: Bantam Books, 1976.

Nadler, J.V., Perry, B.W., & Cotman, C.W. Intraventricular kainic acid preferentially destroys hippocampal pyramidal cells. *Nature,* 1978, **271,** 676-677.

Parmeggiani, P.L. Sleep behavior elicited by electrical stimulation of cortical and subcortical structures in the cat. *Helvetica Physiologica et Pharmacologica Acta,* 1962, **20,** 347-367.

Penfield, W. The role of the temporal cortex in certain psychical phenomena. 29th Maudsley lecture. *Journal of Mental Science,* 1955, **101,** 451-465.

Post, R.M. Progressive changes in behavior and seizures following chronic cocaine administration: Relationship to kindling and psychosis. In E. H. Ellinwood & M. M. Kilbey (Eds.), *Cocaine and other stimulants.* New York: Plenum, 1977.

Rossi, G.F., & Rosadini, G. Experimental analysis of cerebral dominance in man. In C. H. Milikan & F. L. Darley (Eds.), *Brain mechanisms underlying speech and language.* New York: Grune & Stratton, 1967.

Sheehan, G.A. *Advice and philosophy for runners.* New York: Simon & Schuster, 1978.

Sherwood, S.L. Stereotactic recordings from the frontal and temporal lobes of psychotics and epileptics. In E. R. Ramey & D. S. O'Doherty (Eds.), *Electrical studies on the unanesthetized brain.* New York: Hoeber, 1960.

Spencer, W.A., & Kandel, E.R. Hippocampal neuron responses to selective activation of recurrent collaterals of hippocampofugal axons. *Experimental Neurology,* 1961, **4,** 149-161.

Terzian, H. Behavioral and EEG effects of intracarotid sodium amytal injections. *Acta Neurochirurgica,* 1964, **12,** 230-240.

Underwood, A.C. *Conversion: Christian and non-Christian.* London: Allen & Unwin, 1925.

Vinogradova, O.S. Functional organization of the limbic system in the process of registration of information: Facts and hypothesis. In R. L. Isaacson & K. H. Pribram (Eds.), *The hippocampus.* New York: Plenum, 1975.

Waxman, S.G., & Geschwind, N. The interictal behavior syndrome of temporal lobe epilepsy. *Archives of General Psychiatry,* 1975, **32,**

1580-1586.

Weinstein, E.A., & Kahn, R.C. *Denial of illness: Symbolic and physiologic aspects.* Springfield, IL: Charles C. Thomas, 1955.

Winson, C., & Abzug, C. Gating of neuronal transmission in the hippocampus: Efficacy of transmission varies with behavioral state. *Science,* 1977, **196,** 1223-1225.

CHAPTER 20

Endorphins, Neurotransmitters, and/or Neuromodulators and Exercise

Charles E. Riggs

Prolonged exercise such as running produces a variety of physiological responses which are, in fact, required by performance of the activity. Many of the responses are mediated by neurotransmitters and/or neuromodulators. The role of epinephrine and norepinephrine in the exercise response is well documented (Christensen, Galbo, Hansen, Hesse, Richter, & Trap-Jensen, 1979; Galbo, Richter, Hilsted, Holst, Christensen, & Henriksson, 1977), with less known about dopamine (Appenzeller & Schade, 1979; Van Loon, Schwartz, & Sole, 1979) and serotonin (Brown, Payne, Kim, Moore, Krebs, & Martin, 1979). The relatively recent isolation of opiate-like substances from mammalian tissues (Hughes, Smith, Kosterlitz, Fothergill, Morgan, & Morris, 1975; Hughes, Smith, Morgan, & Fothergill, 1975) and investigations concerning their physiological function in the stress response (Appenzeller, Standefer, Appenzeller, & Atkinson, 1980; Baizman, Cox, Osman, & Goldstein, 1979; Lewis, Cannon, & Liebeskind, 1980) has stimulated interest concerning a possible role for these peptides in mediating the exercise response. This chapter will provide a discussion of the function of the neurotransmitters and/or neuromodulators in exercise.

Endorphins and Enkephalins

Endorphin is a term used to indicate any substance that exhibits opiate characteristics when subjected to classic tests. Typical tests include the effect of the substance on electrically stimulated contraction of mouse vas deferens and guinea pig ileum. An opiate-like substance would be expected to inhibit the contraction. The reversability of the inhibitory effect of the substance by naloxone, an opiate antagonist, would also be expected. Several endogenous peptides including met- and leu-enkephalin and alpha- and beta-endorphin as well as others have been shown to meet the necessary criteria. Of those, met-enkephalin and beta-endorphin have received the most attention from researchers, presumably because of the greater biological activity of the two substances.

The enkephalins have been observed in the brain (Hughes et al., 1975a, 1975b) in a pattern of distribution similar to that of the opiate receptors. Clement-Jones, Lowry, Rees, and Besser (1980) measured met-enkephalin in human plasma in picomolar concentrations and suggested that the enkephalins may be secreted by the adrenal gland. Viveros, Diliberto, Hazum, and Chang (1979) demonstrated the storage of met-enkephalin in the adrenal gland and also observed the simultaneous secretion of opiate-like substances and catecholamines. Polak, Sullivan, Bloom, Facer, and Pearse (1977) observed the presence of enkephalins in the gastrointestinal tract.

Many investigations have indicated that the pituitary gland is the source of beta-endorphin (Baizman et al., 1979; Cox, Opheim, Teschemacher, & Goldstein, 1975; Teschemacher, Opheim, Cox, & Goldstein, 1975). Other work has indicated its presence in the brain and the circulation (Wilkes, Watkins, Stewart, & Yen, 1980), although the measured concentrations have been considered by some to be too low to be physiologically significant (Ipp, Dobbs, & Unger, 1978). Suda, Liotta, and Krieger (1978) failed to measure beta-endorphin in the plasma of normal human subjects at all. Grube, Voight, and Weber (1978) measured endorphins in the pancreas.

The precise physiological role of the endorphins remains unclear, and little information is available concerning the interaction of endorphins and the stress of running. In a recent paper, Pargman and Baker (1980) developed the hypothesis that the endorphins are involved in producing the psychological adaptation called the "runner's high" apparently experienced by some long distance runners. The "high," according to Pargman and Baker, is variously described as a euphoric sensation or as "an altered state of consciousness." It apparently occurs in some distance runners who have been regularly running long distances for an extended period of time. The postulated role of endorphins in producing the high is based largely on reports that endogenous and injected endorphins produce an analgesic state (Bloom et al., 1976; Bodnar et al., 1975, 1978; Buscher et al., 1976; Foley et al., 1979; Holaday et al., 1978). The endorphins, in response to stress, typically produce a cataleptic state accompanied by a reduction in responsiveness to external stimuli. Whether this describes the state encompassed by the term "runner's high" is unclear.

Despite one report of no alteration in endogenous opiates in response to a cold stress in humans (Grevert & Goldstein, 1978), it may be possible that the endorphins do play a role in producing the high. Mandell (1979; reprinted in this volume) has postulated that the psychological alterations he calls "the second wind" and "the second second wind," which correspond to the runner's high, are due to the effects of serotonin on the limbic system. If his hypothesis is correct, endorphins may provide the stimulus for the release of brain serotonin during long distance running. A similar hypothesis has been proposed for the hypothermia sometimes caused by the endorphins (Lin, Chern, Chen, & Su, 1979).

Other physiological and biochemical effects of endorphins may be important during distance running. Again, it is necessary to point out that this discussion is speculative, based upon reports of the effects of endorphins under other conditions. Many of the physiological and biochemical changes that occur during running are mediated by the catecholamines' stimulation of adenylate cyclase in various cells. Endorphins also affect adenylate cyclase systems (Klee, 1977) and are also released simultaneously with the catecholamines from the adrenal medulla (Clement-Jones et al., 1980). The endorphins inhibit adenylate cyclase activity (Klee, 1976) and reduce cyclic AMP (Minnemen & Iversen, 1976). Taken together, it is interesting to speculate that during distance running, the endorphins and catecholamines act together in a modulatory way to regulate substrate supply and utilization as well as many other physiological functions.

The endorphins also may plausibly affect other hormonal functions during exercise. Although not universally observed, the endorphins have been shown to cause an increase in the secretion of growth hormone and prolactin (Kato, Iwasaki, Abe, Ohgo, & Imura, 1978; Stubbs et al., 1978). Similar changes in serum concentrations of these hormones occur with exercise. Thus, the endorphins may have a role in mediating the increased levels of these and other hormones during exercise.

A rise in endorphin levels in exercise would be necessary for the endorphins to play a role in the responses mentioned or in others such as thermoregulation during exercise. Appenzeller et al. (1980) has recently shown a statistically significant rise in serum beta-endorphin levels as a result of a long distance run. This increase is intriguing and at least allows for speculation about the interaction of the endogenous opiate-like substances and exercise. The physiological significance of that rise, however, remains unclear and awaits further research.

Other Neurotransmitters and/or Neuromodulators

The physiological changes during exercise including changes in heart rate, blood pressure, circulation, and substrate mobilization and utilization have been attributed at least, in part, to changes in plasma norepinephrine and epinephrine. Exercise clearly affects plasma norepinephrine and epinephrine (Christensen et al., 1979) and also dopamine (Van Loon et al., 1979), and its effect is dependent on the duration and intensity of exercise (Christensen et al., 1979; Hartley et al., 1972; Robertson et al., 1979). Short-term, high-intensity exercise such as vigorous stair climbing has been shown to result in a rise in both plasma norepinephrine and epinephrine (Dimsdale & Moss, 1980). The effect on norepinephrine was greater than on epinephrine, indicating a relatively greater contribution of the sympathetic nervous system. Hartley et al. (1972) examined the effect of short-term bicycle work at mild, moderate, and heavy workloads. Mild exercise had little effect on plasma norepinephrine, but moderate and heavy workloads resulted in significant elevations. Only heavy work significantly elevated epinephrine concentrations. Hickson et al. (1979) observed elevations in plasma norepinephrine and epinephrine following a 200 yd. (182.88 m) exhaustive swim and a less exhaustive 1,000 yd. (914.4 m) swim. Training attenuated both responses, but only the response to the 1,000 yd. (914.4 m) swim was significantly lower after training.

Prolonged exercise results in a rise in both plasma norepinephrine and epinephrine (Christensen et al., 1979; Galbo et al., 1977). The rise in norepinephrine is apparently associated with increasing heart rate and with the pulmonary oxygen saturation (Christensen et al., 1979). The rise in plasma epinephrine is typically associated with more intense work in the later stages of exercise. A relationship also exists between the decrease in plasma insulin in prolonged exercise and the increase in plasma epinephrine.

Plasma dopamine concentrations are reportedly affected by exercise (Van Loon et al., 1979). Significant elevations in plasma dopamine, as well as in norepinephrine and epinephrine, at heart rates of 150% of resting and at maximal were reported. The functional significance of the rise in dopamine, however, is unknown. Appenzeller and Schade (1979), on the other hand, examined dopamine levels before, during, and after a marathon race and reported no changes.

In contrast to the observed reductions in plasma norepinephrine sometimes observed with training (Christensen et al., 1979), Brown and Van Huss (1973) observed an increase in brain norepinephrine with training. In a subsequent study, Brown et al. (1979) attempted to determine the location of increased norepinephrine levels. Following an endurance training program, norepinephrine and serotonin levels in trained animals on a normal diet were higher than for normal sedentary animals in the cerebellum and the midbrain. In the cerebral cortex, the serotonin levels of exercise-trained animals on a high fat diet were elevated. The authors suggested that the higher levels of norepinephrine in the midbrain may have been associated with cardiovascular adaptations. The higher serotonin concentrations were hypothesized to be related to obesity. Although not mentioned, the midbrain catecholamine adaptations may also have been associated with the psychological stress of forced exercise (Porsolt, Bertin, Blavet, Deniel, & Jalfre, 1979). The adaptation may also have been related to changes in substrate regulation. Because plasma serotonin has been shown to be involved in pancreatic secretions (Bryce & Jacoby, 1978), changes in the brain may be associated with a central regulatory process.

Clearly, many questions remain concerning the role of the neurotransmitters and neuromodulators in mediating the responses to exercise. The existing data are provocative and future research may implicate not only the catecholamines but also the endorphins as important components of the exercise response.

References

Appenzeller, O., & Schade, D.R. Neurology of endurance training: III. Sympathetic activity during a marathon race. *Neurology*, 1979, **29**, 542.

Appenzeller, O., Standefer, J., Appenzeller, J., & Atkinson, R. Neurology of endurance training: V. Endorphins. *Neurology*, 1980, **30**, 418-419.

Baizman, E.R., Cox, B.M., Osman, O.H., & Goldstein, A. Experimental alterations of endorphin levels in rat pituitary. *Neuroendocrinology*, 1979, **28**, 402-424.

Bloom, F., Segal, D., Ling, N., & Guillemin, R. Endorphins: Profound behavioral effects in rats suggest new etiological factors in mental illness. *Science*, 1976, **194**, 630-632.

Bodnar, R.J., Kelly, D.D., Spiaggia, A., Ehrenberg, C., & Glusman, M. Dose-dependent reductions by naloxone of analgesia induced by cold-water stress. *Pharmacology Biochemistry and Behavior*, 1978, **8**, 667-672.

Bodnar, R.J., Kelly, D.D., Steiner, S.S., & Glusman, M. Stress-produced analgesia and morphine-produced analgesia: lack of cross-tolerance. *Pharmacology Biochemistry and Behavior*, 1978, **8**, 661-666.

Brown, B.S., Payne, J.T., Kim, C., Moore, G., Krebs, P., & Martin, W. Chronic response of rat brain norepinephrine and serotonin levels to endurance training. *Journal of Applied Physiology: Respiration, Environmental and Exercise Physiology*, 1979, **46**, 19-23.

Brown, B.S., & Van Huss, W. Exercise and rat brain catecholamines. *Journal of Applied Physiology*, 1973, **34**, 664-669.

Bryce, G.F., & Jacoby, J.H. A comparative study of several serotonin receptor antagonists on basal and stimulus induced release of insulin and glucagon in the intact rat. *Life Sciences*, 1978, **22**, 2215-2224.

Buscher, H.H., Hill, R.C., Romer, D., Cardinaux, F., Closse, A., Hauser, D., & Pless, J. Evidence for analgesic activity of enkephalin in the mouse.

Nature, 1976, **261**, 423-425.

Christensen, N.J., Galbo, H., Hansen, J.F., Hesse, B., Richter, E.A., & Trap-Jensen, J. Catecholamines and exercise. *Diabetes*, 1979, **28**, 58-62. (Supplement 1)

Clement-Jones, V., Lowry, P.F., Rees, L.H., & Besser, G.M. Met-enkephalin circulates in human plasma. *Nature*, 1980, **283**, 295-297.

Cox, B.M., Opheim, K.E., Teschemacher, H., & Goldstein, A. A peptide-like substance from pituitary that acts like morphine. *Life Sciences*, 1975, **16**, 1777-1782.

Dimsdale, J.E., & Moss, J. Plasma catecholamines in stress and exercise. *Journal of the American Medical Association*, 1980, **243**, 340-342.

Foley, K.M., Kourides, I.A., Inturrisi, C.E., Kaiko, R.F., Zaroulis, C.G., Posner, J.B., Houde, R.W., & Li, C.H. Beta-endorphin: analgesic and hormonal effects in humans. *National Academy of Sciences of the United States of America*, 1979, **76**, 5377-5381.

Galbo, H., Richter, E.A., Hilsted, J., Holst, J.J., Christensen, N.J., & Henriksson, J. Hormonal regulation during prolonged exercise. *Annals of the New York Academy of Sciences*, 1977, **301**, 72-80.

Grevert, P., & Goldstein, A. Endorphins: Naloxone fails to alter experimental pain or mood in humans. *Science*, 1978, **199**, 1093-1095.

Grube, D., Voight, K.H., & Weber, E. Pancreatic glucagon cells contain endorphin-like immunoreactivity. *Histochemistry*, 1978, **59**, 75-79.

Hartley, L.H., Mason, J.W., Hogan, R.P., Jones, L.G., Kotchen, T.A., Mougey, E.H., Wherry, F.E., Pennington, L.L., & Ricketts, P.T. Multiple hormonal responses to graded exercise in relation to physical training. *Journal of Applied Physiology*, 1972, **33**, 602-606.

Hickson, R.C., Hagberg, J.M., Conlee, R.K., Jones, D.A., Ehsani, A.A., & Winder, W.W. Effect of training on hormonal responses to exercise in competitive swimmers. *European Journal of Applied Physiology*, 1979, **41**, 211-219.

Holaday, J.W., Tseng, L., Loh, H.H., & Li, C.H. Thyrotropin releasing hormone antagonizes beta-endorphin hypothermia and catalepsy. *Life Sciences*, 1978, **22**, 1537-1544.

Hughes, J., Smith, T.W., Kosterlitz, H.W., Fothergill, L.A., Morgan, B.A., & Morris, H.R. Identification of two related pentapeptides from the brain with potent opiate agonist activity. *Nature*, 1975, **258**, 577-579. (a)

Hughes, J., Smith, T., Morgan, B., & Fothergill, L. Purification and properties of enkephalin- the possible endogenous ligand for the morphine receptor. *Life Sciences*, 1975, **16**, 1753-1758. (b)

Ipp, E., Dobbs, R., & Unger, R.H. Morphine and beta-endorphin influence for secretion of the endocrine pancreas. *Nature*, 1978, **276**, 190-191.

Kato, Y., Iwasaki, Y., Abe, H., Ohgo, S., & Imura, H. Effects of endorphins on prolactin and growth hormone secretion in rats. *Proceedings of the Society for Experimental Biology and Medicine*, 1978, **158**, 431-436.

Klee, W.A. Mode of action of endogenous opiate peptides. *Nature*, 1976,

263, 609-611.

Klee, W.A. Opiates and cyclic AMP. In K. Blum (Ed.), *Alcohol and opiates: Neurochemical and behavioral mechanisms.* New York: Academic Press, 1977.

Lewis, J.W., Cannon, J.T., & Liebeskind, J.C. Opioid and nonopioid mechanisms of stress analgesia. *Science,* 1980, **208,** 623-625.

Lin, M.T., Chern, Y.F., Chen, F.F., & Su, C.Y. Serotoninergic mechanisms of beta-endorphin-induced hypothermia in rats. *European Journal of Applied Physiology,* 1979, **382,** 87-90.

Mandell, A.J. The second second wind. *Psychiatric Annals,* 1979, **9,** 57-69.

Minnemen, K.P., & Iverson, L.L. Enkephalin and opiate narcotics increase cyclic GMP accumulation in slices of rat neostriatum. *Nature,* 1976, **262,** 313-314.

Pargman, D., & Baker, M. Running high: Enkephalin indicted. *Journal of Drug Issues,* 1980, **10**(3), 341-349.

Polak, J.M., Sullivan, S.N., Bloom, S.R., Facer, P., & Pearse, A.G.E. Enkephalin-like immunoreactivity in the human gastrointestinal tract. *Lancet,* 1977, **1,** 972-974.

Porsolt, R.D., Bertin, A., Blavet, N., Deniel, M., & Jalfre, M. Immobility induced by forced swimming in rats: Effects of agents which modify central catecholamine and serotonin activity. *European Journal of Pharmacology,* 1979, **57,** 201-210.

Robertson, D., Johnson, G.A., Robertson, R.M., Nies, A.S., Shand, D.G., & Oates, J.A. Comparative assessment of stimuli that release neuronal and adrenomedullary catecholamines in man. *Circulation,* 1979, **59,** 637-643.

Stubbs, W.A., Delitala, G., Jones, A., Jeffcoate, W.J., Edwards, C.R.W., Ratter, S.J., Besser, G.M., Bloom, S.R., & Alberti, K.G.M.M. Hormonal and metabolic responses to an enkephalin analogue in normal man. *Lancet,* 1978, **2,** 1225-1227.

Suda, T., Liotta, A.S., & Krieger, D.T. Beta-endorphin is not detectable in plasma from normal human subjects. *Science,* 1978, **202,** 221-223.

Teschemacher, H., Opheim, K.E., Cox, B.M., & Goldstein, A. A peptide-like substance from pituitary that acts like morphine. *Life Sciences,* 1978, **16,** 1771-1776.

Van Loon, G.R., Schwartz, L., & Sole, M.J. Plasma dopamine responses to standing and exercise in man. *Life Sciences,* 1979, **24,** 2273-2278.

Viveros, O.H., Diliberto, E.J., Jr., Hazum, E., & Chang, K. Opiate-like materials in the adrenal medulla: Evidence for storage and secretion with catecholamines. *Molecular Pharmacology,* 1979, **16,** 1101-1108.

Wilkes, M.M., Watkins, W.B., Stewart, R.D., & Yen, S.S.C. Localization and quantitation of beta-endorphin in human brain and pituitary. *Neuroendocrinology,* 1980, **30,** 113-121.

SECTION SIX

Psychopathology and Running

The previous contributions, for the most part, have emphasized the positive emotional and physical aspects of running. Even the contributors to the section on running addiction were cautious about labeling the phenomenon as pathological; they preferred to see it as a means of dealing with personal or work stress or emphasized the continuum between commitment and addiction. The contributors to this section, however, offer a very different perspective. They express a concern that running may be a symptomatic reflection of an underlying emotional problem of some severity.

The papers by Little and by Colt and his colleagues each deal with important psychiatric considerations in athletic participants. In Chapter 21, Colt and his colleagues demonstrate a high prevalence of primary affective disorder in women runners and a similar (although not statistically significant) trend in male runners. Although the study's sampling method and controls have serious problems, the findings are intriguing. Preceding authors (Greist, Perry and Sacks, Sours, and Altshul) described the antidepressant effect of the running; thus it would make sense to assume that people suffering from depression would gravitate toward running as a means of self-treatment and would persist at it. Colt's paper, however, raises the interesting possibility that, at least in some runners, the runner's high might represent an actual manic or hypomanic elation in individuals who suffer from manic-depressive disease. This switch process from depression to mania has long puzzled researchers interested in the psychopathology of bipolar disease. Running might provide a model for further research on this group.

Little, in Chapter 22, discusses the athlete's neurosis, a neurotic crisis that occurs as a result of aging or of a physical insult. He found that athletic males in their late 30s and early 40s suddenly developed neurotic symptoms, apparently through a "trivial but highly traumatic experience initiating crippling maladjustment . . . (that) can only be understood in relation to the individual's personality and life experiences" (pp. 258-259). Although Little recognizes that the onset of a psychiatric illness in this age period often suggests a primary affective disorder such as manic-depressive disease or unipolar depression, he rejects this possibility. However, the rapid recovery of his patients, together with Colt's findings, does indeed raise this as a question to be more seriously considered.

Chapter 23 by Zira DeFries documents how running became intertwined with the profound psychiatric problems of two young women. Running, for both women, helped to organize a self-image that was severely in conflict over issues of sexual identity and self-worth. Both women suffered from primary affective disorder described by Colt, and interestingly, they also provide an addendum to Oglesby's article. For these young women, the self-image of "I am a woman runner" was more tolerable than their uncertain self-image as sexual women. It suggests that at least for some women an identity as an athlete can provide a refuge from deeper problems. In this regard, they are like the men described in earlier chapters by Joseph, Sacks, and Altshul.

Arnold Cooper, in Chapter 24, explores the issue of pain in running, humorously drawing attention to the readiness of most marathoners to describe the pain and crippling injuries suffered during running. Although these are often presented as the occupational hazards of running, similar to the bad back syndrome suffered by sedentary people, Cooper raises the question of whether the injuries might in themselves be a primary motivation for the runner. From this perspective the runner is actively seeking pain, and it is important to understand the masochism of the activity. Cooper speculates that runners' masochism may relate to their wish to maintain a childlike illusion of omnipotent control over themselves and their fate; in effect, "I suffer from pain but it is a pain that I can control because I produce it." The net result is a negation of those painful experiences in life which are beyond one's control.

These psychiatric evaluations of "hobby" athletes and runners suggest that sports may not always provide the psychological and physiological health espoused by some of its proponents, but may be a way of coping with, or self-treating, an already existing disease. Perhaps these runners are striving to achieve the effects found by Morgan and Pollock (1977) in a select group of world-class marathon runners:

> The psychometric data reveal that elite distance runners resemble other outstanding athletes in other sports such as wrestling and rowing, and their *affect* (or mood) seems to be consistently superior to that of the general population. Further, since they do not differ from the general population on personality traits

such as extroversion-introversion and neuroticism-stability (enduring qualities), it is theorized that the positive affective profiles (states) reflect the *consequence* of involvement in distance running, not an antecedent selection factor. (p. 300)

Reference

Morgan, W.P., & Pollock, M.L. Psychologic characterization of the elite distance runner. In P. Milvy (Ed.), *Annals of the New York Academy of Sciences*, 1977, **301,** 382-403.

CHAPTER 21

A High Prevalence of Affective Disorder in Runners

*Edward W. D. Colt, David L. Dunner,
Kathleen Hall, and Ronald R. Fieve*

During the course of histories and physical examinations of runners who had undergone measurements of body composition or screening blood tests, it was noted that they reported an improvement in mood and a reduction of tension after running; many of them had past histories of depression which had improved since they started running. It seemed that runners might be people with mild to moderate mood disorders who had empirically found that running was beneficial. We decided to test this hypothesis by studying the prevalence of primary affective disorder (PAD) in runners.

Materials and Methods

The 61 runners interviewed were between the ages of 23 and 49. One of the authors, also a runner, asked other runners to participate in a study of body composition, the nature of which was fully explained. Reasons for refusal or acceptance of this request were not documented because they did not seem relevant to body composition. Informed consent was obtained. Subsequently, all

234

of the 19 runners who had undergone body composition studies were asked the question: "Would you be willing to undergo a psychiatric test?" Of the six who did not take the test, one had left the New York area, one appeared but the interviewer did not, and four runners declined without giving a reason. Subsequently, a study of blood chemistry was performed on 130 runners, and the first 43 runners to undergo this survey were asked if they were willing to take a psychiatric test as mentioned earlier. Only one runner declined the test.

A psychiatric diagnosis for each subject was ascertained through use of a structured interview known as "Schedule for Affective Disorders and Schizophrenia—L form" (SADS-L) (Spitzer & Endicott, Note 1) which was administered by a trained rater. The SADS-L forms were scored by a psychiatrist and diagnoses were made according to the criteria of Feighner, Robins, & Guze (1972). PAD diagnoses were made according to the criteria of Fieve and Dunner (1975). Patients termed "Bipolar Other" (BPO) have histories of hypomania and depression and have had outpatient but not inpatient psychiatric treatment. Patients termed "Cyclothymic Personality" (CP) have bipolar affective symptoms but have never been treated. Patients termed "Unipolar Other" (UPO) have depression only, with histories of outpatient but not inpatient treatment, whereas patients termed "Depressive Personality" (DP) have histories of depressed mood without having had psychiatric treatment. We found that slightly over half of the "control" subjects did not have a psychiatric diagnosis by the method employed in this study (Kuyler & Dunner, 1976).

Results

The psychiatric diagnoses in the runners are presented in Tables 1 and 2. Considering only treated cases as having PAD (UPO or BPO), we found that seven of 22 female runners and six of 39 male runners had PAD. We compared these incidences with published control values from an orthopedic surgery sample (Kuyler & Dunner, 1976) in which none of 17 males and 3 of 35 females had PAD: These results are summarized in Table 3. There was a significantly higher prevalence of PAD among women runners than among the orthopedic patients ($\chi^2 = 3.92$, $P < 0.05$). The prevalence of PAD was not significantly greater in male runners than in male controls, although there does appear to be a trend toward significance ($\chi^2 = 3.66$, $P < 0.1$). Interestingly, 21 of the runners were diagnosed by SADS-L as psychiatrically well. Sixteen of the runners had histories of mild mood disturbance (eight with CP and eight with DP).

Discussion

Sampling Problems

In a study of this kind, which reveals a higher prevalence of affective

Table 1

Psychiatric Diagnoses of Male Runners

Age	Miles/Week	Diagnosis	Age	Miles/Week	Diagnosis	Age	Miles/Week	Diagnosis
25	90	UPO	32	100	CP	29	60	Well
32	35	UPO	33	35	CP	35	50	Well
42	10	UPO[a]	26	50	Undiagnosed	35	105	Well
39	55	BPO	36	60	Drug Abuse	32	65	Well
36	100	BPO			Alcoholism	37	35	Well
34	55	BPO	49	75	Drug Abuse, 2° BPO	30	56	Well
33	80	DP	48	55	Alcoholism	37	60	Well
42	70	DP	45	30	Alcoholism	38	60	Well
36	40	DP	38	45	Anxiety Neurosis 2° Depression	36	45	Well
41	40	DP	37	30	Schizophrenia	37	50	Well
31	65	DP	32	90	Well	38	60	Well
41	60	DP	23	90	Well	36	45	Well
27	60	CP				37	50	Well
39	34	CP				39	30	Well

Note. UPO = Unipolar Other; DP = Depressive Personality; BPO = Bipolar Other; CP = Cyclothymic Personality; Mean age = 35.7 ± 5.7 years; Mean mileage = 57.1 ± 21.8 miles/week for 3 months; $n = 39$; Difference in PAD between runners and controls: $X^2 = 3.66$, $P < 0.1$

[a] This runner had been running for 32 years and his mileage has fluctuated markedly from month to month. He bicycles (hard) 40 miles/week. Thus the quoted 10 miles/week gives a misleading estimate of his exercise habits.

Table 2

Psychiatric Diagnoses of Female Runners

Age	Miles/Week	Diagnosis	Age	Miles/Week	Diagnosis
31	19	UPO	41	45	CP
29	25	UPO	31	40	Undiagnosed
31	24	UPO	32	40	{ ECT { Undiagnosed
34	30	UPO			
36	36	UPO	34	60	Drug Abuse
32	30	UPO	26	45	{ Alcoholism { 2° DP
28	50	UPO			
36	55	DP	37	60	Well
34	30	DP	37	32	Well
26	45	CP	27	30	Well
30	55	CP	35	20	Well
23	45	CP	32	17	Well

Note. UPO = Unipolar Other; CP = Cyclothymic Personality; DP = Depressive Personality; Mean Age = 31.9 ± 4.3 years; Mean Mileage = 37.9 ± 13.2 miles/week for 3 months; n = 22; Difference in PAD between runners and controls: χ^2 = 3.92, $P < 0.05$.

disorder in a particular population than in a control group, the fundamental question is: Did this small sample represent the characteristics of runners in general? The answer is the key to the correct interpretation of our findings.

We believe that the sample was not biased toward psychiatric illness because the runners did not know that they were going to take a psychiatric test; originally they took only a laboratory test and neither they nor the individual administering the test had any idea that they would later be asked to undergo a psychiatric test. Furthermore, most of the runners who took the medical tests were willing to participate in the psychiatric testing. A sample bias (of unknown direction), however, would seem to be likely in any study which requires people who hold jobs to travel to and from a medical center and spend at least 1 hour taking a psychiatric test (SADS-L) or 3 hours undergoing a study of body composition. The increased prevalence of primary affective disorder in runners might possibly be even greater when compared to a nonhospitalized group than to an orthopedic surgery sample. Therefore, we conclude that in this relatively small sample, runners had a greater-than-expected frequency of primary affective disorder.

Nonelite Versus Elite Runners

Almost all of the runners in this study were members of the New York City Road Runners Club and were likely to share many of the characteristics of the participants in the New York City Marathon described by Milvy and Thornton (Note 2); that is, they were much better educated than average, with four times the divorce rate of the national average, and a mean income con-

Table 3

Psychiatric Diagnoses of Runners as Compared With Those of Orthopedic Patients

Diagnosis	Runners		Orthopedic Patients (4)	
	Males	Females	Males	Females
Well	16	5	10	13
PAD	6	7	0	3
Difference in				
PAD $X^2 =$	3.66	3.92		
$P =$	< 0.1	< 0.05		
Mild Mood Disturbance				
(DP or CP)	10	6	—	—
Schizophrenia	1	0	1	1
Anxiety Neurosis	1	0	2	0
Hysteria	0	0	0	5
Antisocial Personality	0	0	3	1
Secondary Affective				
Disorder[a]	0	0	1	2
Alcoholism/Drug Abuse	4	2	0	0
Undiagnosed	1	2	0	0
Total Number	39	22	17	25

[a]There were two cases of affective disorder in males secondary to alcoholism and drug abuse in one, and anxiety in the other (see Table 1); they have been listed in the other categories mentioned. There was one case of affective disorder in females secondary to alcoholism; this has been listed in the latter category (see Table 2).

siderably above average. If any group were likely to empirically discover an inexpensive nonpharmacologic treatment for depression, it would be this one.

Morgan and Pollock (1977) studied a group of world-class long distance runners ($n = 19$) and a group of collegiate middle distance runners ($n = 8$). These two groups did not differ significantly from each other in 16 separate psychological variables, but the entire group of runners (as well as groups of oarsmen and wrestlers on the varsity team) did differ significantly from college norms in that they manifested less trait anxiety, tension, depression, fatigue, and confusion. They also demonstrated significantly more vigor than college norms.

These findings might appear to contradict the results of our study; however, we studied nonelite athletes whereas Morgan and Pollock were studying elite athletes, who, a priori, are likely to be different psychologically. It is noteworthy that none of the high-performance runners studied by Morgan and Pollock (1977) became initially involved because of the nature of running or its intrinsic appeal. The reasons these runners gave for their involvement in running were the following: (a) peer influence; (b) parental influence; (c) inability to take part in other sports because of body size; (d) a means of getting into shape for another sport such as basketball; and (e) early success in running races held during grade school or junior high school physical education classes.

Adherence to running among these athletes was found to be related to both extrinsic and intrinsic rewards. The former were related to positive reinforcement resulting from the winning of awards, ability to travel extensively throughout the world, and so on; the latter centered on the sheer joy of running and the sense of well being resulting from training and competing. Each runner reported that he/she would continue running for the remainder of his/her life, regardless of the possibility of competing.

Morgan and Pollock (1977) also found that elite marathoners differed from nonelite marathoners in their cognitive strategy during competition. Unfortunately, they have not reported any psychological testing on nonelite marathoners analogous to the 16 parameters alluded to previously. Nevertheless, the cognitive strategies employed by the elite and nonelite marathoners differ so markedly that it would not be surprising if these groups had other psychological differences, as in, for example, the high prevalence of affective disorder which we have reported in contrast to the low depression scores of the elite group of Morgan and Pollock. The latter reported that the cognitive strategy employed by the elite runners was associative; namely, these runners paid close attention to bodily input, such as feelings and sensations arising in their feet, calves, and thighs, as well as respiration and pace. In contrast, the nonelite runners employed a dissociative strategy which consisted of thinking about life events having nothing to do with running, thereby reducing the pain and discomfort of competition. One runner builds a house when he marathons, another writes letters to everyone he owes a letter to, another listens to a stack of Beethoven records, another steps on the imaginary faces of the two co-workers she detests.

It is important to remember that consistent success in competition is extremely demanding physically and perhaps even more so psychologically, so that low scores in depression, tension, and anxiety would be likely in top performers. One of the runners in our study was a world class marathoner with a best time of 2:12:13. His SADS-L diagnosis was cyclothymic personality; he wished to receive psychiatric help, which had he received, would have put him (by definition) in the category of "bipolar other," i.e., primary affective disorder. Another runner in the study was a top-class professional golfer whose diagnosis was "bipolar other." He was obliged to stop running on account of work pressure and an injury; his bipolar illness then deteriorated and he began lithium therapy. He reported that, at times, he became so depressed that he could not actually start a workout; when he was able to start, his depression would lift by the end of the workout. We encountered another young woman who did not participate in this study but who said that she was able to stop taking lithium when she became a regular runner.

The Psychological Changes Associated with Exercise

Johnson (1962) found improvement in fitness in handicapped children to be associated with improvement in social adjustment, school work, finger skills, speech, functional intelligence, and response to various forms of psychotherapy.

Schultz (1961) found significant superiority in the body image of high school girls of high physical fitness as compared with girls of low fitness.

Bonniwell (1962) reported improvement in confidence, classroom performance, and social adjustment in 16 children with various neuromotor problems after a physical development program.

Jankowski (1976) treated 208 inpatient and outpatient adolescent boys with learning problems, truancy, alcoholism, or drug abuse with either thioridazine, psychotherapy, or hard physical activity. No difference in outcome was observed.

Powell (1974) treated geriatric mental patients with 21 weeks of exercise therapy; they showed significant improvement in the Ravens Progressive Matrices Test and Wechsler Memory Scale compared with an untreated control group and a group participating in social activities.

Buccola and Stone (1975) studied men between 60 and 79 years of age who jogged or cycled for 10 to 40 minutes 3 days per week for 14 weeks. Similar weight and blood pressure decreases in both groups were observed while maximum oxygen consumption increased. Based on the Cattell 16-Personality Factor Questionnaire, the walk-jog group became more sober and self-sufficient, a change not found in the cyclers.

Gary and Guthrie (1972) reported that a group of hospitalized alcoholics who jogged 1 mile per day for 20 days improved their self-esteem and slept better when compared with a group of nonexercising controls who continued usual ward activities.

Dodson and Mullens (1969) studied the effects of jogging on 18 Veterans Administration Hospital inpatients with a variety of psychiatric disorders, including alcoholism, who ranged from being "well-oriented" to "out of contact." Three weeks of daily jogging resulted in a significant decrease in the hypochondriasis and psychasthenia scales of the MMPI during jogging, whereas no change was observed on these dimensions in a control group.

Orwin (1973) described the successful treatment of eight agoraphobic patients using running to compete with the anxiety response of the agoraphobic. He also reported using running close to the limit of toleration in the successful treatment of a specific phobia (1974).

Muller and Armstrong (1975) used running as the major intervention in the successful treatment of a single patient with elevator phobia.

Driscoll (1976) concluded that exertion plus pleasant fantasies produced a significant reduction in self-reports of examination anxiety. When administered alone, exertion and fantasies also reduced anxiety, although not as much as when used in combination.

Morgan (1973) has assessed anxiety by means of the State-Trait Anxiety Inventory before and after vigorous exercise. He found that state anxiety initially fell below the pre-exercise base line with moderate to heavy exercise, whereas no drop was found after light exercise. Six male anxiety neurotics were tested before and following maximal treadmill testing to exhaustion, with a diminution of state anxiety.

Kostrubala (1976) described a thrice weekly running-group psychotherapy treatment which has had positive results in two uncontrolled studies. Individuals with depression, schizophrenia, anorexia nervosa, and "lifestyle changes" all reported symptom reduction and improved functioning in important roles.

Gutin (1966) concluded that the beneficial psychological effects of physical fitness programs are most pronounced in those persons with the lowest initial physical fitness scores.

Ismail and Trachtman (1973) studied a group of 60 middle-aged men who jogged 3 times a week for 4 months using the Cattell 16-Personality Factor Questionnaire. High and low physical fitness groups were isolated and the low fitness group showed significant increases in emotional stability, imaginativeness, guilt proneness, and self-sufficiency on completion of the program and approached the pretest scores of the high fitness group on these measures.

Tillman (1965) believes that basic personality structures do not change as a result of improved physical fitness. He holds, however, that mood variables in particular do appear to be altered by changes in fitness.

Morgan (1976) reported that physical activity modified state variables such as anxiety and depression but did not modify trait variables such as extroversion-introversion.

Morgan and his associates (1970) studied the relationship of depression to a variety of parameters in 67 college faculty members. They concluded that depression and physical fitness were not correlated in normal adult males. Eleven men in this group, however, scored in the depressed range on the Zung depression scale at the outset of a 6-week physical activity study. Each man in the depressed range increased his physical work capacity and scored in the nondepressed range on the Zung scale at the end of the study. None of the other 56 subjects had fallen into the depressed range at the study's completion.

Brown, Ramirez, and Taub (1978) investigated the relationship between thrice weekly exercise and depression in 167 college students. Students rated themselves on the Zung Depression Inventory before and after 8 weeks of either wrestling, tennis, "varied exercises," jogging, or softball. Joggers were unsupervised and averaged 1.24 kilometers per session. The softball players and six control individuals who did not exercise showed no reduction in depression scores, whereas all other subjects did, with joggers showing the greatest reductions. Subjects who initially scored in the range of clinical depression (Zung score greater than 50) also showed a significant reduction in depression with activity ($P < 0.001$).

Kavanagh, Shephard, and Tuck (1975) administered the MMPI to 101 patients 16 to 18 months after myocardial infarction. He isolated a population of 56 with severe depression and followed them for 2 to 4 years. In a regular running program these patients showed significant improvement in the depression score of the MMPI scale, whereas the other indices remained unchanged.

Greist, Klein, Eischens, Faris, Gurman, and Morgan (1979) reported that running was at least as effective as psychotherapy in the treatment of individuals with moderate depression.

Reward and Addiction

If running relieves anxiety and depression as shown by the above studies, it might be that depressed and anxious runners would be more rewarded (by running) than nondepressed, nonanxious runners. Thus, individuals with affective disorder might be "naturally selected" for running.

Furthermore, if the antidepressant and anxiolytic effects of running operate on a dose response principle, the more disordered runners might prefer greater distances. This hypothesis is consonant with the addictive propensity of running first noted by Sheehan in 1975 and later more fully discussed by Glasser (1976), who coined the term "positive addiction"—he described withdrawal symptoms 36 to 48 hours after the last run, which included agitation, restlessness, insomnia, and irritability. All of these symptoms are also the symptoms of depression.

Sacks (Note 3) has stated that running addicts are characterized by a compulsive need to run at least once and sometimes twice a day; if, for some reason, they are prevented from running they become irritable, restless, sleepless, and preoccupied with guilty thoughts that their body will decondition or degenerate in some way. Running addicts often let their running preempt responsibilities toward work and family, frequently fall into daydreams about running, and seek from every run a euphoric sensation known as the "runners' high." The most common reason for running given by 540 regular runners who were interviewed by Sachs and Pargman (Note 4) was that running helped cut down on anxiety, depression, and guilt.

Morgan (1978) has said that running is followed by a state of total relaxation and quiescence that may last for hours, although it is rare for anyone running less than 10 miles a day to consistently experience this altered state of consciousness.

Robbins and Joseph (Note 5) quantified the intensity of withdrawal symptoms experienced by 345 runners when they missed a workout; the results showed that the intensity of the withdrawal symptoms was directly related to the amount of time subjects spent running each week and the distance they ran.

Baekeland (1972) attempted to study changes in sleep EEGs of steady exercisers deprived of their exercise for long periods. Daily exercisers refused to join the study despite substantial monetary inducements, and he had to make do with subjects who exercised only 3 days a week. He concluded that even in this group the month-long period without exercise resulted in impaired sleep.

It would be interesting to see if withdrawal symptoms in runners are correlated with high scores for depression and anxiety and/or primary affective disorder. The fear of not being able to run frequently makes runners continue running despite severe pain. Colt and Spyropoulos (1979) described a young woman who continued to run in spite of developing innumerable stress fractures. When she was finally persuaded to stop running, she lapsed into a depressed and agitated state which lasted until she was able to resume running 4 months later. Reluctance to discontinue running may reach life-threatening proportions as in the six cases of myocardial infarction described by Noakes and his colleagues (1977); one was fatal, all of these runners experienced severe symptoms which they ignored. The runner who died ran 40 miles while experiencing chest pain.

Dienstbier, Crabbe, Johnson, Thorland, Jorgensen, and Sadar (Note 6; published in this volume) have found that following a run, individuals show increased tolerance of sound stress and cold stress.

Black, Chesher, and Stammer (1979) have shown that running increases tolerance of ischemic arm pain which is unaffected by prior administration of naloxone.

As well as relieving depression, running can itself cause depression (which is part of the overtraining syndrome); this has been recognized by coaches in all areas of athletics for decades, if not centuries. Sheehan (1975) has drawn attention to this syndrome which includes the following symptoms: depression, insomnia, fatiguability, irritability, and tachycardia.

Neurochemistry and Neuroendocrinology

There is evidence that intracerebral neurochemical changes accompany exercise. Brown and his colleagues (1979) measured norepinephrine and serotonin concentration in rats following 8 weeks exposure to 30 minutes of treadmill running, 5 days per week. In most brain areas, norepinephrine and serotonin concentrations were significantly greater than in sedentary control rats. The increased concentrations of norepinephrine are consistent with the known modulating action of the brain on sympathetic activity following exercise training. The authors speculated that the increased levels of serotonin in the midbrain might be the neurotransmittal adaptation responsible for decreased appetite and weight loss following chronic endurance exercise.

In humans, Noel, Sah, Stone, and Frantz (1972) have found that running stimulates increases in both prolactin and growth hormone. Colt, Wardlaw, and Frantz (1981) have found that running causes increases in plasma β-endorphin in about 1/2 the subjects tested; during repeat runs at higher intensity, the increase in plasma β-endorphin was considerably augmented. The secretion of these pituitary hormones is known to be influenced by the hypothalamic neurotransmitters, serotonin, dopamine, and norepinephrine. Thus, in humans, there is indirect evidence of exercise-induced alterations in these intracerebral monoamines.

It is interesting that alterations in these monoamines have been implicated in the pathogenesis of affective disorder (Schildkraut, 1965) and amphetamine addiction (Davis & Jankowsky, 1973; Mass, Dekirmajian, & Jones, 1973). Sleep, food intake, thirst, pain threshold, and other autonomic functions are influenced by these monoamines (Reichlin, 1974) which are believed to mediate the effects of antidepressant drugs (Palmer, Robinson, Manian, & Sulser, 1972) and lithium (Singer & Rotenberg, 1973). Now we have evidence that running causes alterations in these monoamines, it is tempting to postulate a unifying intra-cerebral monoamine hypothesis to explain the known psychological consequences of running.

With regard to β-endorphin, increases of which have repeatedly been put forward (if not in the literature, certainly at scientific meetings) as the cause of addiction and the "high" of runners, this laboratory has measured only *plasma* β-endorphin in runners which probably has little if anything to do with intra-cerebral β-endorphin. Thus, our finding that running increases plasma β-endorphin in no way supports the hypothesis that β-endorphin causes the "runners' high." This theory can only be supported by work which shows directly or indirectly that exercise causes increases of intra-cerebral β-endorphin.

Concluding Remarks

This study showed a high prevalence of affective disorder in women runners and a similar (though statistically insignificant) trend in male runners. We hypothesize that these runners were motivated by the mood-improving actions of running to continue running. In addition, there appears to be a remarkable frequency of mild mood disturbance (8 CP and 8 DP) in the 61 runners studied; unfortunately, for purposes of comparison, no control figures are available.

We wonder if the addictive propensity of running is related to its antidepressant effect possibly via a unifying "monoamine hypothesis." In this regard it must be mentioned that most antidepressant drugs are nonaddictive, whereas amphetamines which have some antidepressant effects are addictive.

We have encountered a number of runners who report that they become "revved up" after unusually intense workouts and may then experience insomnia. These symptoms may represent hypomania. One runner with bipolar illness who participated in our study said that a hard workout could make him hypomanic.

We have briefly reviewed the growing body of literature describing the antidepressant and addictive actions of running (and exercise in general). A large number of fascinating questions emerge: What happens to the personalities of athletes who stop exercising? Do they become depressed? Could this explain the suicides of the two ex-world middleweight boxing champions, Freddie Mills and Randolph Turpin, and surely many other athletes besides? Is the increased prevalence of depression among the aged related to decreased activity? Can running switch manic-depressive patients from depression to mania (and vice versa)? Is running as pleasurable to persons of normal mood as it is to those with disturbances of mood? Are those middle-aged golfers (and tennis players) who spend their weekends in the club endlessly describing the last game, suffering from depression? These and many other questions will doubtless become the focus of many studies in the years to come.

Acknowledgements

We would like to thank Dr. John Greist for providing inspiration and a large number of references, as well as Dr. Paul Nassar for reviewing the manuscript and Ms. Robbie Keefer for her secretarial skills. Above all, we would like to thank all those runners who donated their precious time and effort to this work.

Supported in part by Federal Grant MH 21586, The New York State Department of Mental Hygiene, The Columbia-Millhauser Depression Center, the Foundation for Depression and Manic Depression, and the Depression Research Fund, Presbyterian Hospital.

Reference Notes

1. Spitzer, R.L., & Endicott, J. *Schedule for affective disorders and schizophrenia*. Manuscript prepared with the assistance of other participants in a collaborative project on the psychobiology of depressive orders. Sponsored by the Clinical Research Branch of the NIMH.
2. Milvy, P., & Thornton, J. *A demographic description of a group of male marathoners*. Unpublished manuscript, University of New York, 1981.
3. Sacks, M. Paper presented at a Symposium on Running at Cornell University Medical School, New York, October 19, 1979.
4. Sachs, M.L., & Pargman, D. *Personality and the addicted runner*. Paper presented at the International Congress in Physical Education, Trois Rivieres, Quebec, Canada, June 28, 1979.
5. Robbins, J.M., & Joseph, P. *Commitment to running: Implications for the family and work*. Paper presented at a Symposium on Medical Aspects of Long Distance Running, American Medical Joggers Association, New York, October 1979.
6. Dienstbier, R.A., Crabbe, J. Johnson, G.O., Thorland, W., Jorgensen, J.A., & Sadar, M.M. *Running and changes in stress tolerance, mood, and temperament indicators: A bridge to exercise and personality*

change. Paper presented at the Second Annual Psychology of Running Seminar at Cornell University Medical College, October 19, 1979.

References

Baekeland, F. *Practical running psychology.* Mountain View, CA: World Publishers, 1972.

Black, J., Chesher, G.B., & Stammer, G.A. The painlessness of the long distance runner. *Medical Journal of Australia,* 1979, **1**(2), 522-523.

Bonniwell, H. *The effects of participation in a physical development clinic on the body-image of neuromuscularly disorganized children.* Unpublished master's thesis, University of Maryland, 1962.

Brown, B.S., Payne, T., & Chang, K. et al. Chronic response of rat brain norepinephrine and serotonin levels to endurance training. *Journal of Applied Physiology,* 1979, **46**(1), 19-23.

Brown, R.S., Ramirez, D.E., & Taub, J.M. The prescription of exercise for depression. *The Physician and Sports Medicine,* 1978, **6**(12), 34-45.

Buccola, V.A., & Stone, W.J. Effects of jogging and cycling programs on physiological and personality variables in aged men. *Research Quarterly,* 1975, **46,** 134-139.

Colt, E.W.D., & Spyropoulos, E. Running and stress fractures. *British Medical Journal,* 1979, **2**(6192), 706-708.

Colt, E.W.D., Wardlaw, S., & Frantz, A.G. The effect of running on plasma β-endorphin. *Life Science,* 1981, **28,** 1637.

Davis, J.M., & Jankowsky, D. Amphetamine psychosis. In E. Uskin & S.H. Synder (Eds.), *Frontiers in catecholamine research.* Oxford: Pergamon Press, 1973.

Dodson, L.C., & Mullens, W.R. Some effects of jogging on psychiatric hospital patients. *American Corrective Therapy Journal,* 1969, **23**(5), 130-134.

Driscoll, R. Anxiety reduction using physical exertion and positive images. *Psychological Record,* 1976, **26,** 87-94.

Feighner, J.P., Robins, E., Guze, S. et al. Diagnostic criteria for use in psychiatric research. *Archives of General Psychiatry,* 1972, **26,** 57-63.

Fieve, R.R., & Dunner, D.L. Unipolar and bipolar affective states. In F. F. Flach & S. C. Draghi (Eds.), *The nature and treatment of depression.* New York: Wiley, 1975.

Gary, V., & Guthrie, D. The effect of jogging on physical fitness and self-concept in hospitalized alcoholics. *Quarterly Journal of Studies on Alcohol,* 1972, **33,** 1073-1078.

Glasser, W. *Positive addiction.* New York: Harper & Row, 1976.

Greist, J.H., Klein, M.H., Eischens, R.R., Faris, J., Gurman, A.S., & Morgan, W.P. Running as treatment for depression. *Comprehensive Psychiatry,* 1979, **20,** 41-54.

Gutin, E. Effect of increase in physical fitness on mental ability following physical and mental stress. *Research Quarterly*, 1966, **37**, 211-220.

Ismail, A.H., & Trachtman, L.E. Jogging the imagination. *Psychology Today*, 1973, **6**, 78-82.

Jankowski, K. Psychotherapie, Pharmacotherapie und Sporttherapie bei emotional gestorten Jugendichen: Eine vergleichende Analyse von Stationarer und Ambulanter Therapie mit hilfe Physiologischer und Psychologischer. *Methoden Klin Psychol Psychother*, 1976, **24**(3), 251-255.

Johnson, W.R. Some psychological aspects of physical rehabilitation: Toward an organismic theory. *Journal of the Association for Physiological and Mental Rehabilitation*, 1962, **16**, 165-168.

Kavanagh, T., Shephard, R.J., & Tuck, J.A. Depression after myocardial infarction. *Canadian Medical Association Journal*, 1975, **113**, 23-27.

Kostrubala, T. *The joy of running*. New York: J. B. Lippincott, 1976.

Kuyler, P.L., & Dunner, D.L. Psychiatric disorders and the need for mental health services among a sample of orthopedic inpatients. *Comprehensive Psychiatry*, 1976, **17**(3), 395-400.

Maas, J., Dekirmajian, H., & Jones, F. The identification of depressed patients who have a disorder of norepinephrine metabolism and/or disposition. In E. Usdin & S. H. Snyder (Eds.), *Frontiers in catecholamine research*. Oxford: Pergamon Press, 1973.

Morgan, W.P. Influence on acute physical activity on state anxiety. *Proceedings of the National College Physical Education Association for Men*, 1973, 113-121.

Morgan, W.P. Psychological consequences of vigorous physical activity and sport. In *Introduction to Sport Psychology*. St. Louis, MO: C. V. Mosby, 1976.

Morgan, W.P. The mind of the marathoner. *Psychology Today*, April 1978, pp. 38-49.

Morgan, W.P., & Pollock, M.L. Psychologic characterization of the elite distance runner. *Annals of the New York Academy of Sciences*, 1977, **301**, 382-402.

Morgan, W.P., Roberts, J.A., Brand, F.R., & Feinerman, A.D. Psychological effects of chronic physical activity. *Medicine and Science in Sports*, 1970, **2**, 213-217.

Muller, B., & Armstrong, H.E. A further note on the "running treatment" for anxiety. *Psychotherapy: Theory, Research, and Practice*, 1975, **12**(4), 385-387.

Noakes, T., Opie, L., Beck, W., McKechnie, J., Benchimol, A., & Desser, K. Coronary heart disease in marathon runners. *Annals of the New York Academy of Sciences*, 1977, **301**, 593-619.

Noel, G.L., Sah, H.K., Stone, G., & Frantz, A.G. Human prolactin and growth hormone release during surgery and other conditions of stress. *Journal of Clinical Endocrinology and Metabolism*, 1972, **35**(6), 840-851.

Orwin, A. The running treatment: A preliminary communication of a new use for an old therapy (physical activity) in the agoraphobic syndrome. *British*

Journal of Psychiatry, 1973, **122,** 175-179.

Orwin, A. Treatment of a situational phobia—A case for running. *British Journal of Psychiatry*, 1974, **125,** 95-98.

Palmer, G.C., Robinson, G.A., Manian, A.A., & Sulser, F. Modification by psychotropic drugs of the cyclic AMP response to norepinephrine in the rat brain in vitro. *Psychopharmacologia*, 1972, **23,** 201.

Powell, R.R. Psychological effects of exercise therapy upon institutionalized geriatric mental patients. *Journal of Gerontology*, 1974, **29**(2), 157-161.

Reichlin, S. Neuroendocrinology. In R.H. Williams (Ed.), *Textbook of endocrinology*. Philadelphia, PA: W.B. Saunders, 1974.

Schildkraut, J.J. The catecholamine hypothesis of affective disorders. A review of supporting evidence. *American Journal of Psychiatry*, 1965, **122,** 509.

Schultz, L.E. *Relationships between body image and physical performance in adolescent girls*. Unpublished master's thesis, 1961.

Sheehan, G. *Dr. Sheehan on running*. Mountain View, CA: World Publishers, 1975.

Singer, I., & Rotenberg, D. Mechanism of lithium action. *New England Journal of Medicine*, 1973, **289,** 254.

Tillman, K. Relationship between physical fitness and selected personality traits. *Research Quarterly*, 1965, **36,** 483-489.

CHAPTER 22

The Athlete's Neurosis — A Deprivation Crisis

J. Crawford Little

Athleticism

In the clinical investigation of a series of 72 male neurotic patients, referred to a general hospital psychiatric clinic and to private practice over the years 1959-62 in an industrial city in Northern England (Leeds, population 520,000), it was found that these neurotic subjects fell into two extreme categories with respect to "athleticism," i.e., their personal valuation of physical prowess (Little, 1966). On the one hand were the 39% who appeared, to the exclusion of other interests, to overvalue health and fitness, revealing an inordinate pride in their previous sickness-free progress through life and in their excess physical stamina, strength, or skill. In complete contrast were the 42% of the neurotic series who had shown an almost complete lack of awareness of physical wellbeing throughout life and had never shown the slightest interest in sport, games, athletics, or other physical activities.

The two groups were categorised male neurotics of (a) athletic personality ("athletic neurotics") and (b) nonathletic personality ("nonathletic neurotics").

It was evident that such extreme variance with respect to athleticism was uncommon in a group of non-neurotic male control subjects matched with the neurotic subjects for age, social class, and family doctor interviewed in their homes in Leeds in 1965 (Little & Kerr, 1968), for 72% of the controls, but only 18% of the neurotic subjects, revealed attitudes and had followed practices with respect to physical prowess appropriate to their age. Only 9% of controls, compared with 39% of neurotics, were classified as "athletic personalities."

Table 1 and Figure 1 show the essentially dichotomous distribution of the personality variable "athleticism" in neurotic males.

Although "athleticism" may appear a somewhat nebulous and subjective concept, nevertheless independent psychiatrists' rating on a 5-point scale of this personality variable disclosed a high degree of interobserver agreement (product moment correlation, $r = +.93$).

Comparison of Athletic and Nonathletic Neurotic Males

Statistically significant differences emerged in the detailed comparison of the two groups with respect to (A) the circumstances surrounding the onset of the neurotic illness, (B) the nature of the illness itself and (C) the premorbid aspects of personality and life experience.

(A) Onset

(1) Age
Table 2 shows the mean age difference between the two neurotic groups at the time of onset of symptoms and at the time of psychiatric referral.

(2) The Apparent Precipitant
In the 44 athletic subjects a direct threat to their own physical wellbeing, in the form of illness or injury, had initiated the neurotic breakdown in 72.5% of cases, while in the 28 neurotics of nonathletic personality such physical threats had preceded the onset of symptoms in only 10.7% —a highly significant difference as shown in Table 3.

Thus, it can be seen that male neurotics of athletic personality displayed a striking stressor/vulnerability specificity; the men became exquisitely vulnerable, on approaching the fifth decade of life, to threats to their overvalued but *waning* physical prowess, and were relatively insensitive to other types of stressor. Conversely, in nonathletic male neurotics, with their low valuation of physical prowess, only rarely did a physical threat initiate the neurotic symptomatology. The findings reemphasise that an apparently trivial stressor can be a major crisis for an individual, only comprehensible to an observer who has assessed the subject's valuation/vulnerability system.

The neurotic symptoms developed in the great majority of the athletic subjects almost immediately following injury, and in many cases, indeed on the

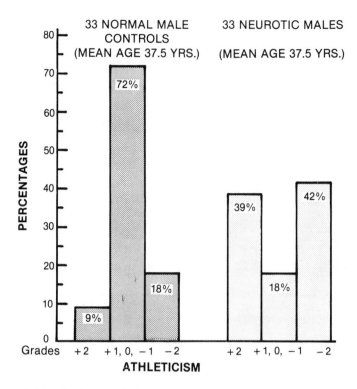

Figure 1. The distribution of athleticism as a personality variable in male neurotics and controls.

Table 1

Athleticism

	N	Grade +2 (Extremely athletic attitudes and practices)	Grades +1,0, −1 ('Normal' athletic attitudes and practices)	Grade −2 (Completely nonathletic attitudes and practices)	Total
Consecutive series of male neurotic patients (1964)	33	13 (39%)	6 (18%)	14 (42%)	33 (99%)
Normal male controls matched for age (1965)	33	3 (9%)	24 (72%)	6 (18%)	33 (99%)

χ^2 (Yates correction) 17.146. df. 2. $p < 0.001$.

Table 2

Age

| | Male neurotics | | | | |
| | Athletic personality | | Nonathletic personality | | |
	N	Mean age	N	Mean age	
Age at onset of the neurotic illness	44	36.36 years	28	29.32 years	t test P< .01
Age at referral to psychiatrist	44	40.3 years	28	34.61 years	t test P< .05

Table 3

Direct Threat to Physical Wellbeing—Male Neurotics

	Present exclusively	Present with other psychological stressors	Not present	Total
Athletic neurotics	23 (52%)	9 (20.5%)	12 (27.5%)	44 (100%)
Nonathletic neurotics	2 (7%)	1 (3.5%)	25 (89.5%)	28 (100%)

χ^2 (Yates correction) 22.75 2 df. p< .001.

same day. Where a physical illness preceded the neurosis, the symptoms of the former became perpetuated and exaggerated along with the emergence of further neurotic symptoms. Rarely was there a symptom-free period between the physical assault and the onset of the neurosis. In most cases the physical assault was a relatively minor one of the sort which must be fairly common in men of this age; it would appear that the magnitude of the vulnerability is more critical than the intensity of the immediate traumatic experience, in which area *relevance* is the conspicuous characteristic.

Physical assaults immediately preceded the onset of neurotic maladjustment in 32 of the 44 subjects of athletic premorbid personality; details are as follows:

Major physical stress—8 cases: Osteotomy; coronary thrombosis; fractured spine, femur and foot; fractured femur; bronchogenic carcinoma; severe leg wound; acute rheumatoid arthritis; pulmonary T.B.

Moderate physical stress—6 cases: In 3 cases the stressors were cumulative with eruption of neurotic symptomatology following the final trauma. In 3 cases the stress was single:

| Cumulative stresses (3) | 3 cumulative events: sciatica-lumbago, diagnosis of prolapsed intervertebral disc, *dental pain;* 4 cumulative events: dental extraction, fractured metacarpal, serious dog bite, *attack of sinusitis;* 3 cumulative events: injury to testicle, hydrocele, *operation on hydrocele.* |
| Single Stress (3) | Hospitalisation with suspected coronary thrombosis; concussion; hospitalisation with renal infection and prolapsed intervertebral disc. |

Minor physical stresses—17 cases: Injury to ankle; attack of lumbago; development of hernia; influenza (3 cases); advice to have surgery for benign parotid tumour; acute awareness of rapid loss of fitness for much-loved active sports; febrile illness; mild encephalitis; two episodes on hockey field: blow on back from ball, and collision with another player; hurt back when lifting at work; feeling no longer strong enough for heavy job; P.U.O.; hypertension revealed by G.P.; several minor injuries on the rugby field; onset of perceptive deafness and tinnitus in the right ear; strained back muscles.

Indirect physical stress—1 case: This patient, a very keen footballer, fainted in the cinema at the moment in the film (*Reach for the Sky*) when the hero's legs (Bader) are to be amputated. An intractable depersonalisation state immediately ensued.

Total 32 cases.

In nine of these athletic subjects with an apparent physical precipitant, there was *in addition* psychological stress of a nonphysical nature present at the onset or shortly before.

In 12 only (27.5%) of the 44 male neurotics judged to have athletic personalities was there absence of a precipitating stress with a component of physical insult. The comparable figures for the male neurotics with nonathletic personalities were 25 out of 28 cases (89.5%).

In the *nonathletic* subjects three types of stressor were associated with the onset of neurosis in 60% of the subjects, viz: difficulties arising from rigid attitudes at work, marital disruption and sexual problems, and death or illness in members of the family group or in friends.

It is of interest that in the entire series of 72 neurotic males (athletic and nonathletic combined) in only 13% was the neurotic illness apparently precipitated by sexual or marital difficulties, while bereavement and illness in family and friends preceded the onset in twice as many.

(B) Nosology

The ensuing neurotic disorders in the athletic subjects were in the main clinically indistinguishable from those seen in the nonathletic subjects, being predominantly anxiety and reactive depressive syndromes. Certain manifestations were significantly more common in the athletic group, viz. general somatic symptoms of hypochondriacal type ($P < .01$) and panic attacks (P <.003), but the pattern of symptoms was not sufficiently constant to justify any attempt to establish a new syndrome. Nevertheless, the existence of two quite distinct aetiological patterns emerged in these male neurotics.

(C) Premorbid Personality and Life Experience

(1) Comparison of athletic and nonathletic male neurotics
    The conspicuous characteristic of the life history of male neurotics of *athletic* personality was the relative absence of neurotic markers. The great majority had enjoyed satisfactory personal relationships, and there was a minimal incidence of psychiatric and *physical* morbidity within the large childhood family. As a group these patients were highly extroverted and sociable and had usually enjoyed excellent health all their lives.
    By contrast, in the *nonathletic group*, neurotic markers were common, interpersonal relationships had been poor, their histories revealed much minor psychiatric morbidity in the family, major *physical* morbidity in the parents during childhood (in characteristically smaller sibling groups), and a much greater number had themselves experienced serious *physical* ill-health during childhood. They were relatively introverted and unsociable.
    These further significant differences between the two groups are shown in Table 4.

(2) Comparison of male neurotics and matched controls
    (a) *The athletic neurotic group differed from the controls* only with respect to their athletic zeal (v.s.) and in the greater number who showed the higher degrees of sociability (Table 5).
    A product-moment correlation of +.79 was found between independent observers' assessments on a 5-point scale of the personality variable "sociability."
    (b) The personalities of the *nonathletic group, however, when compared with the controls*, showed characteristics which conform more to our accepted model of the neurotically vulnerable subject. A greater number had: a family history of mild psychiatric disorder (P< .03), impaired relationship with mother (P<.01), and father (P <.01) during childhood, and, if married, with wife (P <.01), neurotic traits in childhood (P <.01), unhappy childhood (P< .02), and seriously impaired parental health during the patients' childhood (P <.01). A larger number had been members of a smaller sibling group of three and under during childhood (P < .01).
    Age Effect: None of the differences demonstrated between the three groups—athletic neurotics, nonathletic neurotics, and controls—can be attributed to age differences.
    Further results: Space does not permit the elaboration of some further findings, viz. that there were significant differences between athletic and nonathletic neurotics in both mean Neuroticism and mean Extroversion scores of the Maudsley Personality Inventory (Table 6); that the measures of

Table 4

	Male neurotics		χ^2	Y = Yates correction applied	df	P
	With athletic personality	With nonathletic personality				
	N	N				
1. Family history of minor psychiatric illness	41 8 (19.5%)	27 13 (48%)	6.25	—	1	<.02
2. Absence of any known psychiatric illness in the family	41 26 (63%)	27 9 (34%)	5.9	—	1	<.02
3. "Good" relationship with mother	44 33 (75%)	28 12 (43%)	7.54	—	1	<.01
4. "Good" relationship with father	44 28 (63.5%)	28 9 (32%)	6.79	—	1	<.01
5. "Good" relationship with both parents—themselves harmoniously married	44 22 (50%)	28 5 (18%)	6.23	Y	1	<.02
6. Patient a member of a large sibling group numbering four to twelve	44 22 (50%)	28 7 (25%)	4.45	—	1	<.05
	(By method of comparison of two variables)					
7. Presence of neurotic traits in childhood	44 12 (27.5%)	28 17 (60.5%)	7.95	—	1	<.01
8. Childhood recalled as "happy"	44 35 (79.5%)	28 12 (43%)	12.09	—	2	<.005
9. Robust health in childhood	44 41 (93%)	28 19 (68%)	6.18	Y	1	<.02
10. Significant parental illness during patient's childhood	44 4 (9%)	28 14 (50%)	12.67	Y	1	<.001
11. Sociable personality	44 38 (86%)	28 12 (43%)	13.28	Y	1	<.001
12. Marital harmony in those married	36 31 (86%)	19 8 (42%)	9.64	Y	1	<.005

androgyny, using the formula DAS 2 (Tanner, 1951), showed that whereas the bone structure of athletic neurotics was appropriate to their age (Little & Kerr, 1968), that of nonathletic neurotics was characteristic of men 10 to 15

Table 5

Sociability

	N	Grades +2, +1 (More sociable)	Grades 0, −1, −2 (Less sociable)	Total
Athletic neurotics (male)	44	38 (86.5%)	6 (13.5%)	44 (100%)
Normal (control) males matched for age	33	15 (45%)	18 (55%)	33 (100%)

χ^2 (Yates correction) = 12.8 1 df. p < 0.001.

Table 6

Maudsley Personality Inventory Results

	Mean Scores				
	(a) Combined group of 54 neurotic males	(b) 29 athletic neurotics	(c) 25 non-athletic neurotics	Difference between means (b) and (c)	(Students t test)
E Scale	22.13	26.28	17.32	8.96	p < .01
N Scale	29.41	24.69	34.88	10.19	p < .001

Table 7

Results of Anthropometric Investigations

	DAS 2 N	Mean Score	S.D.
Athletic neurotics	29	82.820	4.42
Nonathletic neurotics	26	86.053	5.68

Difference between means 3.233. Value for t 2.367.
df 53. P < 0.05.

years younger (Table 7); and that, despite "good" previous personality and lower Neuroticism scores, the prognosis under treatment for the athletic group was, in general, less favorable.

Incidence of the Athlete's Neurosis

The following figures offer a rough guide and are based on all 387 new psychiatric cases referred to me during 1964. An exclusive diagnosis of "neurotic syndrome" was made in 22% of the 149 males. Approximately 40% of these neuroses occurred in subjects of athletic personality. Thus one in 11 (9%) of new male referrals seen by me over the year was suffering from the athlete's neurosis, a figure close to those for new cases of endogenous depression (13%) and schizophrenia (11%) in males (Little & Lloyd, 1969).

Discussion

Social Influences

The athlete's neurosis, which is no rare, trivial or short-lived reaction, can, and usually does, provoke prolonged and crippling psychological, domestic and economic strains, as many of these men despite previous sound work records subsequently remained unemployable for years. Is this athlete's neurosis yet another disorder contingent on lowered morbidity and mortality levels associated with medical progress and relative affluence when the experience of ill-health can come as a surprise for which the individual may be ill-prepared? The condition is essentially another example of what Hill (1960) has called a "deprivation neurosis" in which conflict appears to play little part. It is a bereavement reaction to loss of part of oneself necessitating, as Lindemann (1944) has said "reorganisations which do not belong to the arsenal of habitual adjustive responses." Thus there are at least three parameters to be considered in assessing a stress-provoking experience: intensity, duration, and relevance to the particular individual's personality and life experience, plus a possible fourth—the surprise effect of the trauma.

Will more men, in advanced societies, fall into the athlete's trap in the future? Perhaps the trend will be as Michael Young (1958) predicts in his provocative book *The Rise of the Meritocracy* in which, retrospecting as from the year 2033, he sees the rise of the new intellectual aristocracy following increasing equality of opportunity and promotion by merit resulting in the striving for prestige through nonintellectual alternatives, among which athleticism increasingly becomes the pabulum of the masses. "The lower classes needed a mythos," he writes, "and they got what they needed, the mythos of muscularity . . . they esteemed physical achievement almost as highly as we of the upper class esteem mental." Furthermore, as Wallach (1960) observes of athletes, "They are destroyed overnight by the concept of mortality . . . these fellows are always and forever twenty-one."

Is Athleticism Neurotic?

The findings of this enquiry present a challenge to Schneider's (1950) dictum "there are no neuroses, only neurotics" and to the viewpoint advocated by Sullivan "that the essence of mental illness lies in a disturbance of interpersonal relationships and that acute illness arises out of a crisis in such relationships" (Davis, 1962). All the evidence in the present study points to exceptionally favorable intra- and extra- family personal relationships in the athletic group.

Furthermore, in this group acute illness does not arise out of a crisis in such relationships, but primarily out of the shock of a threat to overvalued but waning physical prowess. Any disturbance of interpersonal relationship present must be of a very subtle order.

One might well enquire why these subjects became, and remained, so fanatically and exclusively devoted to physical prowess. No one can indefinitely enjoy absolutely ideal interpersonal relationships, and no doubt even deeper probing might well have revealed some defects in these subjects, but would they be sufficient and would they be relevant? Here surely is an occasion for the application of Occam's razor. One may accept the theory of Lorenz (1966) and conceptualise athleticism as a manifestation of the diversion of instinctual aggression into ritualised socially innocuous channels. Whatever its source I would maintain that even excessive athleticism is not in itself "neurotic" for this premorbid behavior is associated neither with suffering in the subject, nor in those with whom he associates. But I would concede that, like exclusive and excessive emotional dependence on work, on key family relationship-bonds, intellectual pursuits, physical beauty, sexual prowess or any other overvalued attribute or activity, athleticism can place the subject in a vulnerable preneurotic state leading to manifest neurotic illness in the event of an *appropriate* threat, or actual enforced deprivation, especially if abrupt or unexpected. The genesis of potentially psychopathological overvaluations does not *invariably* lie in disturbed interpersonal relationships.

Summary

The clinical study here reported reveals a not uncommon psychological aetiology associated with the sudden development of neurotic symptoms in males of apparently robust premorbid personality. This aetiology has not previously been full reported and is characterized by a striking absence of disturbed interpersonal relations.

Conclusion

Although the concept of "neurosis" or "neurotic syndrome" has been fairly narrowly restricted in this study so as to admit only one in five of all male referrals, nevertheless, it has been demonstrated that neurotic maladjustment of acute onset occurs as a manifestation of a deprivation crisis, in the absence of evidence of early or late disturbed interpersonal relations in 40% of such male neurotic subjects, and that the impact of the apparently trivial but highly specific traumatic experience initiating crippling maladjustment in this group can only be understood in relation to the individual's personality and life experiences.

References

Davis, D.R. Family environment and mental illness. In A. T. Welford, M. Argyle, D. V. Glass, & J. N. Morris (Eds.), *Society*. London: Routledge & Kegan Paul, 1962.

Hill, D. In J. M. Tanner (Ed.), *Stress and psychiatric disorder*. Oxford: Blackwell, 1960.

Lindemann, E. Symptomatology and management of acute grief. *American Journal of Psychiatry*, 1944, **101,** 141-148.

Little, J.C. *Physical prowess and neurosis*. Unpublished M.D. thesis, University of Bristol, 1966.

Little, J.C., & Kerr, T.A. Some differences between published norms and data from matched controls as a basis for comparison with psychiatrically-disturbed groups. *British Journal of Psychiatry*, 1968, **114,** 883-890.

Little, J.C., & Lloyd, A.T. A socio-clinical analysis of 1000 new psychiatric referrals, 1969.

Lorenz, K. *On aggression*. London: Methuen, 1966.

Schneider, K. *Psychopathic personalities* (9th ed.). Vienna: 1950.

Tanner, J.M. Current advances in the study of physique. *Lancet,* 1951, **1,** 574-579.

Wallach, I. *Muscle beach*. New York: Dell, 1960.

Young, M. *The rise of the meritocracy*. London: Thames & Hudson, 1958.

Addendum

The psychological motives in sport are complex and fluctuating. Many authors emphasize the aggressive component in sports, and it is not surprising to find that aggression, when turned in on the self, aggravates the depression and anxiety associated with the experience of deprivation.

Prospects for the prevention of athletic neurosis are no more encouraging than the prospects for treatment. One might hope that these fanatical fitness enthusiasts might be identified in advance, warned of the hazards ahead, and encouraged to modify their attitudes and behavior in time to prevent mental illness. But it is my experience that these lemmings do not want to know. If pressed, they become angry and scornful. In correspondence with sports-feature journalists and sports-medicine physicians I have come to believe that the psychological defenses of these enthusiasts are virtually unassailable: the very notion of a neurotic athlete is taboo.

Interest in sports is ever on the increase, even if participation is not. In fact, it has become the "pabulum of the masses." In contemporary Britain many cry for equality, and elitism, for them, is a sin—yet they choose not to see that in an educational system where none must excel academically lest the losers be made to feel inferior, the members of the sports teams are chosen on merit. They see no inconsistency in the fact that, while financial inequality in every other field of endeavor is decried, the most highly skilled sports heroes earn fabulous rewards in money and acclaim. The sports heroes, if wise, retire while in their 30s and retreat into ownership of profitable sports shops. If unwise, their raison d'etre having gone with their youth, many are unable to face social oblivion and break down. Some find final oblivion in suicide, a tragic phenomenon most sports doctors and journalists are reluctant to discuss.

The athlete's neurosis is no rare disorder. It accounted for one out of 11 of all new male referrals to a comprehensive psychiatric service based in a general hospital during the 1960s. I can give no figures for the 1970s, since my clinical commitment has been selectively restricted and the hospital's records give no guide on incidence (the etiologic complex of "athlete's neurosis," if recognized, has not been recorded as such in the diagnosis-oriented system). But former trainee psychiatrists who worked in the team at Leeds, and who are now in senior posts, assure me that they continue to see many such cases and find them still as difficult to treat.

The contemporary craze for jogging and similar exercises must raise questions about the mental-health implications of this phenomenon. I have no knowledge of any jogger's being referred with an unexplained sudden-onset neurotic illness, and I can find no reference to such an event. Among those who jog there will inevitably be some identifiable fitness fanatics, but the psychiatrist with a widespread practice will undoubtedly find that most joggers are so engaged as part of a commonsense response to health-education programs.

A new life style has been deliberately adopted by the American male since the post-World War II era, and it has altered him from the flabby, obese, cigarette-smoking, mechanically mobile figure of that era who was seemingly hell-bent on early self-destruction. The new style entails dieting, exercise, and reduction or cessation of tobacco smoke intake. Just which of these variables has brought about the change in middle-age mortality in the United States is not entirely clear, but the demonstrable positive advantages of the whole "protective packet" far outweigh any speculated psychiatric morbidity from the physical-exercise component (which, if present, is yet to be demonstrated).

In Britain, where regular exercise and other preventive measures are not yet taken seriously, the price is still being paid. To my mind, regular physical exercise to avert or postpone disaster ahead is a far cry from the fanatical pursuit of physical prowess as an exclusive way of life, and I doubt that any significant psychiatric morbidity would ensue.

CHAPTER 23

"Running Madness": A Prelude to Real Madness

Zira DeFries

The omnipresence of runners is testimony to the power of the media to stimulate the latent jogging instincts in a segment of the population that might otherwise be immune to such strenuous physical activity. The stream of new converts to running keeps us well supplied with subjects for investigation of a relatively unexplored form of physical-mental behavior.

That running is more than purely sportive behavior is by now cliche. Its adherents conceive of it as a way of life; others categorize it as a movement. As such, it incorporates a particular ideology that claims the potential for enhancing well being, which in turn confers on it the status of a therapeutic modality. As with any ideology, however, excessive adherence, with exaggeration and distortion, can counteract therapeutic effects and indeed produce pathological ones. An example of a mild form of pathology, a consequence of excessive adherence, is running addiction. However, a far more serious degree of pathology may result if running ideology is used as a primary means of fashioning a self-image. This is especial-

ly true of adolescent females, who are at a crucial stage of identity development and for whom any popular movement (whether it be feminism or running) becomes a means of bolstering self-esteem by providing an opportunity
for identification, which may ultimately aid the development of a secure sense
of self.

Discussed in this paper are two women on the track team of their college.
Their overelaborated perceptions and distorted self-concepts as runners were
used as the basis for self-definition and identity, giving rise to serious mental
illness in which ego disorganization occurred. The special meaning they im-
puted to running, along with their inability to transcend confusion over changing sex roles and masculinity-feminity concepts (a necessary capacity in the
realm of athletic competition for women), created deep-seated conflicts.
Because of their limited sex role adaptability they were particularly vulnerable
to the stress of sport competition, and the identity crises they experienced,
centering on their image as runners, culminated in acute psychotic episodes.

Student A had been, by her description, a star member of her high school
track team. This had given her a feeling of worth and importance and defined
her role vis-a-vis her peers as "a runner." Her running activities in high school
had not been experienced as stressful and had not interfered with her studies.
Shortly after she entered college she joined the track team. Almost immediately, she became aware of uncomfortable feelings of competitiveness
toward her teammates and inadequacy in her social life, particularly with
males. She covered her depression with obsessive thoughts of competition
and track. After one of the team's long distance races, she described the stress
as unbearable and the whole activity as fruitless. A couple of weeks later,
following a race in which she "bombed," her self-concept was badly shaken.
She attempted to restore her tarnished image by intensifying her running
routines and aiming to become the team captain. But she found trying to
keep up with the strenuous demands of both team affairs and academic work
so overwhelming and depressing that she felt herself at the "breaking point."
Nonetheless, she could not relinquish her track team affiliation, because she
was dependent upon it for her "sense of self"—i.e., runner-athlete.

With great difficulty, however, she was finally persuaded to withdraw from
the team. Almost immediately she felt relief; her depression lifted and she
embarked on a series of relationships with men until sex became such "an in-
surmountable problem" that she was forced to "give up men." She promptly
rejoined the team and began fantasizing about the female coach (which she
had done previously), but now she acted out these fantasies with a lesbian
student. She believed that her horizons were being expanded by the combination of sex and running. She was running more intensely than ever at this
point, several hours a day, both with the team and on her own. A progressive
blurring of fantasy and reality occurred, so that she spoke of herself as a living
legend whom all the women in her college envied because of her superior
running capability. In her new-found status as ideal athlete she said she experienced the loneliness of being at the top. Eventually she began to complain

of great fatigue, of inability to concentrate, of being too aware, and too different. Anger at the coach for lack of recognition of her superior ability—she considered herself Olympic material—and a reactivation of an old spastic colon condition provided her with face-saving excuses for leaving the team. Once released from "the power of the coach," her anxiety lessened, but she continued daily long distance runs on her own.

Her former pattern of sexual acting out soon reoccurred, however, and she developed a "cosmic attraction to a guy" described as a perfect replica of herself. She felt she had come to terms with her sexuality, considered herself to be a woman in an athlete's body, and therefore, had no further need to be on the team. No longer perceived by her peers as "the runner" she was now just a student. It was almost as if she had become a real person again. Free to be herself after having overcome the "brainwashing" by the coach who had been her "mentor," her "everything," she thought she could stop running permanently. But the new-found freedom of being "just a person," was short-lived, and the underlying conflicts soon erupted into a series of violent verbal outbursts that she described as a psychological marathon in which she felt her mind racing 100 miles an hour. During one such outburst, she became blatantly psychotic, with disorientation, incoherent speech, grandiose delusional thinking, and uncontrollable rage. She was hospitalized and remained in the hospital for about 6 weeks before being discharged to the care of a private psychiatrist.

Running, and its associated ideology, preoccupied this student throughout her first year of college. In her desire to repair a poorly developed sense of self and a confused sexual identity, she attempted to fashion a self-concept as a runner-athlete. The equation of runner-athlete with acceptable identity was a dominant mode of thought and a standard of reference for her behavior. Her verbalizations were suffused with running language and metaphor. When her sense of herself did not subsume being a runner, she felt she was not a person. Her desperate attempts to overcome the pseudo-identity running provided and to resolve the role confusion she experienced as a female athlete failed, resulting instead in acute psychosis.

Although Student B presents a shorter and less dramatic prologue to her psychotic episode, the drama of her case is heightened by the fact that the psychotic break occurred during a cross-country race and required emergency room treatment at the local hospital.

Student B had begun "serious running" a few months prior to her breakdown. Before that time, she had run sporadically in high school, never more than 2-3 miles. When she entered college, she began daily runs with the track team of 4-5 miles, and soon qualified for the team and participated in races. Her involvement was immediate and intense but it required that she push herself hard in order to keep up with her teammates. This necessitated neglecting her studies and social life. As a consequence, she became tense, anxious, and depressed. Her original reason for running in high school had been to counteract feelings of depression and loneliness. Now these feelings were reactivated and she experienced even greater estrangement from her peers in college than she had in high school. She had hoped that becoming a long distance runner in college would provide her with greater self-confidence and a more positive self-image. In puberty she had thought of herself as a tomboy, in adolescence she considered herself "a sport person," and now she wanted to effect an identity as a female-athlete-*runner*.

Running did bolster her self-esteem initially but only briefly. With the realization of the effort it required, the good feelings and the positive image quickly evaporated. Despite her discouragement, she persevered, because she had come to believe that being a runner was the surest route to improving her self-image. As time wore on, however, she became increasingly phobic about the pain of racing, fixating on her dread and hatred of cross-country running.

She found the aggression and competitiveness of her teammates very disturbing: Women, she felt, were not supposed to be that way. The conflict between her idea of typical female behavior and how she was expected to behave made her want to give up running and become a writer instead. Writing, she reasoned, required similar endurance but was without the associated pain. Nonetheless, she clung to her faltering self-image as runner, all the while feeling desperately alone. Earlier on, boys had always seemed preferable to girls as playmates (she particularly enjoyed beating them up), but in adolescence that preference seemed unnatural. Because she felt disconnected from women—they were "mean, humorless, underhanded and untrustworthy"—her loneliness was acute. Wide mood swings in which she felt happy, frenzied, high one day, and suicidal the next reflected her ambivalence about running. During her third cross country race she suddenly went "berserk." The few memories she retained of that race were of the incredibly difficult course (it was very hilly), the coach screaming at her, and her sudden inability to walk as her "legs left her." Her mind, however, kept racing as her whole life reeled past. She repeated certain words over and over and experienced "the terror of becoming insane." The next thing she remembered was waking up in the emergency room of the hospital.

The following day she complained of feeling confused, strange, listless, and depressed. She was oriented and generally coherent but vague and easily distracted; her speech was sparse and her affect flat. She knew that something serious had happened but felt as though it had happened to someone else; she slept a great deal and had difficulty concentrating. She denied having hallucinations but at times appeared to be listening to inner voices.

Her symptoms disappeared gradually over the next 2 weeks and she felt ready to resume classes. She was guilty about her breakdown and blamed it on not having eaten or slept enough the day prior to the race. She wanted to rejoin the running team, and when told she could not, refused further therapy, which she saw as a deterrent to being allowed back on the team.

This student, like the other, saw running as a way of shoring up a sagging self-concept and gaining a more secure identity. Both had been tomboys in their early years, both had considered themselves athletes of sorts in high school; but neither had made a satisfactory peer group identification, and each had grave doubts about her feminine identity. Both saw running as a means to an acceptable gender identity via the runner-as-female-athlete route. Because they were unable to integrate the stereotypically masculine qualities of aggression and competition essential for running competence, they could not make a proper identification with their running peers. Running, instead of providing the ego boost they needed, exacerbated their feelings of isolation and difference and by eroding their self-esteem further impaired their already negative self-images. The *idee fixe* each had of herself as runner allowed no room for an objective examination of her behavior and prevented resolution of her ambivalence about running. The overwhelming anxiety this created resulted ultimately in a break with reality and in personality disorganization.

The foregoing case reports demonstrate the hazards, for adolescent women with identity problems, of overelaborating the meaning of running and using it as a defense against depression. Despite increasing social acceptance of an athletic personality as appropriate for women, vulnerable females—i.e., those with predisposing idiosyncratic genetic and family background factors—are particularly sensitive to the still existing societal pressures which downgrade aggression and competition as integral aspects of female behavior and are considered inimical to proper female personality development. It is important, therefore, to be cognizant of the dangers implicit in encouraging overzealous, psychologically . vulnerable female adolescents to engage in serious competitive running. Healthier adolescents, with a better developed sense of self, feeling severe stress during strenuous physical activity, would probably curtail their activity rather than risk going beyond the critical point of losing control.

The practical implications of awareness of a critical point by coaches and others in charge are obvious. Premonitory signs of change in individual and team behavior should alert a coach to impending psychological difficulty. Because coaches play a prominent part in the lives of their charges, they are in a position to influence vulnerable students to reduce their athletic load, to seek therapy, or both.

A psychological casuality list of long distance runners has not, to my knowledge, been compiled. A great deal has been written about the therapeutic effects of long distance running for depression, but little or nothing has been described in the running literature concerning its antitherapeutic effects on predisposed depressive adolescents.

Addendum

Diagnostic classification and indications for drugs, omitted from the main body of the paper, require brief comment. Both students described appear to fit the DSM III category of Bipolar Disorder; the second student can be categorized as Atypical Bipolar Disorder.

Student A adamantly refused medication prior to the point of hospitalization, claiming that it would adversely affect her running. Student B was given injectable tranquilizers in the hospital emergency unit but refused subsequent medication, also because of her fear of its negative effect on her running. Interestingly, neither student was adverse to using drugs such as marijuana or cocaine from time to time, but the idea of therapeutic medication was perceived as harmful.

CHAPTER 24

Masochism and Long Distance Running

Arnold M. Cooper

Those of us who don't run much have a constant curiosity, no doubt fueled by envy, about why runners run great distances, often at considerable cost in terms of time and sacrifice of other activities, but most conspicuously to the nonrunner, in terms of bodily and mental pain and anguish. Scratch marathoners once, and they tell you how wonderful they feel. Scratch them twice and they tell you about their latest injuries. In a recent article on sports medicine, this situation is described as follows:

> As America enters its third decade of the Age of Exercise, more and more citizens, men and women of all ages, are subjecting themselves to the glories—and agonies—of some form of vigorous athletic activity. As a result, more and more physicians are being asked to stand by to treat the wounded, and the overall field of sports medicine is suddenly assuming a substantially greater role in the lives of contemporary Americans.

By current estimates, at least one of every three Americans over the age of 16 has been engaging during the last two decades in some form of aerobic (heart-pumping) activity on a regular basis—playing a rapid game of badminton, or volleyball, bicycling, jogging, swimming. Everyone agrees that this kind of activity has been generally healthful—but it also has its dark side. The number of injuries among all athletes has increased dramatically, and it is estimated that 17 million to 20 million injuries are now occurring among weekend athletes alone every year, costing them and their employers [in lost time] some $40 billion. (Conniff, 1980, p.42)

A substantial number of these injuries surely can be assigned to running. Why do people do it? I believe that *one* of the unconscious motivations for distance running relates to narcissistic and masochistic needs; these needs are beautifully gratified by running distances which are clearly beyond the intended uses of the human body. Although the proportions of masochism and narcissism vary for each individual, they regularly contribute a significant, even if not the major, motivation for the runner's activity.

What is narcissism and masochism? Both concepts are fashionable in current psychoanalytic thinking, although details of their meaning and sources provoke great disagreements. In the most general way, narcissism refers to behaviors derived from interest, concern, and satisfaction with oneself. In its healthy forms, narcissism is reflected in high self-esteem following achievement of appropriate goals; it is also shown in the self-confidence which enables one to pursue goals and ideals with pleasure, persistence, and a cooperative, even loving attitude toward at least some other person or persons. In its more pathological forms, narcissism involves an endless series of maneuvers designed to disguise a shaky self-esteem and a faulty inner feeling of a lack of self-worth. This may take the form of grandiose fantasies of self-worth, an intolerance of criticism, an inability to give to others or to recognize their needs, and a tendency to be dissatisfied and depressed because nothing in the real world meets the fantasized expectations of missed gratifications. The image of the body is one of the central features of the sense of self which each of us carries as a partly conscious and partly unconscious mental representation; that is, in general, the more pathological one's narcissistic makeup, the more one is likely to demonstrate a bodily preoccupation, either by an excessive need for maintaining its perfection and beauty or by endless hypochondriacal complaints.

Masochism refers to the strange human propensity for seeming to be able to extract some kind of pleasure or satisfaction out of pain. The most obvious instances are sexual, in which enduring physical pain produces sexual excitement and orgasm. More subtly, but related, are the psychological means by which painful events—humiliations, shame, defeats in life—are arranged, seemingly innocently, but on careful examination, unconsciously and deliberately, for the secret pleasure in pain that masochistic individuals can extract from the situation. We all know individuals who seem never to learn from experience but who continue unrelentingly to pick the precisely mismatched lover or to find new ways to provoke their friends or bosses; these individuals can always snatch defeat from the jaws of victory. Many of them fit the title of "injustice collector" conferred upon them by Edmund Bergler (1949) several decades ago. They endlessly repeat the pattern of unconsciously provoking disappointments or defeats, consciously but ineffectively or inappropriately reacting to the defeat in furious pseudo-aggression (pseudo because it is intended only for display), and finally subside into self-pity and depression.

The tendencies toward narcissism and masochism are linked—fused, even—by the nature of events early in life. Imagine developing infants and children as having two great tasks in order to develop into full-fledged psychological adults. One task is to develop a set of self-images about their body, their assertions, their sexual and aggressive needs, their ideals, their relationships—in short, a self which is basically positive and healthily narcissistic. The second task is to develop autonomy out of the original, total infantile helplessness and dependency on a mother, a dependency so great that infants for some considerable time probably think (or, more probably, feel) that they and the mother are one, and that they have all the powers which in fact she has. Out of this real infantile dependency and fantasized infantile megalomania, along with growing cognitive and muscular capacity and the frustration of some of their needs, infants bit by bit begin to see themselves as separate, enjoying the use of the powers of the giant parents and hoping that one day all those powers will be theirs. Clearly the two tasks of becoming a self, a person, and developing autonomy are related and, at many points, indistinguishable. However, the process of simultaneously trying to keep up some degree of omnipotent fantasy, necessary for developing a healthy self, and simultaneously recognizing that one is separate, helpless, and completely dependent upon an all-powerful parent who periodically does not do what one commands, has certain built-in problems. All infants spend lots of time crying with what we can only interpret as some variety of rage. Forced to recognize that they are not omnipotent and that painful frustrations cannot always be controlled, infants tend to engage in a series of mental maneuvers designed to protect their fantasies, in the face of incontrovertible evidence to the contrary. They first try to construct a black-and-white world in which everything good that happens to them is their doing and all bad things like frustrations are due to someone bad—mother—who is intent on being cruel (the universally fantasized version of a witch). As developing babies begin to recognize that mother is not, in fact, all bad, and that they even love each other, another mode must be found to explain this failure at omnipotence. For this end, infants then manage the strange capacity to turn suffering into pleasure. It is as if they say, "If I am experiencing frustration and pain, it is not because I am helpless to prevent it, and it is not because my mother is unrelentingly cruel. It is because I am still all-powerful and I suffer frustration because I wished my mother to frustrate me because I like it." The operative principle would seem to be "If you can't like 'em, join 'em." By adopting this defense, which is part of all human make-up and varies only in degree, babies fuse their narcissistic needs and masochistic defenses. They maintain their self-esteem by taking credit for actively pursuing and enjoying pains which they cannot avoid. The secondary elaborations of this process are endless, but beyond the purposes of this paper.

From a different point of view, we may ask what the gratifying and constructive aspects of pain are. We have no difficulty in agreeing with every mother's observation that painful frustration, disappointment, and injury are inevitable concomitants of infancy. The most loving and competent mother cannot spare the infant these experiences which, in proper doses, should not be spared. It is likely that painful bodily experiences (particularly with the skin) are important proprioceptive mechanisms which serve not only to avoid damage, but also to provide important developmental components of the forming body-image and self-image. Many cases in the literature are of persons who experience a relief from identity diffusion by inflicting pain upon their skin.

A typical pattern for patients diagnosed as borderline self-mutilators is to cut or otherwise injure themselves in privacy, experiencing little pain in the process, and later to exhibit the injury to the usually surprised caretaker, be it parent or physician, with evident satisfaction in the demonstration that they are sick, suffering, and beyond the caretaker's control. A prominent motivation for this behavior is the need to demonstrate autonomy via the capacity for self-mutilation.

Head-banging in infants, a far more common phenomenon than is usually acknowledged and quite compatible with normal development is also one of the normal, painful ways of achieving necessary and gratifying self-definition. Skin sensations of all kinds, and perhaps moderately painful sensations particularly, are a regular mode of establishing self-boundaries.

Imre Hermann, in a fascinating paper, states:

> In order to understand masochistic pleasure, one has to recognize that it is quite closely interwoven with the castration complex but behind this link is the reaction-formation to the urge to cling—namely the drive to separate oneself. At this point, we have to go far back to early development. Our guess is that the emergence of the process of separation of the mother and child dual unit constitutes a pre-stage of narcissism and painful masochism; normal separation goes along with 'healthy' narcissism. (1935/1976, p. 30)

Hermann describes pain as a necessary concomitant of separation, but a lesser evil than the damage and decay of the self which would result from failure of separation in infancy. He refers to a healing tendency within the psyche and the erotization of pain which facilitates the healing of a damaged psychic area. Hermann views all later self-mutilations, such as self-biting, tearing one's cuticles, pulling hair, tearing scabs, and so on, as attempts to reinforce a sense of freedom from the need to cling. I suggest that running agonies also fulfill that function. "Pain arises in connection with the *separation that is striven for*, while its *successful accomplishment* brings pleasure" (p. 30). Hermann views masochistic character traits as a consequence of failure of successful separation with reactive repetition of separation traumas.

Pain, then, serves the organism's task of self-definition and separation-individuation and is therefore part of a gratifying accomplishment. Mastery—not avoidance—of pain is a major achievement in self-development, and mastery may imply the capacity to derive satisfaction and accomplishment from self-induced, self-dosed pain. That there is a tendency for such an achievement to miscarry is evident.

As far as I know, all cultures at all times have set themselves painful tasks—some form of heroism, accomplishment, endurance, or martyrdom. Achievement alone is not valued unless it was fired in pain. No culture chooses to live without inflicting pain on itself; even cultures seemingly devoted to nirvana-type ideals have painful rituals. Levi-Strauss (1949) has suggested that rites of passage and experiences of mortification are a means of assuring essential aspects of cultural and individual identity. He posits that their effectiveness is directly proportional to their painfulness and sharpness of definition. Perhaps a culture such as ours, lacking appropriate ritual and order, seizes upon any opportunities to provide social unity through shared ritual suffering. It may be no accident that distance running has become popular at the same time that our society has allegedly become more self-centered and narcissistic.

Thus, running, especially distance running, provides a socially sanctioned and relatively harmless method for the gratification of potentially dangerous narcissistic and masochistic tendencies. Runners are, first of all, essentially alone with their body. Runners' reports of their pleasure in running with others seem to me to be thin disguises over their preoccupation with their own bodies and their constant monitoring of their state and performance. Runners are permitted a regression of self-involvement which is reminiscent of children exploring themselves with accompanying grunts of pleasure and concentration. Distance running and swimming are the only sports which provide the opportunities for such single-minded focus, in which there are no teammates, and the activities of one's opponents are far less significant than one's own state. Any relationship to masturbation is not coincidental.

Of even greater importance than the narcissistic aspect, which could be elaborated further, is the clear masochistic element. The inevitable experience of pain and the description, by at least some runners, of the pain as an integral part of the running experience, seems to be a repetition of the infant's desperate need to create everything—even their own pain. Further, the sharp experience of oneself through the bodily pain, concurrent with a blurred awareness of the world, helps to strengthen what may be in runners a weakened sense of clear self-definition. Finally, the combination of doing something that is clearly beyond human capacity—running 26.2 miles—and

thereby demonstrating one's triumph over human frailty, with a secretly enjoyed self-inflicted pain which would otherwise be forbidden by one's inner
conscience and by society, may represent a huge double triumph over inner
guilty restraints on narcissistic and masochistic tendencies; the result is a
hypomanic state experienced as the runner's high. The distance runner
demonstrates omnipotence over the body, overcoming limitations of the real
world, the superego, and the limitations of the inner world. Together these
victories provide illusions of immortality.

We all share pathological narcissistic and masochistic tendencies. Fortunate
individuals find ways to divert these tendencies toward useful or at least
socially sanctioned activities. The runner, almost uniquely, carries on a
useless activity which symbolizes society's need for a special hero who will
enact the infantile triumphs requisite for healthy functioning, and who also
enables us, the audience, to share vicariously in some of his or her forbidden
pleasures. As others have indicated, runners with more than their fair share of
narcissistic and masochistic pathology are likely to use running as an unsuc-
cessful pseudo-solution for avoided problems in life.

Lionel Trilling, in his brilliant (1955) essay, "The Fate of Pleasure," spoke
of the change in cultural attitude from the time of Wordsworth, who wrote of
"the grand elementary principle of pleasure," which he said constituted "the
named and native dignity of man," and which was "the principle by which
man knows and feels, and lives, and moves." Trilling referred to a

> change in quantity. It has always been true of some men that to pleasure they
> have preferred unpleasure. They imposed upon themselves difficult and painful
> tasks, they committed themselves to strange 'unnatural' modes of life, they
> sought after stressing emotions, in order to know psychic energies which are not
> to be summoned up in felicity. These psychic energies, even when they are ex-
> perienced in self-destruction, are a means of self-definition and self-affirmation.
> As such, they have a social reference—the election of unpleasure, however
> isolated and private the act may be, must refer to society if only because the
> choice denies the valuation which society in general puts upon pleasure; of
> course it often receives social approbation of the highest degree, even if at a
> remove of time: it is the choice of the hero, the saint and martyr, and, in some
> cultures, the artist. The quantitative change which we have to take account of is:
> what was once a mode of experience of a few has now become an ideal of ex-
> perience of many. For reasons which, at least, here, must defy speculation, the
> ideal of pleasure has exhausted itself, almost as if it had been actually realized
> and had issued in satiety and ennui. In its place or, at least, beside it, there is
> developing—conceivably at the behest of literature!—an ideal of the experience
> of those psychic energies which are linked with unpleasure and which are
> directed towards self-definition and self-affirmation. (p. 85)

Trilling, with his usual extraordinary perspicacity, described at the level of
culture the same shift which we have experienced in psychoanalysis at the
level of clinical practice. This new type that he described is the same new type
with which psychoanalysis has been struggling now for years, the so-called

narcissistic character. Trilling clearly perceived that this character type struggles to achieve self-definition through the experience of unpleasure. When this occurs within socially acceptable limits, "normal" masochistic-narcissistic character development occurs. The masochistic-narcissistic character as a pathological type of varying severity is marked by the preferential pursuit of suffering and rejection with little positive achievement. Every quantitative gradation occurs between normal and severely pathological or borderline. The long distance runner is probably further along on the narcissistic-masochistic spectrum than the popular press, with its emphasis on the psychological benefits of running, would suggest.

Finally, I think the attempt to describe running as an addiction, with the implication of a physiologic hook which forces one to run, misses the important psychological point. All neurotic activities are continued compulsively and usually cannot be stopped by any ordinary effort of will. We would not term every obsession or every neurotic propensity to establish specifically repetitive damaging interpersonal relationships as an addiction; rather, they are a dynamic expression of neurotic need and attempted defense. The need to inflict pain on oneself in the course of running 26.2 miles is best understood in terms of its contribution to the masochistic psychic balance, with overtones of perverse satisfaction, rather than in terms of addiction, which denies the psychological issues.

References

Bergler, E. *Basic neurosis.* New York: Grune & Stratton, 1949.

Conniff, J.C.G. *The New York Times Magazine,* October 5, 1980, p. 42.

Hermann, I. Clinging-going-in-search. *Psychoanalytic Quarterly,* 1976, **45,** 30. (Originally published, 1935.)

Levi-Strauss, C. *Elementary structures of kinship.* New York: Beacon Press, 1949.

Trilling, L. *Beyond culture.* New York: Viking Press, 1955.

INDEX